Environmental Law

BLACK LETTER OUTLINES

Environmental Law

Jeffrey M. Gaba

Professor of Law,
Southern Methodist University School of Law

FOURTH EDITION

THOMSON
WEST

Mat #40748955

© West, a Thomson business, 2001, 2005
© 2009 Thomson/Reuters
610 Opperman Drive
St. Paul, MN 55123
1–800–313–9378

ISBN: 978–0–314–19443–5

 PRINTED ON 10% POST CONSUMER RECYCLED PAPER

Preface

This "Black Letter" is designed to help a law student recognize and understand the basic principles and issues of law covered in a law school course. It can be used both as a study aid when preparing for classes and as a review of the subject matter when studying for an examination.

Each "Black Letter" is written by experienced law school teachers who are recognized national authorities in the subject covered.

The law is succinctly stated by the author of this "Black Letter." In addition, the exceptions to the rules are stated in the text. The rules and exceptions have purposely been condensed to facilitate quick review and easy recollection. For an in-depth study of a point of law, citations to major student texts are given.

If the subject covered by this text is a code or code-related course, the code section or rule is set forth and discussed wherever applicable.

FORMAT

The format of this "Black Letter" is specially designed for review. (1) **Text.** First, it is recommended that the entire text be studied, and, if deemed necessary, supplemented by the student texts cited. (2) **Capsule Summary.** The Capsule Summary is an abbreviated review of the subject matter which can be used both before and after studying the main body of the text. The headings in the Capsule Summary follow the main text of the "Black Letter." (3) **Table of Contents.** The Table of Contents is in outline form to help you organize the details of the subject and the Summary of Contents gives you a final overview of the materials. (4)

Practice Examination. The Practice Examination in Appendix B gives you the opportunity of testing yourself with the type of questions asked on an exam, and comparing your answer with a model answer.

In addition, a number of other features are included to help you understand the subject matter and prepare for examinations:

Perspective: In this feature, the authors discuss their approach to the topic, the approach used in preparing the materials, and any tips on studying for and writing examinations.

Analysis: This feature, at the beginning of each section, is designed to give a quick summary of a particular section to help you recall the subject matter and to help you determine which areas need the most extensive review.

Examples: This feature is designed to illustrate, through fact situations, the law just stated. This, we believe, should help you analytically approach a question on the examination.

We believe that the materials in this "Black Letter" will facilitate your study of a law school course and assure success in writing examinations not only for the course but for the bar examination. We wish you success.

THE PUBLISHER

Summary of Contents

APPENDICES

*

Table of Contents

Capsule Summary

■ CHAPTER 1. APPROACHES TO ENVIRONMENTAL REGULATION

A. METHODS OF ENVIRONMENTAL REGULATION

There are a number of approaches to regulation that are used in federal environmental statutes. These include:

1. Command and Control

Command and Control regulations are those that directly impose specific obligations on industrial facilities. Limitations on the amounts of pollutants a facility may emit may be a type of command and control regulation. Federal environmental policy relies heavily on this type of regulation.

Command and control regulations that set limits on the amount of allowable emissions are typically established in one of two ways.

a. Technology–Based Regulations

A technology-based regulation is generally a standard or limitation that requires as much pollution control as can be achieved with existing technology.

b. Environmental Quality–Based Regulations

An "environmental quality-based" regulation is generally a standard or limitation that is established to achieve a given level of protection to human health or the environment.

2. Market Incentives

There are a number of regulatory techniques that attempt to use market forces to control environmental pollution. Unlike command and control regulations, market incentives generally allow the operators of individual facilities, rather than the government, to make decisions about the level of pollution control they are willing to achieve. Market incentives include such devices as effluent fees, marketable pollution rights and financial subsidies.

3. Information Disclosure

Some statutes encourage environmental control by requiring publication of information about environmental conditions. The Emergency Planning and Community Right-to-Know Act ("EPCRA"), for example, requires facilities to determine annually the amount of hazardous substances they release and to provide this information to the public. Additionally, the National Environmental Policy Act ("NEPA") requires government agencies to prepare Environmental Impact Statements that describe the environmental consequences of certain proposed government actions.

B. ECONOMIC CONSIDERATIONS

The costs of both environmental pollution and environmental regulations can be considered in a variety of ways. These include: 1) cost/benefit analysis, 2) cost effectiveness analysis, 3) simple identification and consideration of costs or 4) cost obliviousness in which costs are not considered at all.

C. ETHICAL CONSIDERATIONS

In addition to economic considerations, environmental regulations may raise ethical concerns. These include such issues as the extent humans are obligated to protect other species, the obligations one generation has to another, and, increasingly, the issue of whether implementation of environmental statutes has been done in a way that discriminates against the poor or racial and ethnic minorities.

■ CHAPTER 2. CONSTITUTIONAL LIMITS, ADMINISTRATIVE DECISIONMAKING AND JUDICIAL REVIEW

A. CONSTITUTIONAL LIMITS

The federal government does not have any general "police powers" to adopt statutes or regulations to protect human health or the environment; rather, most federal environmental statutes are justified under the authority of the Commerce Clause of the U.S. Constitution. Although Congress' authority under the Commerce Clause has been construed broadly, the Supreme Court in the 1990's began to place new limits on Congress' ability to adopt statutes based on the Commerce Clause. Additionally, the Tenth Amendment places limits on Congress' ability to require states to adopt regulatory programs and the Eleventh Amendment places limits on Congress' ability to create new federal causes of action by private parties against states.

There are also constitutional limits on state authority. The Supremacy Clause provides that federal law will preempt state law and the Dormant Commerce Clause limits states' ability to discriminate against out-of-state goods.

B. ADMINISTRATIVE PROCESS

The Administrative Procedure Act ("APA") defines the procedures that most federal agencies must follow when developing regulations or issuing permits. Some federal statutes, however, contain specific procedures that must be followed when implementing those statutes.

Courts generally review agency regulations under the "arbitrary and capricious" standard. Additionally, the Supreme Court has held that courts must generally defer to agency interpretations of the statutes that they implement.

Federal administrative agencies typically implement and define the general requirements of statutes by promulgating regulations. Most regulations are issued through a "notice and comment" procedure in which the agency 1) proposes a regulation, 2) provides the public an opportunity to comment, and 3) issues a final regulation. Additionally, agencies issue large numbers of interpretations of rules and statutes and other types of policy guidance that are not subject to rulemaking procedures.

Agencies also take actions that focus on individuals, such as issuance of a permit or administrative enforcement actions. These specific actions are typically classified as "adjudications," and under the APA they may require a process similar to a judicial trial.

C. JUDICIAL REVIEW

Agency actions are generally subject to review by federal courts at some point. Most of the federal environmental statutes provide for judicial review of specific actions of the federal agency. Judicial review under these provisions is typically in a U.S. Court of Appeals.

Persons challenging an agency action in federal court must have "standing." To establish that they have standing, plaintiffs must allege, and at some point prove, that 1) they have suffered "injury in fact," 2) their injury was caused by the agency action, and 3) any relief provided by the court will redress or remedy their injury. Additionally, plaintiffs must establish that they are within the "zone of interest" protected by the statute.

■ CHAPTER 3. COMMON LAW TORTS

Environmental pollution is now largely controlled through Federal and State regulatory programs. Common law tort actions, however, still serve an important function. Through tort actions, persons who are injured by exposure to harmful substances may receive compensation for their injury. Additionally, the threat of tort liability encourages better environmental control.

A. CAUSES OF ACTION

There are several common law causes of action potentially available to persons injured by exposure to hazardous substances. These include:

1. Nuisance

A Nuisance typically involves conduct that unreasonably interferes with the use and enjoyment of land.

2. Trespass

A trespass typically involves a physical invasion of another's land.

3. Negligence

Negligence typically involves conduct that falls below some standard of care owed to another.

4. Strict Liability

Strict liability involves a finding of liability without regard to the negligence of the defendant. Strict liability may be found where the defendant's conduct involved "abnormally dangerous" or "ultrahazardous" activity. In Products Liability cases, strict liability may be found if the defendant failed to provide adequate warnings of possible harmful effects.

B. CAUSATION

In all tort cases the plaintiff must prove that the defendant's conduct was the cause in fact of his or her injury. It can be difficult for a plaintiff to prove that exposure to a toxic substance "caused" a disease such as cancer. This arises in part from the lack of scientific knowledge about the causes of cancer. It also arises in part from the fact that cancer may not develop for twenty or more years after exposure to the toxic substance.

C. REMEDIES

1. Availability of Injunctive Relief

Issuance of an injunction is an equitable remedy, and courts may consider a variety of factors, including the adequacy of monetary damages, in deciding whether to issue an injunction. In many jurisdictions, courts will issue injunctive relief to force a facility to stop polluting if the plaintiff can establish that the defendant is committing a continuing tort. In cases such as *Boomer v. Atlantic Cement Co.*, courts have balanced the harm to the plaintiff with the utility of the defendant's conduct in determining whether to issue an injunction.

2. Developing Damage Theories

In many cases it will be difficult for a plaintiff exposed to a cancer causing substance to prove that he or she has suffered injury. Some courts have allowed persons exposed to carcinogens to recover based on theories of 1) cancerphobia, 2) increased cancer risk, and 3) need for medical monitoring.

■ CHAPTER 4. NATIONAL ENVIRONMENTAL POLICY ACT

The National Environmental Policy Act ("NEPA") contains a requirement, in section 102(2)(C), that federal agencies prepare Environmental Impact Statements

("EISs") on "major federal actions that significantly affect the quality of the human environment." NEPA also established the Council on Environmental Quality ("CEQ"). The CEQ has issued regulations defining the requirements for preparation of an EIS.

A. EIS PROCESS

When implementing the EIS requirement, federal agencies typically go through the following steps. They must 1) determine if the action is subject to a statutory or other exemption, 2) prepare an "environmental assessment" ("EA") to determine if the action requires preparation of an EIS, 3) issue a "Finding of No Significant Impact" ("FONSI") if the agency determines that no EIS is necessary, or 4) publish a notice of intent to prepare an EIS and begin to define the scope of the EIS if an EIS is necessary, 5) publish a draft EIS, 6) allow public comment on the draft, and 7) issue a final EIS. The final EIS may be subject to judicial review in federal district court.

B. THRESHOLD ISSUES

In determining whether an EIS is necessary, an agency must determine if the proposed action is:

1. Federal

EIS's are only necessary for federal actions. Private parties are subject to an EIS only if there is some federal involvement.

2. Action

An EIS is only necessary for proposals for action. Preliminary plans of agencies may not yet constitute proposals for action.

3. Major/Significant

The proposal must have a major impact on the environment.

4. Human Environment

The environmental effects must generally involve impacts on the physical environment. Adverse social or economic impacts from a proposed action alone generally will not require preparation of an EIS.

C. SCOPE OF THE EIS

The EIS must address the environmental effects of the proposed action. Issues may arise when an agency attempts to carve a large project into smaller segments and limit the scope of the EIS to each segment. An agency may be prevented from such "segmentation" under some circumstances. In some cases, agencies prepare one general "programmatic" EIS on the overall project and then do specific EIS's on each smaller part. This is known as "tiering."

D. CONTENT OF THE EIS

An EIS must generally contain a description of the proposed action and a discussion of reasonable alternatives. The EIS will also contain an analysis of the environmental effects of the proposed action and, to some extent, the alternatives to the proposed action. The scope of alternatives and effects that must be analyzed is governed by a "rule of reason."

E. SUBSTANTIVE EFFECT OF NEPA

The Supreme Court has described NEPA as "essentially procedural." Although NEPA requires preparation of an EIS, it does not mandate that agencies take any particular action. In other words, an agency's decision to take an action will not be invalidated as a violation of NEPA.

F. JUDICIAL REVIEW

NEPA contains no specific authorization for judicial review. Federal district courts, however, routinely review the adequacy of EIS's under general "federal question" jurisdiction.

G. STATE ENVIRONMENTAL POLICY ACTS

Many states have adopted their own statutes modeled after NEPA. These state environmental policy acts may vary in significant ways from NEPA both in the scope and substantive effect of required EISs.

■ CHAPTER 5. CLEAN WATER ACT

The Clean Water Act ("CWA", also known as the Federal Water Pollution Control Act or "FWPCA") has several distinct programs for the control of water pollution. First, it requires that all "point sources" (sources that directly discharge pollutants into navigable waters) have federal permits (the National Pollutant Discharge Elimination System or "NPDES" program). Second, the CWA imposes requirements on sources that discharge pollutants into municipal sewers (the "pretreatment" program). Third, it contains limited provisions dealing with "non-point sources" of pollution such as agricultural runoff or runoff from city streets. Fourth, it contains an important permit program for persons who dredge and fill navigable waters, including wetlands (the section 404 "Dredge and Fill Permit" program). Finally, it has specific provisions dealing with oil spills to navigable waters.

A. NATIONAL POLLUTANT DISCHARGE ELIMINATION SYSTEM

Every "point source" of pollutants, such as a pipe or ditch, that directly discharges into navigable water must have a National Pollutant Discharge Elimination System ("NPDES") permit. An NPDES permit typically contains limitations on the quantity or concentration of pollutants that the source may discharge. These are known as "effluent limitations." In virtually all cases, effluent limitations are either technology-based limits or water quality standards-based limits. Additionally, the permit will contain requirements that the source test its discharge and report the results to the government. The NPDES permit is issued either by the EPA or by a state if the state has been delegated authority to issue permits.

B. TECHNOLOGY–BASED LIMITS

All point sources must meet technology-based limits. These limits are usually national limitations, promulgated by EPA, that are established for specific industrial categories. They are based on EPA's assessment of the cost and availability of pollution control technology. If EPA has not promulgated national limits, permit writers may develop limits on a case-by-case basis.

The Clean Water Act establishes different types of technology-based limits.

1. BPT

Best Practicable Technology ("BPT") limits were to have been met by all existing industrial sources by 1977. BPT applies to all pollutants.

2. BCT

Best Conventional Technology ("BCT") limits were to have been met by all existing industrial sources by 1989. BCT limits apply only to a limited group of "conventional" pollutants. BCT limits may fall somewhere between BPT and BAT in stringency.

3. BAT

Best Available Technology ("BAT") limits were to be met by existing industrial sources by 1989. BAT applies to a designated group of "toxic pollutants" and to all "non-toxic, non-conventional" pollutants. Most variances are not available from BAT that is set for toxic pollutants. They are the most stringent technology-based limits that apply to existing sources.

4. NSPS

New Source Performance Standards ("NSPS") must be met by new sources and they apply to all pollutants. New sources generally are sources that are constructed after promulgation of NSPS by EPA.

5. Secondary Treatment

Municipal sewage treatment plants (called Publicly Owned Treatment Works or "POTWs") are subject to a minimum technology-based limit called secondary treatment.

6. Variances from Technology–Based Limits

There are several variances from technology-based limits for existing sources. These include, among several others, 1) the "fundamentally different factors" ("FDF") variance, 2) the "cost" variance in section 301(c), 3) a water quality variance in section 301(g), and 4) a "thermal" variance in section 316.

Additionally, persons who violated technology-based limits in their NPDES permit may, in some cases, assert an "upset" defense if they can show that the violation of their permit occurred for reasons beyond their reasonable control.

C. WATER QUALITY STANDARDS–BASED LIMITS

States are required to establish "Water Quality Standards" for all bodies of water within the state. Water quality standards include 1) a designated use, 2) criteria and 3) an antidegradation requirement. NPDES permits must contain limits that are stringent enough to ensure that the water quality standards are not violated. Developing water quality standards and translating them into specific effluent limits involves a number of complex steps.

D. PRETREATMENT PROGRAM

Sources that discharge their wastes into sewers connected to municipal sewage treatment plants (called Publicly Owned Treatment Works or "POTWs") are subject to the pretreatment program in section 307(b). Under the pretreatment program, these "indirect dischargers" must meet 1) applicable technology-based "categorical" pretreatment limits and 2) a "general prohibition" that prohibits discharges that cause a POTW to violate its NPDES permit or that cause the sewage sludge generated at the POTW to violate EPA sewage sludge standards. Indirect dischargers are not required to have an NPDES permit.

E. JUDICIAL REVIEW

Under section 509(b), citizens may seek judicial review of certain enumerated actions of EPA. Judicial review is in a federal court of appeal, and review must be sought within 120 days of the EPA action. Under section 505, citizens may bring action against EPA in federal district court when EPA has failed to perform a "non-discretionary" duty under the CWA.

■ CHAPTER 6. CLEAN AIR ACT

The Clean Air Act is composed of a number of different programs. Each of these programs may be a separate source for limitations on the emission of air pollutants.

A. LIMITS ON AUTOMOBILE EMISSIONS

EPA sets limits on the amount of certain pollutants that may be emitted by automobiles, trucks and other "mobile sources." California is the only state allowed to establish more stringent limits, but other states may require that mobile sources meet these more stringent California standards.

B. NEW SOURCE PERFORMANCE STANDARDS

Under section 111 of the CAA, the EPA promulgates limitations on the amount of air pollutants that may be emitted by new or modified stationary sources of pollutants. These "New Source Performance Standards" ("NSPS") are technology-based standards that must be met by every new source within a given industry. Establishment of NSPS under the CAA is similar to the establishment of technology-based limits in the Clean Water Act.

1. Newly Constructed Facilities

Newly constructed stationary sources are subject to NSPS if the source is constructed after EPA has proposed an NSPS for the industry.

2. Modified Existing Facilities and the Bubble Rule

Modified stationary sources are subject to NSPS if the modification results in the emission of any new pollutant or the increased emission of any existing pollutant.

Section 111 defines a "stationary source" as any "building, structure, or facility" that may emit pollutants. The NSPS might classify individual pieces of equipment within the facility as a source. In that case, any change in equipment could subject the facility to NSPS requirements. Alternatively, NSPS might treat the entire facility, rather than each piece of equipment, as the source. This is known as a "bubble" rule because the entire facility is treated as if it were under a giant bubble with only one smokestack. If EPA uses a "bubble" rule, a modified source may avoid being subject to NSPS if the facility, although increasing its emissions in one part of the facility, decreases them in another such that there is no net increase in pollutants. This is known as "netting out."

In setting NSPS, EPA generally uses a dual definition of "stationary source" which classifies both the entire facility and individual equipment as a source.

C. NATIONAL AMBIENT AIR QUALITY STANDARDS

EPA must publish "criteria documents" for pollutants that satisfy certain conditions specified in section 108(a). Under section 109, EPA must establish National Ambient Air Quality Standards ("NAAQS") for every pollutant that has been designated a "criteria" pollutant.

EPA has promulgated National Ambient Air Quality Standards for six air pollutants: ozone, particulates, sulfur oxides, carbon monoxide, nitrogen oxides and lead. EPA has not added a new pollutant to this list since 1978.

There are two types of NAAQS specified in section 109 of the CAA. Primary NAAQS are set at a level which, allowing an adequate margin of safety, are requisite to protect human health and the environment. Secondary NAAQS are set at a level that is requisite to protect public welfare. Both primary and secondary NAAQS specify the maximum concentrations of these pollutants that can be present in the air.

Promulgation of a primary NAAQS triggers the states' obligation to prepare a State Implementation Plan ("SIP").

D. State Implementation Plans

States are required to develop State Implementation Plans. SIPs contain a variety of provisions. Among these are sufficient limits on the emission of pollutants that ensure that the air quality does not violate NAAQS.

SIPs must be submitted to EPA for review and approval. If a state SIP does not meet the requirements of the CAA, EPA can reject the SIP and publish its own Federal Implementation Plan ("FIP"). Additionally, EPA has several sanctions available that it can impose on states that fail to submit an approvable SIP.

When EPA approves a SIP, it promulgates the SIP as a federal regulation. Once approved, a SIP remains federally enforceable unless both the State and EPA approve a change.

E. Non-attainment Areas

1. General Requirements

Special programs exist for those areas of the country where the air quality has not attained NAAQS. In these "non-attainment areas," the CAA requires that states adopt a number of special requirements. These include the requirement that existing stationary sources of pollution meet a limitation known as "Reasonably Available Control Technology" ("RACT").

Additionally, there are certain special restrictions on the construction of new or modified "major stationary sources" of air pollution. New or modified major stationary sources are required to have a permit. EPA uses a "bubble" rule in the non-attainment program, and modified sources can avoid the permit requirement if they "net out."

In order to obtain a permit, the source must meet several conditions. The two most significant conditions are:

a. Offsets

The source must "offset" its new emissions by a greater reduction of existing emissions. This results in a net reduction of pollutants in the region.

b. LAER

The source must meet an emission limitation known as "Lowest Achievable Emission Rate" ("LAER").

2. **Ozone Non-attainment Requirements**

In the 1990 amendments to the CAA, Congress established new requirements for areas that were non-attainment for ozone. Among other things, the CAA now classifies ozone non-attainment areas as either marginal, moderate, serious, severe, or extreme. Each of these classifications has its own date by which the NAAQS for ozone must be attained, and there are progressively more stringent requirements that apply in each of these classifications.

F. **Prevention of Significant Deterioration**

In areas of the country where the air quality is better than the NAAQS, the CAA establishes special programs to ensure that this air quality is maintained. This is known as the "Prevention of Significant Deterioration" ("PSD") program. The existing air quality for certain pollutants in PSD areas may be degraded by only a certain amount. Additionally, new or modified "major emitting facilities" are required to obtain a permit, and these facilities are subject to emission limitations known as "Best Available Control Technology" ("BACT"). EPA uses a "bubble" rule in the PSD program.

G. **Hazardous Air Pollutants**

Under section 112, EPA must promulgate national limitations on the emission of "Hazardous Air Pollutants" ("HAPs") applicable to a large number of new and existing sources. EPA must first promulgate technology-based limits on hazardous air pollutants for specific groups of industrial sources. These limits are based on "Maximum Achievable Control Technology" ("MACT"). These limitations must be met regardless of where the source is located. EPA is required to determine whether additional, more stringent limitations are necessary to address any "residual risk" to human health.

H. **Acid Rain and Sulfur Trading Allowances**

In 1990, Congress established a program to control acid rain. Under this program, the total amount of sulfur that may be emitted by certain sources is subject to a federal limitation. "Allowances" equal to the total allowable emissions are to be allocated among these sources. Each allowance is the right to emit one ton of sulfur each year, and these allowances will be freely saleable among sources.

I. **Permits**

The CAA contains a requirement that states issue permits to most sources of air pollutants. This permit should contain all of the different limitations applicable to the source.

J.   Other Programs

The CAA also contains a number of specific programs relating to the control of interstate and international pollution, and depletion of stratospheric ozone by chlorofluorocarbons.

■ CHAPTER 7. RESOURCE CONSERVATION AND RECOVERY ACT

The Resource Conservation and Recovery Act is the primary federal statute regulating the management of hazardous waste. Subtitle C of RCRA contains most of the statutory provisions relating to hazardous waste. Subtitle D contains some limited regulation of non-hazardous, solid waste.

A.   THE HAZARDOUS WASTE REGULATORY SYSTEM

Subtitle C, the hazardous waste provisions of RCRA, contains separate requirements applicable to generators, transporters and "treatment, storage, and disposal facilities" ("TSDFs"). Subtitle C has two major mechanisms for ensuring the proper disposal of hazardous waste.

1.   Manifest

A manifest must accompany all shipments of hazardous waste. The manifest is prepared and signed by the generator, and then signed by the transporter and disposal site. If the generator does not receive a signed copy of the manifest from the disposal site within 45 days, the generator must notify EPA. This is intended to ensure that the transporter does not illegally dispose of the waste.

2.   TSDF Permits

All facilities that "treat, store or dispose" of hazardous waste must have a RCRA permit. Facilities must meet certain stringent conditions before they may receive a permit. In most cases, hazardous waste may only be legally disposed of in a permitted TSDF.

B.   DEFINITION OF HAZARDOUS WASTE

Only hazardous wastes are subject to the Subtitle C regulatory program. To determine if a material is a hazardous waste, a generator must 1) determine if it is a solid waste, and 2) determine if the solid waste meets the regulatory definition of hazardous waste.

1. **Definition of Solid Waste**

    Under EPA regulations, a material is a solid waste if it is 1) abandoned, 2) recycled, 3) classified by EPA as inherently waste-like, or 4) a defined "military munition." EPA has promulgated a complex regulation that defines which materials are wastes when recycled.

2. **Definition of Hazardous Waste**

    A material that meets the definition of solid waste is classified as a hazardous waste if 1) it is a "listed" waste or 2) it is a characteristic waste. A listed hazardous waste is a waste that is on one of three specific lists of hazardous wastes promulgated by EPA. A characteristic hazardous waste is a waste that exhibits any one of four characteristics—dignitability, reactivity, corrosivity, or toxicity.

3. **Mixture, Derived–From and Contained–In Rules**

    EPA has also published rules that determine whether mixtures of hazardous and non-hazardous waste are classified as hazardous (the mixture rule), whether residues from the treatment of hazardous waste are classified as hazardous (the derived-from rule) and whether groundwater and soil contaminated with hazardous waste are classified as hazardous (the contained-in interpretation).

C. GENERATOR REQUIREMENTS

Generators of hazardous waste do not need to obtain a permit, but, among other things, they must 1) determine whether they have generated hazardous waste, 2) obtain an EPA I.D. number, 3) properly prepare and transport hazardous wastes for off-site disposal or treatment using a manifest, and 4) store hazardous wastes on site for no more than 90 days in most cases. Facilities that generate less than 100 kilograms of hazardous waste per month are called "conditionally exempt small quantity generators" and are largely exempt from Subtitle C requirements.

D. TRANSPORTER REQUIREMENTS

Transporters of hazardous waste do not need to obtain a permit, but, among other things, they must 1) obtain an EPA I.D. number, 2) only transport properly packaged and labeled hazardous waste that has a manifest, 3) and deliver the hazardous waste only to a permitted TSDF identified on the manifest.

E. TREATMENT, STORAGE AND DISPOSAL FACILITIES

Facilities that treat, store or dispose of hazardous waste must obtain a RCRA permit. The permits are issued either by EPA or states with approved permit programs.

To obtain a permit, a TSDF must meet certain conditions including 1) minimum technical standards (such as liners for landfills or proper equipment for incinerators), 2) groundwater monitoring requirements for landfills, 3) financial responsibility requirements, and 4) plans to close and maintain the site after closure. Facilities that are subject to permit requirements can also be required to undertake "corrective action" to cleanup areas on-site containing hazardous waste or constituents.

F. LAND BAN

RCRA prohibits the land disposal of hazardous waste unless 1) the government has determined that there will be "no migration" of hazardous wastes from the land disposal facility or 2) the hazardous waste has been treated to meet technology-based cleanup levels (called "BDAT").

G. REGULATION OF NON–HAZARDOUS SOLID WASTES

Subtitle D contains limited regulation of non-hazardous solid waste. Solid wastes can only be disposed of in "sanitary landfills" and EPA has promulgated criteria defining what constitutes a sanitary landfill. These criteria are particularly stringent for municipal solid waste landfills. The disposal of non-hazardous waste in sites other than sanitary landfills is known as "open dumping."

■ CHAPTER 8. COMPREHENSIVE ENVIRONMENTAL RESPONSE, COMPENSATION AND LIABILITY ACT

The Comprehensive Environmental Response, Compensation and Liability Act ("CERCLA" or "Superfund") has provisions designed to ensure the cleanup of releases of hazardous substances. It is retroactive in the sense that it applies to hazardous substances that were disposed of prior to its adoption in 1980.

A. APPLICABILITY TO HAZARDOUS SUBSTANCES

Most of the provisions of CERCLA apply to "hazardous substances." The statute defines hazardous substances by reference to other environmental statutes. Hazardous substances include, for example, substances that have been designated as toxic pollutants under the Clean Water Act, hazardous wastes under the Resource Conservation and Recovery Act and hazardous air pollutants under the Clean Air Act. It is important to note that a material may be a hazardous substance even if it is not a hazardous waste under the Resource Conservation and Recovery Act. CERCLA does exclude petroleum, including crude oil and gasoline, from the definition of hazardous substances.

B. NOTIFICATION OF RELEASE OF HAZARDOUS SUBSTANCES

CERCLA requires that the person in charge of a facility notify the government if the person has "knowledge" of a release of a "reportable quantity" of a hazardous substance.

C. OPTIONS FOR PROMOTING THE CLEAN UP OF HAZARDOUS SUBSTANCES

The government has two basic options to cleanup releases (or threats of release) of hazardous substances. First, EPA may cleanup the hazardous substances using money from the Hazardous Substances Trust Fund (known as Superfund). EPA may then sue a defined group of "potentially responsible parties" ("PRPs") under section 107(a)(4)(A) to recover its expenses. Second, EPA can issue an order to persons, generally PRPs, compelling them to cleanup the hazardous substances. Persons who receive a cleanup order may not obtain "pre-enforcement review."

Private parties who incur costs for the cleanup hazardous substances can sue PRPs to recover an equitable portion of their "response costs.". Private parties, including PRPs, who voluntarily cleanup property can bring a private party cost recovery action under section 107(a)(4)(B). PRPs who have been sued under § 107 or who have entered into approved settlements with the government can sue for contribution under section 113(f). Under CERCLA, private parties cannot get a court order to compel someone else to cleanup hazardous substances.

D. LIABILITY PROVISIONS

"Potentially Responsible Parties" are liable to the government or private parties for costs of cleaning up a facility if there was a release (or threat of release) of hazardous substances from a facility.

The group of PRPs is defined in section 107(a) and includes 1) the current owner or operator of a facility, 2) the persons who owned or operated the facility at the time of disposal of hazardous substances, 3) the persons who "arranged for disposal" of hazardous substances at the facility, and 4) persons who transported the hazardous substances to the facility if they selected the site.

Under CERCLA, PRPs are strictly liable for cleanup costs. This means that they are liable even if they were not negligent or if they legally disposed of hazardous substances. PRPs are also "jointly and severally" liable. This means that they are generally liable for 100% of the cost of cleanup regardless of their share of hazardous substances at the site.

In private cost recovery or contribution actions and in settlement with the government, PRPs may be able to allocate the cleanup costs. Typically, allocation is based on the percentage of hazardous substances that the PRP contributed to the site.

E. DEFENSES TO LIABILITY

There are several statutory defenses to liability under CERCLA. Section 107(b) provides a defense to liability if the release was caused by an 1) act of God, 2) act of war, or 3) acts of third parties. To assert a third party defense, the PRP must prove that the release was caused by a third party, that the PRP did not have a direct or indirect contractual relationship with the third party, and the PRP took steps to prevent foreseeable acts of third parties.

The "innocent landowner" defense arises from the definition of "contractual relationship." Landowners can assert the defense if they purchased property without knowledge of the existence of hazardous substances and if they undertook "all appropriate inquiry" at the time they purchased the property.

Congress has also established protection from liability for "bona fide prospective purchasers." Parties purchasing land after January 2002 who, among other things, undertake "all appropriate inquiry" before they buy the property may not be liable under CERCLA even if they buy with knowledge of the existence of hazardous substances.

EPA has promulgated regulations defining what actions constitute "all appropriate inquiry." These include visual inspections, interviews with landowners and checks of government records. This type of review is sometimes referred to a "Phase I environmental audit."

Parties cannot, by contract, avoid CERCLA liability. They can, however, enter contracts in which a person waives claims under CERCLA or agrees to indemnify personss if they incur CERCLA liability. Such contracts are common in sales of property.

F. ELEMENTS OF A COST RECOVERY CLAIM

In order for the government or a private party to recover their costs under section 107(a)(4), they must prove that 1) there was a release or threat of release of a hazardous substance from a facility, 2) the defendant is a PRP, 3) the plaintiff has incurred some costs prior to bringing the action, and 4) the costs were incurred in a manner that is consistent with the "National Contingency Plan."

G. EXTENT OF CLEANUP—HOW CLEAN IS CLEAN

CERCLA contains some provisions defining how clean a site must be made when hazardous substances are removed. Additionally, EPA has promulgated the "National Contingency Plan" ("NCP") which contains substantive and procedural requirements for cleaning up hazardous substances under CERCLA. EPA has published the "National Priorities List" ("NPL") that contains the list of the worst sites in the country. EPA has regulations that limit its ability to undertake long-term cleanups at a site that is not on the NPL.

In general, CERCLA cleanups must meet "Applicable or Relevant and Appropriate Requirements" ("ARARs"). ARARs are standards found in other environmental statutes. Additionally, cleanups standards may be based on risk assessments and, in some cases, state law.

The NCP contains procedural requirements, including public participation requirements, that apply when determining a proper level of cleanup.

H. SETTLEMENT OF CERCLA CLAIMS

The government frequently enters into settlement agreements with PRPs in which the PRPs agree to undertake the cleanup and the government agrees to 1) require a PRP to pay for only its allocated share of the cleanup, 2) give some release to the PRPs for liability for future costs and 3) give protection from contribution claims by non-settling PRPs. Most government settlement agreements must be approved by a court.

■ CHAPTER 9. ENFORCEMENT

A. Government Enforcement

The Clean Air Act, Clean Water Act and the Resource Conservation and Recovery Act all authorize the federal government to issue compliance orders, impose administrative penalties for violations without going to court, seek civil penalties in federal district court, or seek criminal penalties, in most cases, for "knowing" violations of the statute.

B. Citizen Suits

The CAA, CWA and RCRA all provide for citizen suits in which a private party can sue another private party for violation of the requirements of the statute. Available remedies include injunctive relief and civil penalties paid to the federal government, but not damages for personal injury or property loss.

Plaintiffs must satisfy constitutional requirements with regard to standing, but there are also several statutory prerequisites to bringing a citizen suit:

a. Notice and Delay

Plaintiffs must give notice of their intent to file the citizen suit to the violator, state and EPA at least 60 days before filing suit.

b. Diligent Prosecution

The citizen suit cannot be brought if the government has commenced and is diligently prosecuting an enforcement action prior to filing the citizen suit.

c. Wholly Past Violations

In most cases, a citizen suit can only be brought if the defendant is "in violation" at the time of filing and the violation is not "wholly past."

■ CHAPTER 10. REGULATION OF TOXIC SUBSTANCES

Federal environmental regulation increasingly focuses on toxic substances, particularly carcinogens. There are a number of general problems that arise when regulating such substances.

A. UNCERTAINTY

In most cases, there is little scientific information about the effects of exposure to low levels of toxic substances. Regulators usually must make decisions even thought there is uncertainty about the health effects of the substances.

B. DEFINING SAFETY

Regulators generally assume that there is no safe level of exposure to carcinogens. This means that any exposure will increase a person's risk of getting cancer. In such a case, there is no safe level of exposure. Some statutes, however, require an agency to determine whether exposure to a toxic substance is unsafe, and this may require a regulator to make a value judgment as to what level of increased risk is acceptable or significant. Other statutes require regulation of "unreasonable risk." Determining whether a risk is unreasonable typically involves a balancing of the costs of regulation against the risk from the substance.

C. RISK ASSESSMENT METHODOLOGY

Agencies may attempt to quantify the risks of exposure to toxic substances through a "risk assessment." Risk assessment methodology typically includes 1) Hazard Identification, 2) Dose—Response Assessment, 3) Exposure Assessment, 4) Risk Characterization.

D. TREATMENT OF TOXIC SUBSTANCES UNDER FEDERAL STATUTES

Numerous federal environmental statutes give special treatment to toxic substances. Section 112 of the Clean Air Act has special provisions for "hazardous air pollutants." Various provisions of the Clean Water Act give special treatment to "toxic pollutants."

The Federal Insecticide, Fungicide and Rodenticide Act ("FIFRA") provides for the registration and cancellation of pesticides. It contains complex provisions that, among other things, require EPA to determine if a pesticide will have "unreasonable adverse effects" on the environment.

The Toxic Substances Control Act ("TSCA") gives EPA broad authority to regulate toxic substances. TSCA gives EPA authority to require manufacturers of chemicals to test the effects of the chemicals and provide information to EPA. TSCA also gives EPA authority to impose regulations on the use of chemicals. This broad authority has not been widely used.

■ CHAPTER 11. REGULATION OF NATURAL RESOURCES, REGULATION OF LAND USE AND REGULATORY TAKINGS

There are a large number of federal and state laws and common law doctrines that affect the development and preservation of natural resources. The primary constitutional limit on the imposition of government land use restrictions is the "takings" clause of the Fifth Amendment of the U.S. Constitution.

A. Regulation of Wetlands under Section 404 of the Clean Water Act

Section 404 of the Clean Water Act prohibits the discharge of dredge or fill material into wetlands without a permit. The definition of "wetlands" is broad and focuses on the capacity of the land to support types of wildlife that live in saturated soils. There have been a number of Supreme Court cases dealing with the scope of waters that may be regulated as "wetlands." Section 404 permits are issued by the Army Corps of Engineers, and to obtain a permit persons must consider alternatives that have less impact on wetlands and may have to mitigate the impact of their activities on wetlands.

B. Endangered Species Act

The Endangered Species Act ("ESA") protects endangered and threatened plant and animal species.

1. Listing of Endangered and Threatened Species and Designation of Critical Habitat

Under section 4 of the ESA, the Secretaries of the Interior and Commerce are responsible for designating species as either "endangered" or "threatened" and for designating "critical habitat" for endangered species.

2. Limitations on Actions by the Federal Government

Under section 7 of the ESA, the federal government is prohibited from taking any action that is likely to "jeopardize" the continued existence of an endangered species or result in destruction of designated "critical habitat." Section 7 requires federal agencies to consult with the Department of Interior before taking actions that might jeopardize endangered species. Section 7(b)(4) allows federal agencies to "take" individual endangered species if the taking is "incidental," the agency mitigates impacts, and the action is unlikely to jeopardize the continued existence of the species.

3. Limitations on Actions by Private Parties

Under section 9, private parties cannot by their actions "take" an endangered species. A "take," as defined under the ESA, includes not only intentional killing of a member of an endangered species, but it also may include "significant habitat modification" that results in the actual death of an endangered species.

Section 10 authorizes the Department of the Interior to authorize "incidental" takes by private parties under certain restrictions. Authorization is implemented through the issuance of "habitat conservation plans." Although section 7 only applies to the federal government, it may indirectly apply to private parties if their actions require federal authorization.

C. Public Trust Doctrine

The public trust doctrine may provide federal and state governments authority to regulate certain lands, primarily water bodies, submerged lands and tidal land adjacent to water. These lands may be subject to a public trust held by the federal and state government.

D. Federal Land Policy

There are a large number of statutes that affect the use of lands owned by the federal government. Development on some lands, such as national parks, is prohibited; other federal lands are subject to "multiple use."

E. Takings

The Fifth Amendment prohibits the government from taking private property for pubic use without just compensation. The Supreme Court has held that regulations affecting private land may be prohibited as a "regulatory taking" under the Fifth Amendment. The Supreme Court has not been able to develop a clear test to distinguish a proper regulation from an improper taking.

1. Per Se Tests

The Supreme Court has held that regulations that result in a "physical invasion" of private property or that result in a "total deprivation" of all value of the property are per se takings.

2. Ad Hoc Balancing Tests

Most regulations are judged through an ad hoc, case-by-case balancing test that considers such factors as the magnitude of the loss, the extent to which the regulation affects "distinct investment backed expectations," the extent to which the regulation prevents a public harm, or the reciprocity of benefits and burdens imposed by the regulation.

■ CHAPTER 12. INTERNATIONAL ENVIRONMENTAL LAW

The field of environmental law is increasingly focusing on global environmental problems. Two important international conferences, the Stockholm Conference in 1972 and the Rio Conference in 1992, produced important "declarations" of global environmental principles.

A. Sources of International Law

There are several recognized sources of international law including:

1. Treaties. Treaties can specifiy obligations between treaty members. Treaty obligations arise only through the consent of the parties.

2. Custom. "Customary International Law" can establish binding norms of conduct on nations. Customary internal law is established by examination of whether certain obligations are generally followed by nations and whether countries recognize their legal obligation to comply with these obligations.

3. General Principles. "General Principles of Law" consist of legal doctrines that are widely recognized as binding on nations. This may consist of procedural obligations, such as res judicata, or substantive obligations arising from "natural law."

4. Judicial Decisions and Writings of Highly Qualified Publicists. Judicial decisions and writings of academics are recognized as sources for determining international obligations.

B. International Environmental Institutions

There are a number of important institutions that have a role in shaping international environmental law. These include international tribunals (such as the International Court of Justice), international organizations (such as the United Nations Environment Programme, trade organizations (such as the World Trade Organization), financial institutions (such as the World Bank) and non-governmental organizations ("NGOs").

C. Issues in International Environmental Law

The field of international environmental law includes a wide range of issues. Transboundary pollution, pollution from one country that adversely affects another, may be addressed through treaty or customary international law. Ozone depletion, the reduction in the amount of ozone in the upper atmosphere, is the subject of an international agreement, the Montreal Protocols.

Global warming refers to the potential increase in the average temperature of Earth from the release of "greenhouse" gases as a result of human development. Global warming is addressed in the UN Framework Convention on Climate Change (UNFCCC). The Kyoto Protocols were adopted under the UNFCCC and impose specific obligations to reduce emissions on greenhouse gases by certain industrial countries that have ratified the Protocol. Although the U.S. ratified the UNFCCC, it did not ratify the Kyoto Protocol.

D. International Trade and the Environment

There is a potential tension between international agreements to encourage free trade and environmental concerns about the effect of development. Under the General Agreement on Tariffs and Trade/World Trade Organization Agreement ("GATT/WTO"), nations are generally prohibited from imposing discriminatory barriers to the importation of foreign products. Although there are certain exceptions that allow countries to impose restrictions relating to protection of human health and the environment or preservation of natural resources, these exceptions have generally been narrowly construed by the trade organization, currently the World Trade Organization, that implements the GATT/WTO. For example, U.S. efforts to restrict the import of tuna caught in ways that injure dolphins were found to violate U.S. obligations under GATT/WTO.

*

Perspective

A. INTRODUCTION TO ENVIRONMENTAL LAW

There are two things you need to know about the study of environmental law. First, it is extremely complicated. Environmental law, like tax, involves detailed analysis of the language of statutes and regulations. It also frequently involves discussions of complex issues of biology, geology and engineering. Second, environmental law, unlike tax, is (or should be) fun. Among other things, the study of environmental law requires you to think about important economic and ethical issues. Although most of the time the study of environmental laws focuses on the trees (or little tiny pieces of bark) rather than the forest, environmental law should challenge your views about proper national and international environmental policy.

B. ORGANIZATION OF ENVIRONMENTAL LAW COURSES

The survey course in Environmental Law is in a state of flux. The number and complexity of federal environmental statutes and regulations have grown, and there is on-going debate among teachers of environmental law over the appropriate coverage in a survey environmental law course. Some attempt to address a specific statute in detail and others try to address broad organizing principles. Everyone agrees that issues of administrative law and statutory interpretation are important parts of environmental law, but there is disagreement over the extent to which these should be addressed in an environmental law course. Most of us end up trying to do everything.

There is also a growing number of casebooks in environmental law. Virtually all of these books present materials on the basic federal statutes, but there are differences in emphasis on such areas as regulatory policy, environmental land use issues, regulation of toxic substances and international law.

At a minimum, your course will likely include discussion of the Clean Air Act ("CAA"), Clean Water Act ("CWA"), Resource Conservation and Recovery Act ("RCRA") and the Comprehensive Environmental Response Compensation and Liability Act ("CERCLA"). Additionally, your course will require you actually to read statutes and regulations, and deal with problems of administrative implementation of complex and vague statutes. You will also be required to learn something of the specialized language (the strange acronyms) that is a part of environmental law.

Beyond that your survey or specialized environmental law course might emphasize any of a wide range of issues.

C. ORGANIZATION OF THIS BOOK

This book is organized to reflect the approach adopted in the majority of environmental law survey casebooks. It is largely statute specific with a separate chapter on each of the major federal environmental statutes. If your course is organized differently, you will still find the material you need. To aid you, this book has an index to statutes and a table correlating the sections of this book with the page coverage in the major environmental law casebooks.

This book is intended to help you understand the issues raised in your environmental law course. It will also help you quickly identify the relevant statutory provisions dealing with those issues. It is obviously not a substitute for reading the statutes, regulations and other materials provided by your professor.

D. HINTS ON SURVIVING ENVIRONMENTAL LAW

Here are a few pointers that might assist you in your study of environmental law.

1. Statutes

Although the common law is an important part of environmental law, the main focus of most environmental law courses is on federal environmental statutes. This involves an analysis of the language of the relevant statute. There is *absolutely no alternative* to reading the appropriate statutory provisions as you review issues for class. In this book, relevant statutory citations are included in bold faced type. Read them.

a. Why Are There Two Different Numbers Referring to the Same Section of a Statute?

As part of your training as lawyers, you have become familiar with the U.S. Code. The U.S. Code is a compilation of statutes adopted by Congress which have been organized and given section numbers. For example, the citation to the section of the Clean Water Act that requires certain polluters to have permits is 33 U.S.C. § 1311.

Most environmental law practitioners, however, do not refer to the Code sections. Rather, they refer to the original section numbers included in the statute before it was codified. 33 U.S.C. § 1311, for example, was originally section 301 of the statute. The Environmental Protection Agency and most courts and lawyers routinely refer to section 301 of the Clean Water Act rather than 33 U.S.C. § 1311.

You need to be familiar with both methods of referring to statutory provisions. It is part of the language of environmental law. The *West Selected Environmental Law Statutes* provides both citations.

b. What Are the Proper Names of Statutes?

It can also be difficult to know the appropriate name of a statute. The Resource Conservation and Recovery Act ("RCRA") was adopted in 1976 as an amendment to the Solid Waste Disposal Act. You will sometimes, but rarely, see the statute called the Solid Waste Disposal Act. It is uniformly referred to as RCRA.

Sometimes, significant amendments to statutes keep their own name. For example, RCRA was amended by the Hazardous and Solid Waste Amendments of 1986 ("HSWA"). RCRA still is the name of the statute, but practitioners refer to the HSWA amendments.

The various chapters of this book contain a description of the names used to describe statutes.

2. Regulations

Much of environmental law involves an analysis of regulations promulgated by federal agencies such as the Environmental Protection Agency. Just like statutes, study of regulations requires close attention to the specific language of the regulations. Many questions raised by ambiguous statutory language are answered by referring to the implementing regulations.

a. What Are Regulations?

Many statutes give an administrative agency the authority to adopt regulations that implement and explain statutory provisions. Regulations can have the force of law, and a person can be prosecuted for violating provisions of a regulation.

Since much of environmental law involves regulations, it is important to have a basic idea about how they are adopted and how they may be challenged in court. Chapter II gives a brief description of rulemaking procedures, but a course in Administrative Law would be helpful for someone wishing to specialize in environmental law.

b. Where Do You Find Regulations?

Federal regulations, when first promulgated, are published in the Federal Register. The Federal Register is a daily publication of the federal government that includes, among other things, proposed and final regulations and other notices or announcements. A search to find the most current regulations would involve a check to see if a new or revised regulation has appeared in the Federal Register. In addition to the text of the regulation, the Federal Register will also contain a discussion of the agencies explanation of the regulation. This is contained in the "preamble" to the regulation. The preamble to a regulation is similar to legislative history of a statute. The preamble can contain important information that an effective lawyer can use.

Federal regulations are annually codified in the Code of Federal Regulations ("CFR"). EPA regulations are contained in Title 40. The EPA regulation, for example, which defines "solid waste" under RCRA is 40 C.F.R. § 261.2. The CFR is, however, only compiled on an annual basis, and even the current CFR may not include changes to regulations that have occurred within the last year.

Many states have their own versions of both CFR and the Federal Register.

3. Acronyms

Environmental lawyers speak their own language. This language includes a mind-numbing array of acronyms. Once again, there is no way around dealing with these acronyms. In order to learn environmental law, you have to learn the language. The description of acronyms at the end of this book should help you with your study.

E. RESEARCH TOOLS

The study and practice of environmental law requires the same legal skills and involves the same types of legal research that are used in other areas of the law. There is nothing special about statutory or regulatory interpretation in environmental law.

Nonetheless, there are some specialized research tools that help to deal with issues in the field.

1. Internet

The internet has dramatically affected the availability of information relating to environmental law. The Environmental Protection Agency (*www.epa.gov*) and state environmental agencies have "web sites" that provide access to an enormous amount of information and documents that were previously of limited availability. Environmental organizations, industry trade associations, academic institutions, and international organizations have web sites with useful information. Every student of environmental law should spend some time surfing the web for environmental sites and, at a minimum, review the EPA web site.

2. Commercial Computer Databases

Perhaps the most important available research tool is on-line legal databases like Westlaw. Westlaw has a separate environmental library which contains an enormous amount of information. This includes not only environmental cases and regulations, but numerous EPA documents and even law reviews. It is helpful to be familiar with the type of environmental information available through a service like Westlaw.

3. CFR and Federal Register

As discussed above, federal regulations are contained in the Code of Federal Regulations and the Federal Register.

4. Reporter Services

There are a number of specialized environmental reporter services such as BNA Environment Reporter. Some of these services contain updated and current cases, regulations and statutes; some contain weekly news reports on important environmental developments. These services can be very helpful research tools.

CHAPTER 1

Approaches to Environmental Regulation

■ ANALYSIS

A.   METHODS OF ENVIRONMENTAL REGULATION
   1.   Command and Control
        a.   Technology–Based Regulation
             (1)   Strengths
             (2)   Weaknesses
        b.   Environmental Quality–Based Regulation
             (1)   Strengths
             (2)   Weaknesses
   2.   Market Incentives
        a.   Types of Market Incentives
             (1)   Effluent Fees
                   (a)   Strengths
                   (b)   Weaknesses
             (2)   Marketable Pollution Rights

A. Methods of Environmental Regulation

There are a number of different techniques that could be used to regulate environmental pollution. Each of the following approaches has its strengths and weaknesses, and each approach is used to some extent in federal environmental regulation.

1. Command and Control

Regulators could simply specify the amount of pollutants a facility may emit or the type of pollution control equipment it must use. Much of federal environmental regulation employs this type of "command and control" regulation. There are two primary approaches to determining how much pollution control will be required.

a. Technology–Based Regulation

A technology-based regulation is a standard or limitation that basically requires as much pollution control as can be achieved with existing technology. Technology-based regulations are based on an assessment of the types of available control technologies and their costs. In most cases, technology-based regulations are set without considering the effect of the emissions on the environment.

Example: EPA determines that a type of pollution control equipment, a carbon filter, is now used by the least polluting facilities in an industry. The Agency determines that the carbon filter could be used by other facilities within that industry and the cost of the equipment is not unreasonable. EPA then sets a technology-based regulation based on the amount of pollutants a typical plant in the industry would emit if it used the filter.

Statutory language requiring use of a technology-based limitation typically includes such terms as "available," "practicable," or "feasible." The "Best Available Technology" ("BAT") limitations under the Clean Water Act are examples of a technology-based limitation. Chapter 5 describes the process of establishing a technology-based limitation.

In some cases, Congress has required industries to meet limitations that can not be achieved by existing technologies. For example, Congress imposed automobile emission limitations under the Clean Air Act that required automakers to develop new technology. This is called "technology forcing."

In most cases, technology-based limitations are expressed as "performance standards." A performance standard sets a target which may be met by source in any way it chooses. An effluent limitation like BAT is a form of performance standard. EPA sets the limits based on its assessment of available technology, but they are expressed as maximum amounts of pollutants that a facility may discharge. This means that a facility is free to use any type of pollution control equipment or other means of reducing pollution that it wishes as long as the standard is met.

A limitation may also be expressed as a "design standard." A design standard specifies the design of equipment that a facility must use. In effect this may require industry to use a particular piece of equipment selected by the government.

(1) Strengths

Technology-based regulations include a consideration of the cost of compliance; a regulator may conclude that technology which is "too" expensive is not "available." Thus, compliance with technology-based regulations, although expensive, should not force an entire industry out of business. Additionally, technology-based regulations have some advantages to the regulatory agency. Development of technology-based regulations requires judgments about technology and cost which, though difficult, are less controversial than setting limits based on health or environmental effects. Technology-based standards merely require judgments about achievable levels of pollution; they do not require a judgment about acceptable levels of pollution.

(2) Weaknesses

Technology-based regulations are set with little or no consideration of their environmental impact; pollution is controlled to the extent technologically and economically possible. The actual level of control required by a technology-based regulation may be either too strict or too lenient to reach an environmental goal. This approach has been criticized as "pollution control for pollution control's sake."

b. Environmental Quality–Based Regulation

Environmental quality-based regulations are set to ensure that a given level of environmental quality is achieved. This may include consideration of the impact of pollutants on human health, environmental ecosystems or both. Statutory provisions requiring an environmental quality approach typically require regulations that are adequate "to protect human health and the environment." The National Ambient Air Quality Standards ("NAAQS") under the Clean Air Act are examples of environmental quality-based standards, and individual limits on air emissions are set to ensure that these standards are not violated.

(1) Strengths

Environmental-quality standards are set to achieve a goal that we care about—protection of human health and the environment. If properly set, they should ensure that the "right" amount of pollution control is required.

(2) Weaknesses

Scientific data about the health and environmental effects of pollutants are usually inadequate to allow regulators to set standards with any degree of confidence in their accuracy. Even if adequate data are available, establishing environmental quality-based regulations, especially health-based regulations, may require the regulator to make difficult value judgments about who is to be protected and the degree of protection to be provided.

2. Market Incentives

There are a number of regulatory techniques that attempt to use market forces to control environmental pollution. In general, these techniques are intended to provide incentives for the reduction of pollution by sources that can do so most cheaply and to allow owners of individual facilities, rather than the government, to make decisions about the level of pollution control they are willing to achieve.

a. Types of Market Incentives

(1) Effluent Fees

Taxes or other fee could be imposed based on the amount of pollution produced by an industry. The more the industry pollutes, the more taxes or fees it would pay. This would create an incentive to reduce its pollution. Effluent fees have not been widely used in the U.S. The Clean Air Act, however, contains an escalating tax on the production of chlorofluorocarbons to encourage their replacement by other chemicals that are not taxed.

(a) Strengths

Effluent fees allow the facility to choose between reducing pollution or paying the tax, and the facility should make the decision that is individually most cost effective. Effluent fees also raise money that could be used to improve the environment or enforce the system. Increasingly, fees are being charged to issue environmental permits (based on the amount of pollution from the facility) with the money being used to administer the government's environmental program.

(b) Weaknesses

It is difficult to set the amount of the tax or fee. Ideally, the amount would be set at a level that would encourage industry to reduce its pollution to an "acceptable" level. If the tax were too high it might encourage facilities to reduce pollution more than is environmentally necessary; if the tax were too low it would not provide adequate incentive.

(2) Marketable Pollution Rights

Marketable pollution rights also attempt to use market forces. This approach, for example, may involve 1) establishing a given level of allowable pollution, 2) allocating to industrial facilities the right to emit pollutants at a level that will achieve this level, and 3) allowing facilities to freely buy and sell their allocated right to pollute. If a facility reduces its emissions to a level below its allocated right, it may sell to another facility a "right to pollute" equal to this reduction. The other facility will buy the right to pollute if it can do so more cheaply than its cost of actually reducing pollution. This should result in the desired level of pollution being achieved at the lowest cost. The main purpose of marketable pollution rights is to encourage pollution control at facilities that can reduce their pollution most cheaply.

It is important to understand that marketable pollution right approaches do not address the setting of environmental goals. Marketable rights are intended to assure that whatever environmental goal is established is met at the cheapest possible cost.

The sulfur trading program and the "offsets" program under the Clean Air Act, discussed in Chapter 7, are perhaps the most developed examples of marketable rights programs. The general concept of marketable pollution rights, including "cap and trade" programs, is discussed in Chapter 7.B

(a) Strengths

Marketable rights programs allow facilities to make individual decisions to either reduce pollution or pay for the right to pollute. This avoids problems that arise when the government tries to decide how much each individual facility may pollute. Instead, the combined independent decisions made by each facility should result in the most cost-effective allocation of controls.

(b) Weaknesses

Marketable rights raise difficult questions of implementation. Among other things, some system is necessary to ensure that willing buyers and willing sellers are brought together. This may result in "pollution banking" or the creation of markets to buy and sell pollution rights. Additionally, any sales must result in enforceable restrictions on the buyer and seller. Other issues in implementing a marketable rights program are addressed in in Chapter 7.B.

Marketable rights programs also raise troubling ethical questions about whether the right to pollute the environment should be treated as a property right or commodity to be traded like hog bellies.

(3) Subsidies

In some cases, the government can encourage pollution control by giving an economic subsidies to those controlling pollution. For many years, for example, the government paid up to 75% of the cost of building municipal sewage treatment plants. In many cases, tax deductions are also provided for certain expenditures for pollution control equipment. This, in effect, subsidizes the cost of the equipment.

3. Information Disclosure

Improvement in environmental quality may also be achieved by requiring the production and publication of environmental information. Informational approaches do not require that any specific level of environmental pollution be achieved or that the information result in specific control measures. Rather, it is the fact of compiling and publicly disclosing the information that is intended to produce beneficial results; the information can result in political or economic incentives to reduce environmentally harmful behavior.

a. Types of Information Approaches

(1) Reporting

Industrial facilities may be required to provide public information about the types and amounts of pollutants they emit. The Emergency Planning and Community Right-to-Know Act ("EPCRA") requires such reporting.

(2) Study and Planning

In some cases, statutes require persons to study and report on the environmental effects of proposed activities. The requirement that the federal government prepare Environmental Impact Statements ("EISs") under the National Environmental Policy Act ("NEPA") is perhaps the clearest example of this approach.

b. Strengths

Informational approaches assume that publication of information will generate pressure to reduce environmental harm. Rather than publicly reporting under EPCRA that it releases large quantities of hazardous substances, a facility may chose to reduce the amount it releases or to switch to the use of less hazardous substances. These decisions will be made without a government mandate.

c. Weaknesses

Although information may be published, there is no guarantee that it will have any affect. Although NEPA has resulted in the publication of numerous, lengthy EIS's, there is considerable controversy as to whether NEPA has actually mitigated the environmental affects of government decisions.

B. Economic Considerations

1. The Issue of "Externalities"

Many economists view environmental regulation as a device for addressing "externalities." An externality is a cost associated with production of a good that is not reflected in the price of the good. Externalities result in economic inefficiency. For example, when making a widget, a company may have to pay for raw materials and labor (which then affect the price of the widget), but may not have to pay for the costs to neighbors resulting from air or water pollution produced in making the widget. These costs to neighbors are externalities.

Environmental regulation, by forcing the company to pay for equipment to reduce the pollution, is reducing these externalities. Although the price of the widget may rise, economists would view this as an efficient use of resources.

If the goal of regulation is to prevent externalities, the cost imposed by regulation should not exceed the cost of the harms caused by the pollution.

2. Types of Economic Analysis

A major issue in establishing environmental regulations is the way in which the costs and benefits of the regulation are to be evaluated. There are several approaches that can be used to consider costs.

a. Cost–Benefit Analysis

A cost-benefit analysis compares the cost of a regulation with the benefits of the regulation. If the value of the benefits exceed the costs, the regulation could be viewed as economically efficient.

There are two major problems in performing cost-benefit analyses. First, a strict cost-benefit analysis requires that all of the costs and all of the benefits be expressed in dollars so that they can be compared. This raises difficult issues because it requires that dollar values be given to the benefit of preventing death or injury. Although there is no consensus, there are techniques that economists use to place a dollar value on a human life or a dollar value on reducing the risk of death. There are also difficult problems in placing a dollar value on environmental values, such as beautiful views or preservation of endangered species.

Second, cost-benefit analysis requires that all future costs and benefits be discounted to present value. There are formulas for calculating what the present cost is of the requirement to spend money in the future. It is far more difficult to determine the present value of lives saved in the future.

Consider a regulation will cost an industry $50 million dollars in capital costs and $2 million dollars per year in operating costs. It is projected that the regulation will save 20 lives over the next 15 years. A strict cost-benefit analysis requires that the present and future costs be discounted to present value. It also would require placing a dollar value on the 20 lives that would be saved and may require discounting the value of lives saved in the future to their present value. Only if the present discounted dollar value of the lives saved exceeds the present discounted dollar value of the cost would this regulation be considered "efficient" under cost-benefit principles.

Few environmental statutes require a strict cost-benefit analysis. Presidents, however, have issued "Executive Orders" that require federal agencies to prepare cost-benefit analyses of major regulations.

b. Cost Effectiveness Analysis

A cost effectiveness analysis compares the cost of two options to achieve a given goal. The least costly method of achieving the goal is more cost effective.

Example: Assume that the government has set a goal of reducing emissions from an industry by 90%. One piece of equipment, Option One, will achieve this goal for $10,000 and a different piece of equipment, Option Two, will achieve the goal for $20,000. Option One is more cost effective.

Some statutes require some form of cost effectiveness analysis. The cleanup method selected by the government under the Comprehensive Environmental Response, Compensation, and Liability Act must be cost-effective. Additionally, most marketable rights programs involve attempts to meet a given goal in the most cost-effective manner.

c. Cost Consideration

In some cases, statutes require costs to be considered without giving any guidance on how the cost information should affect the final decision. In setting BAT limits under the Clean Water Act, for example, the statute requires EPA to consider "costs," but the statute does not give any guidance on what weight EPA is to give to cost considerations. In these cases, the Agency has substantial discretion in deciding how much a regulation may cost.

d. Cost Oblivious

In some cases, regulations are supposed to be established without considering the costs at all. A statute may, for example, require that a standard be set at a level that is necessary to protect human health. In setting the health based level, the Administrator may not be authorized to consider the costs of meeting the standards. For example, EPA need not consider costs when it sets National Ambient Air Quality Standards under the Clean Air Act.

C. Ethical Considerations

Economic analysis does not directly consider the ethical implications of regulation. Ethical concerns pervade the field of environmental law, and there usually no clear answers to the ethical questions that are raised.

1. Protecting Nature

A major element of environmental law is the protection of the natural environment. Serious ethical questions are raised about the value of "nature" (independent of its economic benefit to humans) and the inherent value of non-human species.

2. Protecting Future Generations

Environmental regulation also raises ethical questions relating to our obligation to future generations. How much money, for example, should the current generation spend for environmental controls in order to provide a better environment for future generations?

3. Environmental Justice

The areas of "environmental justice" or "environmental racism" focus on the growing concern that environmental regulations impose disproportionate adverse impacts on the poor or on racial or ethnic minorities. A series of studies have suggested that waste disposal facilities and other environmentally harmful industries are disproportionately located in areas with large populations of African–Americans. Interpretation of these studies is still a matter of some controversy.

There are a number of legal theories that are potentially available to address environmental justice concerns. These include:

a. Equal Protection

Constitutional challenges to state action that disproportionately affect racial minorities are potentially available under the "Equal Protection" Clause of the Fourteenth Amendment. The U.S. Supreme Court, however, has required that plaintiffs prove "intentional discrimination" to establish a violation of the Equal Protection Clause.

b. Executive Order 12898

In 1994, President Clinton issued an executive order that requires federal agencies to consider environmental justice issues, but the order itself creates no private right of action and provides no new authority to federal agencies.

c. Title VI of the Civil Rights Act of 1964

Title VI of the Civil Rights Act of 1964 prohibits discrimination by certain parties receiving federal funds. Title VI has been used, for example, to petition the EPA to determine whether state environmental agencies receiving federal funds are using discriminatory policies. The Supreme Court has held that Title VI does not create a private cause of action allowing private parties to directly sue fund recipients.

d. Specific Environmental Laws

Specific environmental statutes may contain authority to consider environmental justice concerns.

CHAPTER 2

Constitutional Limits, Administrative Decisionmaking and Judicial Review

■ **ANALYSIS**

A. **CONSTITUTIONAL LIMITS ON FEDERAL AND STATE REGULATORY AUTHORITY**
1. Potential Limits on Federal Regulatory Authority
   a. Commerce Clause
   b. Tenth Amendment
   c. Eleventh Amendment
2. Potential Limits on State Regulatory Authority
   a. Supremacy Clause and Preemption
   b. Dormant Commerce Clause
B. **ADMINISTRATIVE PROCESS**
1. Environmental Protection Agency

A. Constitutional Limits on Federal and State Regulatory Authority

1. Potential Limits on Federal Regulatory Authority

a. Commerce Clause

The federal government does not have any general "police powers" to adopt statutes or regulations to protect human health or the environment; rather, federal statutes must be justified under an enumerated power granted in the U.S. Constitution. The Commerce Clause provides that Congress may regulate "commerce among the several states," Art. I, § 8, cl. 3, and virtually all of the major federal environmental statutes are justified under this authority. Although Congress' authority under the Commerce Clause has been construed quite broadly, the Supreme Court in a series of cases in the 1990's began to impose new requirements on Congress to justify the interstate nature of problems regulated by federal statute. In *United States v. Lopez*, 514 U.S. 549, 115 S.Ct. 1624, 131 L.Ed.2d 626 (1995), for example, the Supreme Court held that Congress does not have authority under the Commerce Clause to prohibit the possession of firearms near schools. The Court stated that the regulation did not have a "substantial relation" to interstate commerce since the regulated activity did not "substantially affect" interstate commerce. Although the issue has been raised, the Supreme Court has not ruled that any major environmental program is not justified under the Commerce Clause.

b. Tenth Amendment

Under the Tenth Amendment, the federal government may be prohibited from requiring states to adopt and implement regulatory programs. In *New York v. United States*, 505 U.S. 144, 112 S.Ct. 2408, 120 L.Ed.2d 120 (1992), the Supreme Court, reviewing a state challenge to a federal statute requiring states to take title to certain low-level radioactive wastes, held that Congress could provide incentives for state action but was limited in its ability to compel state regulation.

Most federal environmental statutes do not require states to adopt federal regulatory programs; rather they provide that the federal government will regulate if the state fails to act. Under the Clean Water Act, for example, water pollution permits are issued by the federal government unless a state requests delegation of the permit program. Under the Clean Air Act, states must adopt "state implementation plans," but if they do not do so the sanctions include loss of certain federal money or the adoption of implementation plans by the federal government.

c. Eleventh Amendment

Under the Eleventh Amendment, federal courts may not have jurisdiction to hear certain actions by private parties against a state. In other words, the Eleventh Amendment acts in certain cases as a constitutional statement of state sovereign immunity. The Supreme Court has invalidated several federal statutes that authorized private federal causes of action against state governments. In *Seminole Tribe of Florida v. Florida*, 517 U.S. 44, 116 S.Ct. 1114, 134 L.Ed.2d 252 (1996) the Supreme Court stated that the Eleventh Amendment barred cost recovery actions against states by private parties under the Comprehensive Environmental Response Compensation and Liability Act. This Eleventh Amendment protection does not, however, apply to counties and municipalities.

2. Potential Limits on State Regulatory Authority

a. Supremacy Clause and Preemption

The U.S. Constitution can also limit the authority of states to adopt certain environmental regulations. Under the "Supremacy Clause," federal statutes "shall be the supreme law of the land," Art. VI, cl. 2., and federal statutes can preempt state laws. The Federal Insecticide, Fungicide and Rodenticide Act (FIFRA), for example, preempts states' authority to regulate federally registered pesticides. Most of the major federal environmental statutes, however, expressly allow states to adopt requirements more stringent than required by federal law.

b. Dormant Commerce Clause

The Supreme Court has held that the Commerce Clause prohibits states from adopting certain types of restrictions that discriminate against out-of-state products. This is known as the "dormant commerce clause." The Supreme Court has applied a two-tier approach in assessing the constitutionality of state laws under the dormant commerce clause. Under the first tier, a patently discriminatory law (one, for example, which expressly treats out-of-state products differently) is virtually per se a violation of the dormant commerce clause. Under the second tier, a state law that does not facially discriminate against outofstate products may still violate the dormant commerce clause based on its indirect effects on interstate commerce. In such a case the court will employ a balancing test to see if the burden on interstate commerce is excessive in relation to the local benefits. Applying a dormant commerce clause analysis, the Supreme Court, in *Philadelphia v. New Jersey*, 437 U.S. 617, 98 S.Ct. 2531, 57 L.Ed.2d 475 (1978), for example, held that New Jersey could not expressly prohibit the importation of out-of-state wastes for disposal in New Jersey. In a series of "dormant commerce clause" cases in the 1990's, the Supreme Court invalidated a variety of other state restrictions that indirectly discriminated against out-of-state wastes.

B. Administrative Process

Much of environmental law involves the implementation of statutes by administrative agencies. Therefore, it is important to understand how administrative agencies operate and the basic rules of law which govern how agencies make decisions. Students who wish to practice environmental law should seriously consider taking a course in Administrative Law.

1. Environmental Protection Agency

The Environmental Protection Agency ("EPA") is responsible for implementation of most of the major federal pollution control statutes discussed in courses on Environmental Law. EPA was created in 1970, and many of the environmental statutes adopted since that date give EPA specific responsibility for promulgation of regulations, issuance of permits and enforcement.

EPA is currently headed by an Administrator appointed by the President. EPA has a headquarters, located in Washington, D.C., and several regional offices located around the country. The Washington office of EPA is responsible, among other things, for promulgation of regulations implementing statutes. The regional offices are primarily responsible for issuance of permits to individual sources and for initiating enforcement actions.

There are, however, numerous other federal administrative agencies with environmental responsibilities. These include, among many others, the Department of Interior, the Department of Energy, the Occupational Safety and Health Administration (part of the Department of Labor), and the Food and Drug Administration (part of the Department of Health and Human Services).

2. Administrative Decision-making

a. Administrative Procedure Act

Much of the process of federal administrative law is governed by the Administrative Procedure Act ("APA"). The APA defines the procedures that agencies must follow and establishes procedures for judicial review. Specific environmental statutes may, however, contain procedures that agencies must follow instead of those specified in the APA.

b. Rulemaking

Federal administrative agencies typically implement and define the general requirements of statutes by promulgating regulations. Regulations, when properly adopted, have the force of law, and persons may be civilly and criminally liable for failure to comply with these agency developed "laws."

Most regulations promulgated by EPA are issued through a process called "informal rulemaking" or "notice and comment rulemaking." Section 553 of the APA specifies the requirements of informal rulemaking. **5 U.S.C. § 553(b)**. These include 1) publication of the proposed rule, 2) providing an opportunity for the public to submit comments on the proposal, 3) issuance of a final regulation, and 4) preparation of the Agency's explanation of why it adopted the final rule and how it responds to major comments received during the public comment period. Federal regulations are published in the Federal Register and the textual discussion of the regulation, the "preamble," typically contains the Agency's explanation of the regulation. The Federal Register is a daily publication which contains proposed rules, final rules and other notices issued by the federal government.

In some limited cases, where required by statute, agencies will engage in "formal rulemaking" which involves holding a trial-type hearing on the proposed rule. Formal rulemaking is time-consuming and complex, and it is required by very few statutes.

Additionally, agencies issue large numbers of interpretations of rules and statutes or other policy guidance. These are not typically issued through either informal or formal rulemaking, and they are not binding as a matter of law. As a matter of fact, however, agency statements of policy are taken seriously by affected persons.

c. Adjudication

Regulations involve general requirements typically affecting large numbers of people. Agencies also take actions that focus on a single person, such as issuance of a permit or administrative enforcement actions. These specific actions are typically classified as "adjudications" and are subject to different procedures than are applicable to rulemaking. Where statutes require than an adjudication be held "on the record" and "after an opportunity for an agency hearing," the APA establishes formal requirements for conduct of the hearing. **5 U.S.C. §§ 554, 556, 557.** Other adjudications are governed by agency regulations and the requirements of the Due Process Clause.

Adjudications involve a process similar to a judicial trial. Persons objecting to a permit or contesting an administrative penalty are typically given an opportunity to contest the decision before an impartial "administrative law judge" ("ALJ"), to be represented by lawyers, and to cross-examine witnesses.

C. Judicial Review

Parties, in most cases, have the opportunity to seek judicial review of actions of the EPA.

1. Jurisdiction

In order to obtain judicial review in federal courts, parties must establish that the federal court has jurisdiction over the matter. There are typically three sources of jurisdiction to review actions of EPA. First, most of the federal environmental statutes provide for judicial review of specific actions of the Administrator. Review under these judicial review provisions are typically in a U.S. Court of Appeals. Second, most of the statutes contain "citizen suit" provisions which allow citizens to sue EPA when the Agency has failed to take a non-discretionary action required by the statute. Typically, this involves an action to force EPA to promulgate a regulation required by statute. These suits are brought in the U.S. District Court. Finally, if an action is not subject to judicial review under the specific provisions of an environmental statute, citizens may claim jurisdiction under the "federal question" provisions of 28 U.S.C. § 1331 which give district courts jurisdiction over disputes arising under the "Constitution, laws, or treaties" of the United States.

Judicial review under specific environmental statutes is discussed in other chapters.

2. Standard of Review

The issue of "standard of review" deals with how stringently a court will review a decision by an agency. Under section 706 of the APA, courts review most regulations issued by federal agencies under the "arbitrary and capricious" standard of review. **5 U.S.C. § 706**. Most "formal adjudications" are reviewed under the "substantial evidence" standard. It is not clear what difference, if any, exists between these standards, but the "arbitrary and capricious" standard is typically seen as more deferential to the Agency's decisions.

Regardless of the specific standard of review, most courts claim that they will defer to the judgments of the Agency. Some courts, however, developed a "hard look" doctrine which, at a minimum, means that the courts would ensure that the agency has thoroughly reviewed all information in the record and has adequately explained its decision in light of applicable statutory factors and the relevant information.

In *Chevron, U.S.A. v. NRDC*, 467 U.S. 837, 104 S.Ct. 2778, 81 L.Ed.2d 694 (1984), the Supreme Court reaffirmed that courts should defer to agency interpretations of statutes unless the Agency's construction was contrary to the explicit intent of Congress or is not a reasonable interpretation of the statute.

3. Standing

Not all persons may seek judicial review of an agency action. The doctrine of "standing" prevents persons from litigating unless they have a sufficient stake or interest in the litigation. Standing in federal litigation is, in large part, a constitutional requirement, and arises from the "case or controversy" provisions of Article III of the U.S. Constitution.

In a series of cases, the Supreme Court has stated that persons must satisfy a number of elements to have standing.

a. Zone of Interest

The Supreme Court has stated that parties must establish that they are within the "zone of interest" of the statute under which they are litigating. This requires the court to determine whether Congress intended to protect the type of interest asserted by the plaintiff. In *Bennett v. Spear*, 520 U.S. 154, 117 S.Ct. 1154, 137 L.Ed.2d 281 (1997), the Supreme Court held that the "zone of interest" requirement was generally satisfied in citizen suits brought under environmental statutes that authorize such suits by "any person."

b. Injury in Fact

Persons must also establish that they have suffered an "injury in fact" from the agency action. In *Sierra Club v. Morton*, 405 U.S. 727, 92 S.Ct.

1361, 31 L.Ed.2d 636 (1972), the Supreme Court indicated that, if properly pleaded, allegations of environmental or aesthetic harm would be sufficient to establish injury in fact. Typically, environmental groups will allege that individual members of the group have suffered injury from the actions of the agency.

In recent years, however, the Supreme Court may have become more demanding in regards to injury in fact. The Court has stated that injury must be "concrete and particularized" and "actual or imminent, not conjectural or hypothetical." *Lujan v. National Wildlife Federation*, 497 U.S. 871, 110 S.Ct. 3177, 111 L.Ed.2d 695 (1990), involved a challenge by an environmental group to actions of the Department of Interior which opened certain public lands to mining activities. The group had submitted affidavits from two of its members alleging that the members visited "in the vicinity" of certain affected federal land and that their aesthetic enjoyment was injured by the agency actions. The court indicated that these vague allegations were not adequate to establish standing.

Reversing the trend of more stringent treatment of standing requirements, the Supreme Court in *Friends of the Earth v. Laidlaw Environmental Services (TOC), Inc.,* 528 U.S. 167, 120 S.Ct. 693, 145 L.Ed.2d 610 (2000) found that citizens had standing based on allegations that the citizens had ceased using waters as a result of their concern for discharges into the water from an industrial facility. Although the evidence of actual environmental impact was limited, the Court noted that injury in fact was satisfied by evidence of injury to the plaintiff and not necessarily to the environment. Evidence of actual past use and prospective use of a natural resource by the plaintiff together with a lessening of the resource's recreational or aesthetic value seemed enough to satisfy "injury in fact."

c. Causation and Redressability

There are two other, related, requirements to establish standing. Persons seeking standing must establish that the defendant's action caused their injury. This means that their injury is "fairly traceable" to the action they are challenging.

Additionally, persons must establish that judicial relief would "redress" their injury. In other words, they must show that relief would be effective in correcting their injuries.

d. Organizational Standing

Many environmental lawsuits are brought, not by individuals, but by organizations. In *Hunt v. Washington Apple Adv. Comm'n,* 432 U.S. 333, 97

S.Ct. 2434, 53 L.Ed.2d 383 (1977), the Supreme Court established three elements that an organization must prove to have standing to sue on behalf of its members. These are 1) some of its members must have standing to sue in their own right, 2) the interests it seeks to protect are germane to the organization's purpose and 3) the suit does not require participation of individual members.

CHAPTER 3

Common Law Torts

■ **ANALYSIS**

A. Introduction

Historically, the common law provided the primary legal mechanism for controlling environmental pollution. Through tort actions against persons engaged in harmful conduct, the legal system provided a means both to discourage this conduct and compensate persons who were injured. Today, industrial pollution is largely controlled through statute and regulation, but tort still serves a significant supplementary role. Tort actions are particularly important since they may be the only means for recovering financial compensation for personal injury or property damages.

B. Causes of Action

Facilities which pollute the environment may be liable under a number of different theories. Consider, for example, a hazardous waste landfill which releases "toxic substances" into the groundwater. Neighbors of the landfill who drink water containing the hazardous substances may be able to bring a tort action for compensation under any of the following theories.

1. Nuisance

a. Private Nuisance

A private nuisance is conduct which "unreasonably" interferes with the use and enjoyment of another's land. A private nuisance is essentially a land use tort since it involves a claim that the offensive conduct interferes with rights stemming from property ownership. A nuisance can exist if defendant's conduct is either negligent or intentional; the key issue is whether the conduct unreasonably interferes with the use and enjoyment of land.

Jurisdictions have differing standards over what constitutes a nuisance. Some say that any "substantial" interference with a person's interest in property may be a nuisance. Others, including the Restatement (2d) of Torts, require that the court balance various factors to determine whether the defendant's conduct was "unreasonable." This may involve a determination as to whether the utility of the defendant's conduct outweighs the harm it causes.

b. Public Nuisance

You should distinguish a private nuisance action, brought by private citizens, from a public nuisance action, typically prosecuted by the government. A public nuisance is a common law cause of action that may be brought, generally by the government, against a person whose conduct "unreasonably" interferes with a right common to the public. Thus, the government may have an action against a party who pollutes public waters or the air. Like private nuisances, finding a public nuisance may require a court to balance the utility of the defendant's conduct with the extent of the harm the conduct causes. In some jurisdictions, a public nuisance may only be brought if the defendant is violating a statute or administrative regulation; in other jurisdictions this is merely one factor to consider.

Private parties generally may not bring an action alleging a public nuisance unless they have suffered damages different in kind from those suffered by the public at large. Thus, a private party may not recover under a public nuisance theory for damages from air pollution if the party has not suffered any different type of damage (or in some cases suffered damages substantially greater) than the type of damages the general public has suffered from exposure to air pollution.

2. Trespass

A trespass typically involves a physical intrusion onto the property of another. It therefore may be available in some cases of environmental contamination where, for example, a person's actions have resulted in pollutants entering a neighbor's land. Courts have split over how "tangible" or visible the physical invasion must be, and whether chemical pollution of the water or air will give rise to a trespass action.

3. Negligence

Environmental contamination may give rise to an action based on negligence if the defendant's conduct falls below the standard of care owed the plaintiff. Among other things, an action in negligence requires that the plaintiff prove the defendant's act (or failure to act) was negligent or otherwise did not conform to some minimum standard of conduct. In some cases, statutes or regulations may define the standard of conduct.

4. Strict Liability

In some cases, the common law has imposed tort liability on parties without regard to whether they were negligent or otherwise at fault. Strict liability with regard to environmental contamination or exposure to toxic substances generally arises in two situations.

a. Ultrahazardous Activity

Since the English case of *Rylands v. Fletcher*, the common law has recognized the possibility of strict liability where a party engages in an "ultrahazardous" or "abnormally dangerous" activity. Operation of a hazardous waste landfill in a residential area may, for example, give rise to a claim that the operators should be strictly liable for damages because they engaged in ultrahazardous or abnormally dangerous activity. Liability in such a case could be imposed without regard to whether the defendants were negligent in construction or operation of the landfill.

Courts have differed in their approach to determining which conduct is subject to strict liability. In some cases, courts may consider whether the dangerous activity was "unnatural" to the location. This would involve an assessment of whether an activity which was otherwise acceptable was conducted in an inappropriate location. Second 520 of the Restatement (2d) of Torts provides for consideration of a variety of factors in judging whether an activity should be subject to strict liability as an "abnormally dangerous" activity. These factors include, in addition to the appropriateness of the location, the risk of harm from the conduct, the ability to minimize the harm, and the extent to which the benefits from the activity outweigh the harms.

b. Products Liability

A distinct claim for strict liability arises in product liability cases. Manufacturers or sellers of products may be strictly liable for damages arising from use of the products if, for example, there is some "design defect" in the product or, more commonly in toxic tort cases, they failed to warn of the risks involved in use of the product.

C. Causation

All private tort actions require the plaintiff to show that the defendant's actions were the proximate cause of some injury. In tort actions involving exposure to environmental pollutants this can be a difficult element to satisfy.

Proving that a "toxic substance" caused a physical injury can be difficult. Plaintiffs generally have the burden of showing by a "preponderance of the evidence" that the exposure caused injury.

There are several problems in proving injury. First, there are typically long periods of time between exposure to a toxic substance and development of a disease like cancer. This is called the "latency period." Thus, persons exposed to toxic substances may not yet have developed any demonstrable injury. Damage claims, such as "cancerphobia," discussed below, have been advanced to deal with this problem.

Second, even if a plaintiff has contracted a disease such as cancer, it can be extremely difficult to prove that the exposure to the toxic substance caused the disease. "Scientific" evidence relating to the effects of low level exposures to toxic substances is usually limited. Evidence may consist of epidemiological studies showing a statistical association between exposure to a substance and increased rates of a disease such as cancer. There are, however, several problems with the use of epidemiological evidence. First, there may not be any existing studies, and it can be extremely expensive to perform them. Second, if the studies show only a small association (i.e., the substance increases the risk of cancer by only a few percent), the evidence may not be adequate to demonstrate that exposure to the toxic substances "more likely than not" caused the plaintiff's injuries.

Plaintiffs may also attempt to rely on expert testimony. Some experts may be willing to testify that, based on their knowledge and experience, they believe that the plaintiff's injuries were caused by exposure to the toxic substances. There are significant evidentiary questions as to when such testimony meets standards of admissibility and relevance. In *Daubert v. Merrell Dow Pharmaceuticals*, 509 U.S. 579, 113 S.Ct. 2786, 125 L.Ed.2d 469 (1993), the Supreme Court held that for expert testimony to be admissible the trial court judge must determine if it meets some standard of "scientific" validity.

D. Remedies

1. Availability of Injunctive Relief

In many cases involving on-going environmental pollution, plaintiffs are seeking to enjoin the defendants from continuing their injurious activities. An injunction is an equitable remedy, and traditionally courts have considered a variety of factors, including the adequacy of monetary damages, in determining whether it is appropriate to issue an injunction which may shut down an on-going industrial operation.

In many jurisdictions, however, plaintiffs who establish that the tortious conduct is continuing are entitled to an injunction as of right. The economic efficiency and fairness of such a rule has been questioned when the effect of the injunction is to close an existing business that provides employment and other economic benefits.

Boomer v. Atlantic Cement Co., 26 N.Y.2d 219, 309 N.Y.S.2d 312, 257 N.E.2d 870 (1970), is widely cited for its analysis of whether to issue an injunction to prohibit operation of a cement company which was causing continuing and substantial damages to neighboring property from its air pollution. The court, among other things, balanced the benefits from continued operation of the facility with the harm to the neighbors and concluded that an injunction requiring that the plant close immediately was inappropriate. Instead, the court issued a "conditional" injunction which required the plant to close only if the owners failed to fully compensate the injured neighbors for present and future damages.

2. Developing Damage Theories

Traditionally, a plaintiff may recover damages for his or her personal injuries that exist at the time of trial and damages for additional injuries that the plaintiff can establish are likely to occur in the future. In only limited cases has the common law allowed recovery where the plaintiff cannot establish some physical injury at the time of trial.

In many cases, however, persons exposed to toxic substances will not exhibit injuries until decades after exposure. Persons who have tried to bring a tort action at the time of exposure have advanced theories to attempt to recover without demonstrating an existing physical injury.

a. Cancerphobia

Some plaintiffs exposed to carcinogenic substances have claimed that they have suffered an immediate harm by being subjected to fear that they may later develop cancer. This has been described as "cancerphobia."

Traditionally, plaintiffs in tort actions have not been able to recover for emotional distress unless they can demonstrate some existing physical injury or some physical manifestation of their distress. Courts have been reluctant to allow plaintiffs to recover for their subjective fear or distress without some objective manifestation of injury. Courts have been concerned that this would make it too easy for plaintiffs to bring unwarranted tort actions based on their allegation of distress. For this reason, most courts have been reluctant to allow plaintiffs to recover based on allegations of "cancerphobia."

b. Increased Risk of Cancer

Plaintiffs have also alleged that they have suffered an immediate injury from exposure to carcinogens by being placed at an increased risk of developing cancer in the future. Most courts have not allowed plaintiffs to recover for this alleged injury without demonstrating, with a reasonable medical certainty, that they are likely to contract cancer in the future as a result of the exposure. Given the state of knowledge about the development of cancer, plaintiffs are unlikely to be able to meet this burden.

c. Medical Monitoring

Some plaintiffs exposed to toxic substances have sought to recover the cost of periodic medical examinations to identify diseases that may occur in the future as a result of the exposure. In other words, plaintiffs claim that the costs of medical monitoring are damages that they have immediately suffered as a result of the exposure. Some courts have recognized this claim and have allowed recovery for future medical monitoring where the plaintiff demonstrates that the monitoring is reasonably necessary. Other courts have rejected the claims unless the plaintiffs can demonstrate some existing physical injury.

E. Procedural Issues

1. Statute of Limitations

Statutes of limitation place a limit on the time in which a person may commence a tort action. For many toxic pollutants, however, a long latency period may exist between exposure to the toxic pollutant and the occurrence of a disease. If the statute of limitations period began to run when the defendant committed the act giving rise to the exposure, the potential plaintiff may not learn of the injury until after the statute of limitations period has run. In such cases, statutes of limitation may create an obstacle to a tort action by an injured person.

Most, but not all, jurisdictions minimize this problem through some version of the discovery rule. In many jurisdictions, the discovery rule starts the statute of limitations period running at the time the potential plaintiff discovers or should have discovered the injury. Other jurisdictions have adopted variations of the rule which start the time period running when potential plaintiffs discover sufficient facts to alert them of injury and the possible existence of a cause of action.

2. Splitting Causes of Action

Most jurisdictions require that all claims arising from a common set of facts be brought in one action. Plaintiffs are not allowed to "split" their claims by suing for some damages in one action and later bringing an action for different damages arising from the same set of facts. This can create a problem for plaintiffs seeking to recover for damages arising from exposure to a toxic substance. If the plaintiff is allowed to sue immediately after exposure but before the occurrence of the disease, the plaintiff may be later barred from bringing an action for damages when the disease actually occurs. Some jurisdictions which allow recovery of costs of medical monitoring may allow a later action if a disease actually develops.

*

CHAPTER 4

National Environmental Policy Act

■ ANALYSIS

A. **INTRODUCTION**
    1. Background
    2. Structure of NEPA
        a. National Environmental Policies
        b. Environmental Impact Statements
        c. Council on Environmental Quality
            (1) Implementing Regulations
            (2) Coordination Among Federal Agencies; EPA Review of EIS's
            (3) Preparation of an Annual Report
B. **EIS PROCESS**
    1. Exemptions From EIS Obligation
        a. Generally
        b. Environmental Protection Agency

A. Introduction

1. Background

The National Environmental Policy Act of 1970 ("NEPA") was the first of the modern federal environmental statutes. Among other things, this short statute established environmental policies and goals for the country and created the President's Council on Environmental Quality. The most important provision of NEPA, however, is section 102(2)(C) which requires that a federal agency prepare a "detailed statement" when it proposes to take a "major federal action significantly affecting the quality of the human environment." This detailed statement is known as an "environmental impact statement" or "EIS."

Unlike the Clean Air Act, Clean Water Act or Resource Conservation and Recovery Act, NEPA is not a regulatory statute. It does not impose pollution control requirements on anyone. Rather, NEPA is largely an information statute. It requires the federal government to prepare and publish information about the environmental effects of and alternatives to actions that the government may take. NEPA is premised, in large part, on the assumption that providing information to the decision-maker and the public will improve the quality of final decisions.

2. Structure of NEPA

a. National Environmental Policies

Section 101 of NEPA establishes certain broad national policies relating to protection of the environment. **§ 101, 42 U.S.C. § 4331.**

b. Environmental Impact Statements

As discussed below, section 102(2)(C) of NEPA requires a federal agency to prepare an EIS when it is proposing to take certain major actions. **§ 102(2)(C), 42 U.S.C. § 4332(2)(C).** The EIS is supposed to describe the proposed federal action, discuss the environmental impacts of the proposed action, and consider alternatives and their environmental impacts. The EIS is to be an "interdisciplinary" document that provides the decision-maker, the public and Congress with information about the environmental consequences of federal actions. The EIS has been described as the "action forcing" provision of NEPA. At a minimum, it does force agencies to consider the environmental consequences of their actions.

c. Council on Environmental Quality

NEPA also establishes the Council on Environmental Quality ("CEQ") to advise the President on environmental issues. **§ 202, 42 U.S.C. § 4341**. The role of the CEQ is limited. The CEQ has not generally had a strong role in shaping U.S. environmental policy.

The CEQ has three major functions.

(1) Implementing Regulations

The CEQ is responsible for overseeing the implementation of NEPA, and it now publishes regulations that direct other federal agencies on how they must implement NEPA. The authority of the CEQ to promulgate regulations has been unclear, but courts have given substantial deference to the CEQ's interpretation of NEPA. The CEQ regulations are a good place to start when you have questions about implementation of NEPA.

(2) Coordination Among Federal Agencies; EPA Review of EIS's

Federal agencies that prepare EIS's are required to submit them, not to CEQ, but to the Environmental Protection Agency. EPA then makes judgments about the adequacy of the EIS and the environmental impact of the proposed federal action. EPA's authority to review EIS's is contained in section 309 of the Clean Air Act. **CAA § 309(a), 42 U.S.C. § 7609(a)**. If there are disputes between EPA and other federal agencies, the dispute may be referred to CEQ for resolution. **CAA § 309(b), 42 U.S.C. § 7609(b)**. Neither CEQ nor EPA has the power to alter the decisions of other agencies, but they do have the power to focus attention on environmental concerns.

(3) Preparation of an Annual Report

The CEQ also publishes an annual report that summarizes the state of environmental conditions in the U.S. This annual report is a useful reference.

B. EIS Process

In general NEPA requires that agencies 1) identify whether they are required to prepare an EIS, 2) prepare a draft EIS, if necessary, and offer the draft for public comment, and 3) prepare a final EIS that is part of the record of the final agency decision.

This general process is implemented through a series of actions.

1. Exemptions From EIS Obligation

a. Generally

As discussed more fully below, some agency actions are exempt from the EIS requirement of NEPA. These exemptions may be specific statutory exemptions adopted by Congress or "categorical exemptions" that apply to classes of actions that the agency has determined will not trigger the requirement to prepare an EIS. If the agency determines, on either of these bases, that the action is exempt from the EIS process, it does nothing further.

b. Environmental Protection Agency

Most actions of the EPA are exempt from the requirement to prepare an EIS. Some of these exemptions are statutory. All actions of EPA under the Clean Air Act, for example, are exempt from the EIS requirement. This exemption is contained, not in the Clean Air Act, but in the Energy Supply and Environmental Coordination Act of 1974. **15 U.S.C. § 793(c)(1).** Additionally, EPA actions under the Clean Water Act, except for providing grants to municipal wastewater treatment systems and issuing NPDES permits to new sources, are exempt from the EIS process. **CWA § 511(c)(1), 33 U.S.C. § 1371(c)(1).**

Additionally, courts have generally held that EPA does not have to prepare an EIS on actions where the agency prepares a "functional equivalent" of an EIS. EPA is the only agency that has successfully asserted the functional equivalence argument.

2. Environmental Assessment

If a proposed action is not exempt, the agency must determine whether it meets the threshold for preparation of an EIS—whether it is a "major federal action significantly affecting the quality of the human environment." In order to make this determine, the agency typically prepares an "environmental assessment" ("EA"). The EA is a concise document that describes the proposal and contains information, including a limited discussion of alternatives, that aid the agency in deciding whether a full EIS is necessary. In many ways, the EA is a shorter and less formal version of an EIS.

3. Finding of No Significant Impact

If the agency determines that no EIS is necessary, it prepares a "Finding of No Significant Impact" ("FONSI"). The FONSI is a short document, based on the EA, which explains the agency's reasons for concluding that no EIS is necessary. If the agency issues a FONSI, it will typically take no further action under NEPA.

4. Notice of Intent and Scoping

If, based on the EA, the agency determines that an EIS is necessary, it will publish a "Notice of Intent" to prepare an EIS. The agency will then go through a process of "scoping" in which it identifies the scope of the EIS and the significant issues that will be addressed. If more than one federal agency is involved, one will be designated the "lead agency" and the others will be "cooperating agencies."

5. Draft EIS

The lead agency will prepare a "draft EIS" which contains a full analysis of the project. The content of the EIS is discussed below, but essentially the draft contains a description of the proposed action, a discussion of alternatives to the action, including actions to mitigate adverse effects, and a discussion of the environmental consequences of the action and alternatives.

6. Public Comment

The draft EIS must be made available for comment by the public. The agency has some discretion as to whether to hold a public meeting to discuss the draft EIS. Additionally, the agency must solicit the comments of cooperating agencies and other agencies with jurisdiction over the action or special expertise with respect to the environmental impacts involved. Comments on the draft EIS are part of the administrative record of the agency's action.

7. Final EIS

After receiving comments, the agency will prepare a final EIS. The agency is required to respond to comments and, if necessary, modify the draft to reflect its response to comments. Although the agency may, it is not usually required to resubmit a modified EIS for public comment.

8. Judicial Review

Final agency actions are typically subject to judicial review for compliance with NEPA. Courts may review 1) the decision not to prepare an EIS, including review of a FONSI, and 2) whether the final EIS was prepared in compliance with the procedural requirements of NEPA. NEPA has been described by the Supreme Court as "essentially procedural," and the issue of whether a court may review the substance of an agency decision under NEPA is discussed below.

C. The Threshold Issue: When Must an EIS Be Prepared

An EIS is only required for "proposals for legislation and major federal action significantly affecting the quality of the human environment." § 102(2)(C), 42

U.S.C. § 4332(2)(C). Before it prepares an EIS, an agency must determine whether its proposed action meet this threshold requirement. This threshold question is often controversial and virtually every word in the statutory phrase has been the subject of litigation.

1. Federal Actions

Only "federal" actions are subject to EIS requirements. Purely private activities or activities of state or local governments are not subject to NEPA. Nonetheless, determining whether an action is "federal" raises significant issues.

a. Actions by the Federal Government

Most simply, activities which the federal government undertakes itself are federal actions. Thus, construction of federal facilities or issuance of federal regulations or proposals for legislation will all satisfy the federal requirement.

b. Federal Authorization of Actions by Private Parties

The activities of private parties may also be subject to EIS requirements if there is sufficient federal involvement. If, for example, the activity of a private party needs a federal permit or other federal authorization, the entire private project may be subject to review in an EIS. It is the issuance of the permit or authorization that is the federal action that triggers the EIS requirement.

Example: Company A is leasing federal land from the Department of the Interior for oil and gas exploration. The possible environmental impact of the company's activities may evaluated in an EIS before the federal government leases the land.

This raises what is called the "small handle" problem. If the federal authorization is only a small part of a larger private activity, the federal approval may not trigger an EIS. Thus, in *Winnebago Tribe of Nebraska v. Ray*, 621 F.2d 269 (8th Cir.1980), the court held that an EIS was not required for construction by a private party of a major power transmission line when the only federal action was issuance of a right of way for the power line to cross navigable water.

c. Federal Funding

In some cases, activities funded by the federal government may become federal actions. Where the federal government provides a major share of the funding for a specific project, the project is likely to be "federal" for purposes of NEPA. Where, however, the federal government provides money without specifying how the money is to be used, the answer becomes less clear. In general, the more "strings" that the federal government keeps on use of the money, the more likely that the funded project will be consider federal for purposes of NEPA.

2. Actions

Only a "proposals for legislation and other major federal actions" are subject to the EIS requirement. Determining whether agency activity rises to the level of an "action" or "proposed action" can be difficult.

a. Proposals

Agencies consider and plan activities all the time, and it can be difficult to determine when an activity is no longer just a "gleam" in the agency's eyes but an actual proposal for action. In determining the point at which NEPA applies, courts must consider whether the proposal has reached a stage that is sufficiently concrete and definite to constitute an actual proposal for action by the agency. Challenges to an agency's failure to prepare an EIS on a proposal are frequently analyzed as "ripeness" questions.

In *Kleppe v. Sierra Club*, 427 U.S. 390, 96 S.Ct. 2718, 49 L.Ed.2d 576 (1976), the Supreme Court dealt with the issue of when and whether agency activity is a "proposal" subject to NEPA requirements. The case involved a claim that the Department of Interior ("DOI") must prepare an EIS on coal development in the Northern Great Plains. DOI had prepared an EIS on its national program and intended to prepare EIS's on each specific coal leasing decision. Plaintiffs argued, however, that DOI assessments of coal development in the Northern Great Plains constituted a regional program requiring an EIS.

The Supreme Court rejected this argument and held that an EIS was required only if there is an actual "proposal" for action put forth by the agency. The Supreme Court indicated that an EIS only need be prepared at the stage that the agency actually proposes the action and not when it is considering or formulating possible proposals.

Note the dilemma raised by this issue. On the one hand, an EIS must be prepared early enough in the process to be useful in shaping the alternatives that the agency considers. On the other hand, the EIS need not be prepared too early before the agency has actually formulated its proposal.

b. Inaction

Federal agencies may also decide to take no action even though they may have the statutory authority to act. An issue under NEPA is whether this "inaction" is subject to the EIS requirement. In *Defenders of Wildlife v. Andrus*, 627 F.2d 1238 (D.C.Cir.1980), the court held that an EIS did not need to be prepared on the Department of Interior's decision *not* to stop a wolf kill planned by the State of Alaska. The court held that only an "overt act" by the government is a federal "action" subject to NEPA.

Although the CEQ regulations classify a "failure to act" as federal action if that inaction is reviewable under the Administrative Procedure Act, the courts, in general, have not required preparation of an EIS for agency inaction.

c. Proposals for Legislation

The EIS requirement applies to "proposals for legislation," but the CEQ regulations make clear that this applies to a federal agency and only if a federal agency has prepared a specific legislative proposal for submission to Congress. There is limited case law on this requirement, and few courts have required preparation of an EIS on agency proposals or recommendations to Congress.

3. Major/Significantly Affecting

The EIS requirement applies to "major" federal actions that "significantly" affect the quality of the human environment. Some courts have suggested that these are two separate standards. Most courts and the CEQ regulations provide that "major" and "significantly" deal with the same issue and are analyzed together.

There are few general criteria for determining whether an action is "major" or "significant," and the issue typically involves a fact specific assessment of the particular action. At a minimum, the determination involves an assessment of the extent of possible environmental impacts of a proposed action. Additionally, the significance of a proposal can also be based on the cumulative effects of a number of smaller but related actions. Thus, an action which itself does not have significant impacts may be subject to the EIS requirement if it is part of a broader pattern of actions that together have significant impacts. This issue is similar to the question of "segmentation" discussed below.

4. Human Environment

The EIS requirement may be triggered by effects on the "human environment." In general, this means that an EIS is required only if the proposal will have an effect on the physical environment. An EIS would not be required if the effects were purely social and economic. This distinction is not easily made.

In *Hanly v. Kleindienst (II)*, 471 F.2d 823 (2d Cir.1972), the court considered whether an EIS must be prepared for a proposal to build jail facilities in a residential neighborhood in downtown Manhattan. The court indicated that psychological or sociological effects on neighbors were not covered by NEPA, but suggested that possible increases in crime were the type of effect on the environment covered by NEPA.

Similarly, numerous courts have rejected the argument that an EIS must be prepared because a project will result in people of a different racial or socioeconomic class entering a neighborhood. In other words, they have rejected treating "people as pollution." Note, however, that an EIS might be required to address the increased traffic and pollution resulting from an influx of people into a neighborhood.

In *Metropolitan Edison v. People Against Nuclear Energy*, 460 U.S. 766, 103 S.Ct. 1556, 75 L.Ed.2d 534 (1983), the Supreme Court held that psychological harm due to the fear of nuclear power was not of the type of harm covered by NEPA. Thus, while actual adverse environmental effects must be addressed in an EIS, fear of those adverse effects need not.

D. Scope of the EIS

If a proposal for action requires preparation of an EIS, difficult questions still remain about the scope of that EIS.

1. Segmentation

One of the most difficult questions under NEPA involves whether a number of small and related actions must be comprehensively addressed in a single EIS. If an agency were allowed to address each action separately, the total cumulative effect of the series of actions might never be considered. This issue is referred to as "segmentation" since an agency may carve a larger project into a number of smaller segments. The most typical case of segmentation involves construction of small stretches of a long highway. Courts have frequently dealt with the issue of whether an EIS need only address each individual segment or whether a single EIS must be prepared on the entire highway.

There are no simple criteria to determine whether an EIS can be limited to a single segment of a larger project. The courts and the CEQ regulations have identified some factors that will be considered. First, it is relevant whether the series of actions are closely related. This may include an assessment of whether the actions affect the same geographic area or whether the first action automatically triggers later actions. Second, it is relevant whether the first action has "independent utility." If, for example, a highway segment is not useful unless later segments are built, it is likely that an EIS must address subsequent actions. Finally, if there are cumulative impacts of a number of small similar actions, the EIS may need to address those cumulative impacts.

Note that this issue may be closely related to the issue of whether an EIS need be prepared at all. In some cases, smaller portions of a larger project will not themselves "significantly" affect the environment. An EIS may be required if the "proposal" for action is seen to be the larger project or if the cumulative effects of the smaller projects are considered.

2. Tiering and Programmatic EIS's

The CEQ regulations allow an agency to "tier" the preparation of impact statements. The agency may prepare a large or "programmatic EIS" on the overall project. In this programmatic EIS, it may consider the cumulative effect of smaller actions and identify alternatives to the overall project. In site specific EIS's, it may consider the local effects of the smaller component and limit the discussion of alternatives to those relating to that component. In this way, the agency does not need to reconsider general issues in each individual EIS.

The courts and the CEQ regulations give agencies substantial discretion to determine whether to prepare a programmatic EIS. Note, however, the issue of whether a programmatic EIS is necessary is closely tied to a determination of whether a specific overall "proposal" exists.

In *Kleppe v. Sierra Club*, 427 U.S. 390, 96 S.Ct. 2718, 49 L.Ed.2d 576 (1976), the Supreme Court upheld the Department of Interior's decision to prepare a programmatic EIS on the entire national coal leasing program as well as separate EIS's on each individual coal lease or other specific project. The Court largely left the decision on whether to address overall issues in a programmatic EIS to the discretion of the Agency.

E. Content of the EIS

In general, NEPA requires that an EIS address both the environmental effects of and alternatives to proposed actions. The EIS is required to be "interdisciplinary," and the responsible agency is required to consult with other federal agencies which have jurisdiction or which have special expertise with respect to any environmental impact.

A number of issues routinely arise with respect to the adequacy of the content of an EIS.

1. Alternatives

An EIS must address alternatives to the proposed action. This requirement is contained in both section 102(2)(C)(iii) and section 102(2)(E). **§ 102(2)(C)(iii), 42 U.S.C. § 4332(2)(C)(iii); § 102(2)(E), 42 U.S.C. § 4332(2)(E)**. CEQ regulations describe the requirement to consider alternatives as the "heart" of the EIS.

In general, the courts and CEQ have applied a "rule of reason" in determining the scope of alternatives that must be considered. Only reasonable alternatives must be identified and considered in an EIS. This includes at a minimum, a discussion of 1) the "no action" alternative (i.e., not taking any proposed action), 2) reasonable alternatives that would eliminate or minimize the need for the proposed action and 3) alternatives that would mitigate the environmental impact of the proposal. The agency must also discuss environmental impacts of the alternatives including direct, indirect and cumulative impacts.

Determining what are "reasonable" alternatives can be difficult.

NRDC v. Morton, 458 F.2d 827 (D.C.Cir.1972), was an early and influential case which discussed the alternatives issue. The case involved the scope of an EIS prepared by the Department of Interior for an offshore oil and gas lease sale. DOI claimed that it did not need to consider speculative alternatives or alternatives it did not have authority to implement that would lessen the need for offshore oil and gas. The court indicated that the scope of alternatives that must be considered was to be judged by a "rule of reason." The court held that "remote and speculative" technologies, such as coal degasification or geothermal energy, did not need to be considered. But the court held that other actions, including eliminating oil import quotas, did need to be addressed even if they could not be implemented by DOI. The court noted that DOI's leasing activity was part of a broader government energy policy and emphasized that one of the purposes of the EIS was to provide information to decision-makers, including Congress, who could act.

In *Vermont Yankee Nuclear Power Corp. v. NRDC*, 435 U.S. 519, 98 S.Ct. 1197, 55 L.Ed.2d 460 (1978), the Supreme Court may have narrowed the scope of alternatives that must be considered in an EIS. *Vermont Yankee* involved a claim that the Nuclear Regulatory Commission ("NRC") should have considered energy conservation as an alternative to issuance of a specific license to a nuclear power plant. Although the Supreme Court reaffirmed the "rule of reason" the Court held that the agency did not need to consider every possible alternative including energy conservation. The court seemed to limit the agencies independent obligation to identify and consider alternatives, and seemed to place the burden on the opponents of a proposed action to present the alternatives to the agency.

2. Mitigation

Agencies are required to consider reasonable alternatives that will mitigate the adverse environmental impact of a proposed action. In *Robertson v. Methow Valley Citizens Council*, 490 U.S. 332, 109 S.Ct. 1835, 104 L.Ed.2d 351 (1989), the Supreme Court held that a "reasonably complete" discussion of mitigation measures was necessary in an EIS prepared on a Forest Service permit for a ski resort in a national forest.

The Court further held, however, that the Forest Service had no substantive obligation to adopt any mitigation measures as long as the issues were adequately discussed in the EIS.

3. Uncertainties and New Information

In many cases there is inadequate scientific information to determine what the environmental effects of a proposed action will be. At a minimum, CEQ and the courts require the agencies to publicly disclose that the information is lacking.

The extent to which agencies must affirmatively generate new information is less clear. The CEQ regulations require agencies to include "incomplete information" that is "essential" to a reasoned choice among alternatives if "the overall costs of obtaining it are not exorbitant." 40 C.F.R. § 1502.22(a). The Agency must disclose the fact that "relevant" information has not been included because the costs of obtaining the information is exorbitant or the means to obtain it are not known. 40 C.F.R. § 1502.22(b).

In *Alaska v. Andrus*, 580 F.2d 465 (D.C.Cir.1978), the court upheld a decision of the Department of the Interior to undertake a sale of offshore oil and gas leases off Alaska although the environmental effects of oil and gas activity were not known. The court held that agencies do, in some cases, have an affirmative duty to acquire information and that they cannot avoid considering uncertain or unknown effects by labeling them "crystal ball inquiry." The court noted that NEPA does not specify the "quantum of information" that agencies must have before they proceed, but held that the agency must at least weigh the cost of delay with the cost of going forward in light of the uncertainties.

4. Worst Case Analysis

Preparation of a "worst case analysis" is one way of dealing with unknown environmental effects or effects that have a low probability of occurring but catastrophic consequences if they do occur. A worst case analysis identifies the environmental consequences of the worst possible outcome.

At one time, CEQ regulations required preparation of a "worst case analysis" when information was uncertain or incomplete. The worst case regulation was withdrawn in 1986, and the regulations now require consideration of "reasonably foreseeable" impacts if supported by credible scientific evidence and is within the rule of reason. In *Robertson v. Methow Valley Citizens Council*, 490 U.S. 332, 109 S.Ct. 1835, 104 L.Ed.2d 351 (1989), the Supreme Court upheld revocation of the worst case regulation.

5. Supplemental EIS

In some cases, new information or changes in the design of a proposal may raise issues not addressed in the original EIS. In these cases, agencies may be required to prepare a "supplemental" EIS that addresses the effect of this new information. The CEQ regulations require a supplemental EIS if the change in the project is "substantial" or if new information is "significant." In *Marsh v. Oregon Natural Resources Council*, 490 U.S. 360, 109 S.Ct. 1851, 104 L.Ed.2d 377 (1989), the Supreme Court stated that courts may review an agency's decision not to prepare a supplemental impact statement but held that the standard of review of the agency's decision was a limited "arbitrary and capricious" standard.

F.   Substantive Effect of NEPA

The Supreme Court has described NEPA as "essentially procedural." While it is clear that agencies must comply with NEPA's procedural obligations in preparing an EIS, it is far less clear what legal effect NEPA has on the substantive decisions made by federal agencies. The issue of NEPA's "substantive effect" generally involves the question of whether an agency's final decision (as opposed to its preparation of an EIS) violate the requirements of NEPA.

In considering the issue of the substantive effect of NEPA it is useful to distinguish between arguments that NEPA *requires* agencies to reach a specific decision and arguments that NEPA *authorizes* agencies to reach a decision.

1. Must an Agency Reach a Specific Decision Under NEPA

If an agency prepares an adequate EIS, can the final action that the agency takes be challenged as violating the substantive requirements of NEPA? In other words, does NEPA impose any substantive requirements to reject environmentally harmful actions or to mitigate the adverse environmental effects of an action?

This issue has been largely resolved by several decisions in which the Supreme Court rejected challenges under NEPA to the substantive decisions made by federal agencies. *Strycker's Bay Neighborhood Council, Inc. v. Karlen*, 444 U.S. 223, 100 S.Ct. 497, 62 L.Ed.2d 433 (1980), involved a challenge to a decision of the federal Department of Housing and Urban Development ("HUD") to construct low income housing in Manhattan. HUD had prepared an environmental assessment, and the Court of Appeals specifically found that the assessment was procedurally adequate and the consideration of alternatives was not arbitrary and capricious. The Court of Appeals nonetheless rejected the decision apparently based on HUD's improper weighing of environmental factors. The Supreme Court reversed. The Court held that NEPA requires no more than an adequate consideration of environmental factors, and strongly implied that a court could not reject an agency decision under NEPA based on the court's assessment of the agency's weighing of information contained in an otherwise adequate EIS.

The Supreme Court reaffirmed the limited substantive content of NEPA in *Robertson v. Methow Valley Citizens Council*, 490 U.S. 332, 109 S.Ct. 1835, 104 L.Ed.2d 351 (1989). In this case, the Supreme Court held that an agency had no obligation to adopt mitigation measures identified in an EIS. Thus, the agency decision could not be rejected under NEPA as long as the EIS was procedurally adequate. The Court stated that NEPA prohibits "uninformed—rather than unwise—agency decisions."

Although the Supreme Court has limited the substantive effect of NEPA, NEPA still may play a significant role in any challenge to agency decisions. First, many agencies are acting under the authority of statutes that contain substantive environmental provisions. For example, when the Department of Interior issues offshore oil and gas leases it is operating under the authority of the Outer Continental Shelf Lands Act ("OCSLA") which specifically requires a weighing of environmental factors in the leasing decision. If DOI prepares an EIS on a leasing decision, the information contained in the EIS may be important in a claim that DOI violated the substantive provisions of OCSLA. Although not a challenge under NEPA, NEPA can significantly affect litigation over the issue. It is very important to look for statutes other than NEPA which may provide a substantive basis for challenging the environmental decisions made by an agency.

Second, under the federal Administrative Procedure Act, a court may reject a federal decision if it is "arbitrary and capricious." NEPA ensures that information about the environmental consequences of an action are in the administrative record of the agency's action. If the agency does not adequately explain why it is reaching a decision and does not respond to issues raised during the EIS process, a court may conclude that the agency decision is "arbitrary and capricious."

2.   May the Government Reach a Specific Decision

Does NEPA expand an agency's legal authority to base its decisions on environmental factors? In one of the earliest and most important NEPA cases, *Calvert Cliffs' Coordinating Committee, Inc. v. United States Atomic Energy Commission*, 449 F.2d 1109 (D.C.Cir.1971), the court specifically held that NEPA authorized the Atomic Energy Commission to consider non-nuclear environmental factors in determining whether to issue a license for a nuclear power plant. The court stated that under NEPA the AEC was "not only permitted, but compelled, to take environmental values into account." Similarly, in *Environmental Defense Fund v. Mathews*, 410 F.Supp. 336 (D.D.C.1976), the court specifically held that NEPA provided "supplementary" authority to base its substantive decisions on environmental factors even if those factors were not specified in other legislation authorizing the agency's actions.

The continuing validity of these cases may be in question in light of such cases as *Strycker's Bay* and *Methow Valley* in which the Supreme Court limited the substantive effect of NEPA.

G.   International Application of NEPA

There has been a persistent dispute as to whether NEPA applies to federal actions taken abroad. In general, federal statutes are not presumed to have "extraterritorial" effect unless there is clear indication that Congress intended the statute to be applied abroad. The case law on the international application of NEPA is limited, but courts have not been willing to hold that Congress clearly intended NEPA to apply abroad.

In 1979, President Carter issued Executive Order 12114 that extended requirements similar to those found in NEPA to federal actions that have significant environmental effects abroad. Private citizens, however, may not sue for violations of the Executive Order.

H. Judicial Review

NEPA does not contain a "citizen suit" provision, and it does not specifically authorize judicial review of agency compliance. Nonetheless, courts routinely review agency compliance with NEPA and judicial review has been crucial in developing the requirements of NEPA.

1. Source

Jurisdiction for courts to review agency compliance with NEPA arises under 28 U.S.C. § 1331. This section is the general grant of "federal question" jurisdiction which authorizes federal courts to review issues "arising under" federal law. In *Calvert Cliffs' Coordinating Committee, Inc. v. United States Atomic Energy Commission*, 449 F.2d 1109 (D.C.Cir.1971), the D.C. Circuit held that the courts have an important role to play in ensuring compliance with NEPA, and this decision set the stage for active judicial review of agency actions under NEPA.

2. Standard of Review

The Administrative Procedure Act ("APA") establishes the standard of review that courts will apply in judging most federal actions. Virtually all of the actions reviewed under NEPA are considered to be informal agency decision-making and are judged under the APA's "arbitrary and capricious" PERSPECTIVEstandard.

3. Scope of Review

Courts will review agency actions to ensure full compliance with NEPA. In practice, this means that agency decisions not to prepare an EIS are subject to judicial review. In addition, courts have been willing to determine whether agencies have fully complied with the procedural obligations of NEPA and whether the content of the EIS satisfies the obligations of NEPA. Thus, a court will determine whether an agency has adequately defined the scope of the EIS and whether the agency has adequately addressed alternatives in the EIS. As discussed above, however, NEPA may not have "substantive" requirements, and thus a court will generally not determine that the final decision reached by an agency violates NEPA.

4. Relief

NEPA does not authorize civil penalties against agencies for violation of its provisions, and, in general, the remedy for violation of NEPA is an injunction which prohibits further federal action until the Agency complies with NEPA. Issues relating to injunctive relief most frequently arise when plaintiffs seek a preliminary injunction to enjoin agency actions until resolution of the NEPA issue. Federal courts typically are required to "balance the equities" before issuing an injunction, and this would typically require some showing of "irreparable harm" if the injunction is not issued and, in the case of preliminary injunctions, a showing of "probable success on the merits."

In a number of cases, courts have been willing to presume "irreparable harm" when NEPA has or is likely to be found to have been violated. Given a presumption of irreparable harm, courts have generally been willing to grant injunctive relief for claimed violations of NEPA. Several cases suggest, however, that courts may be unwilling to continue automatically to grant injunctions for violations of NEPA without some showing of irreparable harm.

I. State Environmental Policy Acts

A majority of states have adopted legislation modeled on NEPA. These statutes, generally known as "little NEPAs" or state environmental policy acts ("SEPAs") mimic the basic structure of NEPA by requiring some form of environmental analysis prior to taking an action. In many cases, state courts look to interpretations of the federal NEPA to determine the content of state SEPAs.

Note, however, that the SEPA's may differ in important respects from NEPA. Some SEPA's, for example, apply to private as well as government actions. Additionally, they may provide greater substantive authority than NEPA and they may specify a different scope or content to the environmental review. It is important to evaluate the specific state statute when determining the requirements of a SEPA.

J. Criticisms of NEPA

NEPA has resulted in a great deal of paperwork and a great deal of litigation. It is less clear whether NEPA has resulted in any improvement in the environment. Critics of the NEPA process have charged that federal agencies do not seriously consider the environmental issues or recommendations found in EIS's. They charge that the bureaucratic process within "mission" agencies (those agencies with the responsibility to accomplish a particular mission—i.e., promotion of housing at Housing and Urban Development, development of nuclear power at the old Atomic Energy Commission) tends to discount alternatives that will interfere with the Agency's mission. In this view, NEPA results in elaborate

Environmental Impact Statements that are not part of the real decision-making process by the Agency.

Supporters of NEPA argue that the generation of information in EIS's does affect the substantive outcome of agency decisions. Even if the most protective environmental option is not selected, some of the worst environmental problems are avoided when information about those problems is contained in the administrative record of the agency's decision. You should note that simply placing information before an agency can affect agency decision-making since, to avoid a determination by a court that the agency's action was arbitrary and capricious, the agency must explain its response to the information.

Perhaps the most significant effect of NEPA has been to delay agency actions. Opponents of agency actions have frequently been successful in delaying a project based on the agency's failure to comply with the procedural requirements of NEPA. Delaying a project may result in the project being canceled or altered.

There have been few studies of the actual effect of NEPA on agency decision-making, and those few studies are equivocal on whether NEPA has improved the quality of agency decisions.

K. Review Questions

1. T or F   EPA is authorized to prohibit any proposed federal action subject to § 102(2)(C) of NEPA if, after review of the EIS, EPA determines that the environmental effects of the proposed action are unsatisfactory.

2. T or F   The citizen suit provision of NEPA authorizes citizens who meet the constitutional requirements for standing to challenge the adequacy of an EIS in federal district court.

3. T or F   When EPA issues a permit to a "major source" under Title V of the Clean Air Act, EPA will be required to prepare an EIS if operation of the source will "significantly affect the quality of the human environment."

4. T or F   Although a federal agency must review existing information about the environmental effects of a proposed federal action subject to § 102(2)(C), an agency is never required to undertake new studies or generate new information about possible environmental effects.

5. T or F   A federal agency is not required to undertake any environmental review or assessment of a proposed action if the agency determines

that the action will not significantly affect the quality of the human environment.

6. **T or F** Since § 102(2)(C) applies only to "major federal actions" activities of private parties are never subject to an assessment in an EIS.

7. **T or F** Under NEPA, a federal agency is required to mitigate, to the greatest extent practicable, the adverse effects of a proposed project that are identified in an EIS.

8. **T or F** If an agency determines that it should consider the cumulative effects of a number of small projects, the agency may address the common environmental impacts in a "programmatic" EIS and address the local impacts in a "site specific" EIS.

9. **T or F** Once an agency has prepared an EIS that complies with NEPA, it is never obligated to "reopen" the EIS to consider newly generated information about the environmental effects of the proposed action.

10. **T or F** In order to obtain information about environmental effects and alternatives at the earliest possible stage in agency deliberations, an agency must prepare an EIS at the point when it first formulates the idea that could lead to a final agency action.

CHAPTER 5

Clean Water Act

■ ANALYSIS

G.   REVIEW QUESTIONS

A. Background

The Clean Water Act is the primary federal statute dealing with water pollution. It consists, as described below, of a variety of different and quite distinct programs. However, most casebooks focus attention on those portions of the statute which regulate the direct discharge of pollution from industrial and municipal sources. This is the "National Pollutant Discharge Elimination System" or "NPDES" permit program.

1. Name of the Statute

You will see this statute referred to as either the Clean Water Act (CWA) or the Federal Water Pollution Control Act (FWPCA). Both are correct. The basic structure of the statute was originally adopted in the Federal Water Pollution Control Act Amendments of 1972, but EPA and most practitioners refer to the statute as the Clean Water Act.

2. Structure

The Clean Water Act has several distinct programs that deal with control of water pollution.

a. Direct Dischargers—NPDES Point Source Program

The Clean Water Act requires that every industrial and municipal facility that directly discharges pollutants into streams, lakes or the ocean have a permit. § 301(a), 33 U.S.C. § 1311(a). This permit is called a "National Pollutant Discharge Elimination System" or "NPDES" permit. This permit generally contains limitations on the quantity or concentration of pollutants that the facility can discharge.

b. Indirect Dischargers—Pretreatment Program

Facilities that discharge their wastes down a sewer to be treated by a municipal sewage treatment facility are called "indirect dischargers." They are required to meet "pretreatment" requirements that apply to the wastes they put in the sewer. § 307(b), 33 U.S.C. § 1317(b). These restrictions are established either by the federal government or the local municipal sewage treatment authority. Indirect dischargers are not, in most cases, required to have an NPDES permit.

c. Non-point Sources—Areawide Controls

Some pollution, such as agricultural runoff or runoff from city streets, is neither discharged by point sources nor put down a sewer. This type of pollution is called "areawide" or "non-point source pollution." Several sections of the CWA require local planning to control this type of pollution, but there is almost no effective regulatory controls for this type of pollution under the Clean Water Act. **§ 208, 33 U.S.C. § 1288, § 319, 33 U.S.C. § 1329**.

d. Dredge and Fill Program

Section 404 of the CWA establishes a separate national permit program for activity that results in dredging or filling of "wetlands." **§ 404, 33 U.S.C. § 1344**. Criteria for permit issuance have been established by EPA, but the permit itself is issued by the Army Corps of Engineers. This program is typically not addressed in detail in environmental law casebooks, but the dredge and fill program is one of the more significant federal programs regulating land use.

e. Oil Spill Program

Section 311 of the Clean Water Act contains provisions relating to reporting and cleanup of spills of oil and hazardous substances to navigable water. **§ 311, 33 U.S.C. § 1321**. This program is totally distinct from other provisions of the CWA. It has many elements in common with the Comprehensive Environmental Response, Compensation and Liability Act ("CERCLA"), but, unlike CERCLA, it applies to oil and it applies only to releases or threats of releases into navigable water.

3. History

Prior to 1972, Congress enacted a number of federal statutes dealing with water pollution, but the current structure of the CWA was established by the Federal Water Pollution Control Act Amendments of 1972. The 1972 Act established two of the major elements of the existing statute—a national permit program and the requirement that industrial dischargers meet progressively more stringent technology based limits. The 1972 Act continued, with significant modifications, a water quality standards program that had been established in 1965.

The statute has been the subject of several significant sets of amendments since 1972. In 1977 the statute was amended to create, among other things, the "Best Conventional Technology" ("BCT") limitation on industrial dischargers. The statute was subsequently amended by the Water Quality Act of 1987 which, among other things, increased controls on toxic pollutants. Additionally, in the Oil Pollution Act of 1990, Congress amended section 311 of the CWA to establish a more effective program to respond to oil spills.

4. Outline of Major Statutory Provisions

Section 101, 33 U.S.C. § 1251. General goals and policies of the Act.

Section 301, 33 U.S.C. § 1311. Prohibition on discharge without a permit and obligation to meet Best Practicable Technology ("BPT"), Best Available Technology ("BAT"), Best Conventional Technology ("BCT"), and Secondary Treatment requirements.

Section 302, 33 U.S.C. § 1312. Provision for establishing water quality related effluent limitations. This is a different source of authority from water quality standards, and section 302 has rarely, if ever, been used.

Section 303, 33 U.S.C. § 1313. Provisions relating to water quality standards.

Section 304, 33 U.S.C. § 1314. Provisions specifying factors for establishment of BPT, BCT and BAT limits and requirements relating to toxic hot spots.

Section 306, 33 U.S.C. § 1316. Provisions relating to new source performance standards.

Section 307, 33 U.S.C. § 1317. Provisions for designating toxic pollutants and establishment of toxic effluent standards. Also requirements for establishment of pretreatment program.

Section 311, 33 U.S.C. § 1321. Provisions dealing with spills of oil and hazardous substances into navigable waters.

Section 401, 33 U.S.C. § 1341. Requirement for states to certify that a discharge will comply with state laws.

Section 402, 33 U.S.C. § 1342. Provisions dealing with issuance of NPDES permits and delegation of permit issuance authority to states.

Section 403, 33 U.S.C. § 1343. Ocean discharge criteria.

Section 404, 33 U.S.C. § 1344. Provisions relating to issuance of dredge and fill permits.

Section 405, 33 U.S.C. § 1345. Provisions relating to sewage sludge criteria.

Section 502, 33 U.S.C. § 1362. General definitions.

Section 505, 33 U.S.C. § 1365. Citizen suit provisions.

Section 509, 33 U.S.C. § 1369. Provisions relating to judicial review of EPA actions.

Section 510, 33 U.S.C. § 1370. Provision generally preserving states' authority to adopt water pollution requirements that are more stringent than the federal requirements.

B. National Pollutant Discharge Elimination System Permit Program

1. Basic Structure

The NPDES permit program could not be simpler. If you discharge pollutants from a point source, such as a pipe, into water, such as a stream, you must have an NPDES permit. The permit will typically contain limits on the quantities of pollutants that can be discharged. Those limits are either "technology-based," limits based on what pollution control technology is available, or "water quality standards-based," limits set to ensure your discharge will not violate state water quality standards. If you violate the limits in your permit you can be sued for substantial penalties either by the government or by private citizens. The rest is simply detail.

2. Scope

The key to understanding the NPDES permit program is section 301(a) of the CWA. **§ 301(a), 33 U.S.C. § 1311(a)**. That section prohibits the "discharge of pollutants" unless authorized by a permit. The definition of "discharge of pollutant" is found at § 502(12), and it has several key elements. **§ 502(12), 33 U.S.C. § 1362(12)**. To be a discharge of pollutants there must be the "addition of any pollutant" from a "point source" into "navigable waters."

a. Addition of a Pollutant

Pollutant is broadly defined by the CWA to include almost any physical substance and even non-physical substances such as heat. **§ 502(6), 33 U.S.C. § 1362(6)**. The discharge of a pollutant will trigger the permit requirement. There is no requirement that the pollutant cause adverse environmental effects. In other words, pollutants are regulated not pollution.

Additionally, the pollutant must be added to the water. In some cases, facilities that take water out of a stream and return that water to the same stream without adding new pollutants do not need a permit. In other words, there must be a net increase in pollutants not simply the gross addition of pollutants. This is called the "net/gross" rule.

b. Point Source

The NPDES permit program applies to discharges from point sources. This is defined as "any discernible, confined and discrete conveyance," including such things as pipes or ditches. **§ 502(14), 33 U.S.C. § 1362(14).** An industrial facility, for example, may collect its wastewater and discharge the wastewater from a pipe into a local stream. The pipe is a point source, and the facility may be required to obtain an NPDES permit for its discharge of wastewater.

In some cases, natural channels or gullies through which water flows may be a point source. Rainwater, for example, may collect into natural channels on industrial property and then flow into a local stream. The channel may be a point source, and the facility may be required to obtain an NPDES permit for its stormwater runoff.

c. Navigable Water

The NPDES permit requirement applies to all discharges into "navigable waters." These are defined to include "waters of the U.S, including the territorial seas." **§ 502(7), 33 U.S.C. § 1362(7).** The territorial seas include waters three miles from shore. Additionally, facilities other than boats, such as oil platforms, that discharge into the ocean beyond three miles are required to have an NPDES permit.

A key point to recognize is that the terms "navigable waters" and "waters of the U.S." are not defined by whether boats can actually float on them. Rather, EPA ha defined such waters broadly to include, among other things, 1) traditionally navigable waters, 2) tributaries of traditionally navigable waters, 3) waters "the use, degradation or destruction of which could affect interstate or foreign commerce," and 4) wetlands. EPA defines "wetlands" to include not only swamps or marshes but also areas which support types of plant life that biologists characterize as living in saturated soil. The Corps of Engineers has promulgated a comparable definition of "waters of the U.S." for purposes of applying the § 404 dredge and fill permit program. **§ 404, 33 U.S.C. § 1344.**

In a series of cases, the Supreme Court has dealt with the jurisdictional scope of the terms "navigable waters" and "waters of the U.S." In *United States v. Riverside Bayview Homes*, 474 U.S. 121, 106 S.Ct. 455, 88 L.Ed.2d 419 (1985), the Supreme Court upheld the government's definition of "wetlands" that was based on this biological assessment of the life supported in the area. In *Solid Waste Agency of Northern Cook Cty. v.*

United States Army Corps of Engineers, 531 U.S. 159, 121 S.Ct. 675, 148 L.Ed.2d 576 (2001), the Supreme Court held that Clean Water Act jurisdiction did not extend to isolated, intermittent bodies of water that might be used by migratory birds. In *Rapanos v. United States,* 547 U.S. 715, 126 S.Ct. 2208, 165 L.Ed.2d 159 (2006) a divided Supreme Court was unable to produce a majority opinion interpreting the scope of "waters of the U.S." Four justices held that the term only applies to waters that are navigable in fact, relatively permanent bodies of water that are connected to traditional navigable waters, or wetlands that that have a substantial surface connection to such waters. Four justices held that the term includes waters that affect interstate commerce as specified in the EPA regulation. One justice, Justice Kennedy, held that "waters of the U.S." include wetlands that have a "significant nexus" to other waters of the U.S. Proving a "significant nexus" would involve a case-by-case assessment of whether the wetland "significantly affects the chemical, physical or biological integrity" of other covered waters. Most courts are applying Justice Kennedy's "significant nexus" test.

3. Imposition of Conditions

a. Types of Conditions

An NPDES permit can contain several types of conditions. The most important conditions are limitations on the quantities or concentrations of pollutants that the facility can legally discharge—these are called "effluent limitations." Additionally, a permit will typically require the facility to test the discharge to see if it meets the specified effluent limitations. These tests must be reported to the appropriate government body. This report is known as a "discharge monitoring report" or "DMR."

b. Sources of Authority to Impose Conditions

The CWA requires point sources to meet technology-based effluent limitations and to meet effluent limitations based on water quality standards. These are the most important sources of authority for including effluent limitations in permits. Virtually all effluent limits are either technology or water quality standards based. Additionally, there are several other sources of authority to place restrictions in the permit. These are far less significant than technology-based or water quality standards-based limits.

(1) Technology–Based Limits

The permit writer may include "technology-based" limitations in an NPDES permit. **§ 301(b), 33 U.S.C. § 1311(b) and § 306, 33 U.S.C.**

§ 1316. These limitations are based on an assessment of the "best" type of pollution control equipment which that type of facility could use.

Determining the "best" technology typically involves an assessment of the cost and availability of pollution control technology. As described below, there is an alphabet soup of acronyms describing the various levels of technology-based limits—for industrial sources, these include Best Practicable Technology ("BPT"), Best Available Technology ("BAT"), Best Conventional Technology ("BCT"), and New Source Performance Standards ("NSPS"). The technology-based limitation applicable to municipal sewage treatment plants, known as "publicly owned treatment works" or "POTWs," is "secondary treatment."

All facilities must meet applicable technology-based limits; they are a floor or minimum level of control.

(2) Water Quality Standards—Based Limits

Alternatively, limits may be "water quality standards-based." § 301(b)(1)(C), 33 U.S.C. § 1311(b)(1)(C). These limitations are set at a level which will ensure that state water quality standards are not violated. Water quality standards-based limits (sometimes referred to as "water quality standards-based effluent limitations" or "WQBELs") are included in an NPDES permit when technology-based limits are not sufficiently stringent to ensure that state water quality standards are not violated.

(3) Ocean Discharge Criteria

Facilities that discharge into the territorial sea, contiguous zone or ocean are also subject to limits based on the "ocean discharge criteria." § 403, 33 U.S.C. § 1343. These are intended to prevent "unreasonable degradation" of the marine environment. This source of authority can be important for coastal or offshore facilities.

(4) Toxic Effluent Standards

The CWA authorizes EPA to promulgate stringent national limits on the discharge of designated toxic pollutants. § 307(a)(2), 33 U.S.C. § 1317(a)(2). Although EPA has listed 65 toxic pollutants, it has, for various reasons, promulgated toxic effluent standards for only six of these pollutants. EPA has not published any since 1977. Be careful to distinguish the six section 307(a) toxic effluent standards from other technology-based or water quality standards-based effluent limitations on toxic pollutants.

(5) Water Quality Related Effluent Limitations

EPA is authorized under section 302 to establish stringent limits to ensure that local water quality is preserved. **§ 302, 33 U.S.C. § 1312**. This section, among other things, requires EPA to perform some type of cost-benefit analysis in establishing the limits. Under the CWA EPA can more easily impose the same limits through the water quality standards program, and EPA does not impose limitations using the authority under section 302. Again, be careful. EPA and state frequently establish water quality standards based effluent limitations (WQBELs) under the water quality standards program of § 303. Section 302 "water quality related effluent limitations" sound the same, but they are completely different.

4. Permit Issuance

a. Federal or State Permit Issuance

Under the CWA, the EPA was initially required to issue all NPDES permits. **§ 402(a), 33 U.S.C. § 1342(a)**. The CWA, however, allows EPA to delegate permit issuing responsibility to a state if the state adopts a permit program substantially equivalent to the federal program. **§ 402(b), 33 U.S.C. § 1342(b)**. If a state has been delegated authority, it, rather than EPA, issues the NPDES permit. If a state has not been delegated authority, EPA still issues the permit. To date, approximately 90% of the states have been delegated permit authority.

Even when the state issues NPDES permits, EPA retains a role in the process. Under section 402(d), EPA has the authority to veto a state issued permit that is "outside the guidelines and requirements" of the act. **§ 402(d), 33 U.S.C. § 1342(d)**. If the state does not revise the permit in response to EPA's veto, EPA may then issue the permit. Additionally, a state's authority to issue NPDES permits may be revoked if EPA determines that the state is not administering the program in accordance with the requirements of section 402. **§ 402(c), 33 U.S.C. § 1342(c)**.

b. Individual or General Permits

Most NPDES permits are individually issued to particular facilities. EPA regulations also authorize issuance of "general" permits that apply to large numbers of similar facilities. EPA, for example, has issued one general permit that applies to most off-shore oil platforms in the Gulf of Mexico. Additionally, EPA has issued general permits that apply to "stormwater runoff" from large numbers of industrial facilities and construction sites.

c. Procedural Issues

When issued by EPA, an individual NPDES permit is typically issued following a number of steps: 1) A draft permit is prepared, 2) a public meeting on the draft may be called in some cases, 3) a final permit is issued, and 4) if the permittee or other citizen objects to the final permit, an administrative hearing may be called (this hearing, held before an Administrative Law Judge (ALJ), is similar to a mini-trial), 5) following a determination by the ALJ, parties may appeal the final decision to the Administrator of the EPA. Following appeal to the Administrator, the permit is final for purposes of judicial review.

Facilities that are covered by a "general permit" do not need to go through the normal permit issuance process. Rather, they simply submit a "Notice of Intent" to be covered by the general permit and then must comply with the conditions contained in the permit.

d. Effect of Permit—Permit Shield

Section 402(k) of the CWA provides that compliance with an NPDES permit is "deemed compliance" with virtually all of the requirements of the act. § 402(k), 33 U.S.C. § 1342(k). This is known as a "permit shield." This means that if a facility is meeting the specific requirements of its permit, it cannot, with few exceptions, be prosecuted for violating the Clean Water Act. This provision is widely misunderstood. EPA has for many years taken the position that it is legal to discharge a pollutant even if that pollutant is not specified in an NPDES permit. Therefore, the permit shield protects a facility if it discharges a pollutant even if the permit does not contain a specific limitation on that pollutant. If EPA wants to control the discharge of that pollutant, it must modify the permit to include a limitation. Compare section 402(k) of the CWA with section 504(f) of the Clean Air Act.

C. Technology–Based Limits

1. Role of Technology–Based Standards

Every point source that discharges pollutants is required by sections 301 and 306 to meet applicable technology-based limitations.

Technology-based limitations are derived based on a consideration of the cost and availability of pollution control technology. One of the major elements of the CWA is a requirement that sources use the "best" technology available regardless of whether the government demonstrates that the discharge is causing adverse environmental harm. Technology-based standards for industrial sources are intended to become progressively more stringent, and EPA is required to review the standards every five years. **§ 301(d), 33 U.S.C. § 1311(d).**

Different types of technology-based limitations are described by a shorthand of acronyms. As described below, BPT, BAT, BCT and NSPS all refer to types of technology-based limits. These differ with respect to 1) when they must be achieved, 2) what types of sources they apply to, 3) what pollutants they cover, and 4) their level of stringency.

2. Sources Covered

a. Existing Sources

Existing sources of pollution, other than municipal sewage treatment plants (called "publicly owned treatment works" or "POTWs"), are subject to technology-based limitations, known as Best Practicable Technology ("BPT"), Best Conventional Technology ("BCT") and Best Available Technology ("BAT") limits. Typically, controls on existing sources are based on technology that can be added at the "end of the pipe" rather than controls that require modification of the industrial process itself.

b. New Sources

New sources of pollution (other than POTWs) are subject to a different, and potentially more stringent, technology-based requirement than existing sources. These are known as NSPS or BADT limits. New source limits could be more stringent since newly constructed facilities can "design" pollution control into their process itself. Thus, new source limitations may require more process modifications, such as recycling of wastewater, than existing source limitations.

A key point to understand is that classification of a facility as a new source depends on whether EPA has promulgated applicable new source limitations. Under section 306, a new source is defined as a facility that commences construction *after* EPA proposes a new source performance standard (if the standard is thereafter promulgated in accordance with the section). § 306(a)(2), 33 U.S.C. § 1316(a)(2). Thus, if a facility were built tomorrow it would still technically be an existing source if EPA has not yet proposed, and promulgated, a new source standard that applies to that type of facility.

Although the statute and caselaw is somewhat confusing, EPA has taken the position that, under the Clean Water Act, a facility is not a new source unless it commenced construction after *promulgation* of final new source standards. Compare the definition of new source in section 306 of the CWA with the definition of new source in section 111 of the Clean Air Act.

c. Publicly Owned Treatment Works

A final class of facilities subject to their own technology-based standards are municipal sewage treatment plants called "publicly owned treatment works" or "POTWs." POTWs are subject to the relatively non-stringent, technology-based limitation known as "secondary treatment." § 301(b)(1)(B), 33 U.S.C. § 1311(b)(1)(B).

3. Pollutants Covered

The CWA divides pollutants into three categories—toxic pollutants, conventional pollutants and the remaining group of "non-toxic, non-conventional" pollutants. There are two main consequences associated with the category of pollutant being regulated. First, most variances are not available from limitations that apply to toxic and conventional pollutants. Second, a different cost test applies to certain limitations on conventional pollutants.

a. Toxic Pollutants

Under the CWA, EPA may designate a pollutant as a "toxic pollutant" based on its harmful effect on the environment. Just because a pollutant is harmful, however, does not mean it is a toxic pollutant. It is a toxic *only* if EPA has formally listed the pollutant as toxic. § 307(a)(1), 33 U.S.C. § 1317(a)(1). There are now approximately 65 of these toxic pollutants. You may sometimes see a list of hundreds of toxic pollutants, but this includes subclassification of this basic list.

As described below, toxic pollutants are subject to BPT, BAT and NSPS effluent limitations. A facility may be eligible for a "fundamentally different factors" variance for limits on toxic pollutants, but it may not get a § 301(c) cost variance or § 301(g) water quality variance from a restriction on a toxic pollutant.

b. Conventional Pollutants

EPA may designate certain pollutants as "conventional pollutants." § 304(a)(4), 33 U.S.C. § 1314(a)(4). These pollutants include non-toxic pollutants, with well understood environmental effects, that have been the focus of traditional water pollution control efforts. The list of conventional pollutants includes biological oxygen demanding pollutants ("BOD"), suspended solids, fecal coliform, pH and oil and grease.

As described below, conventional pollutants are subject to BPT, BCT and NSPS effluent limitations. There are no BAT limits on conventional pollutants. A facility may be eligible for a "fundamentally different factors" variance for limits on conventional pollutants, but a facility may not get a § 301(c) cost variance or § 301(g) water quality variance from a restriction on a conventional pollutant.

c. Non-toxic, Non-conventional Pollutants

All remaining pollutants that are not specifically classified as toxic or conventional pollutants are "Non-toxic, non-conventional" pollutants. As described below, these pollutants are subject to BPT, BAT and NSPS effluent limitations. A facility may be eligible for all available variances from limitations on these pollutants.

4. Development of National Technology–Based Standards

a. Developing Technology–Based Limits

Section 304(b) of the CWA specifies factors that EPA must consider in developing effluent limitations guidelines for existing sources. § 304(b), 33 U.S.C. § 1314(b). Section 306 specifies factors for establishing NSPS for new sources. § 306(a)(1), 33 U.S.C. § 1316(a)(1). Although the factors vary for BPT, BAT, BCT and NSPS, particularly with respect to cost, all of the guidelines include some consideration of the cost of employing technology and the availability of technology within the category or subcategory.

In developing national effluent limitations guidelines, EPA goes through a number of steps including 1) collection of data about the industry, 2) determination of appropriate subcategories within the industry, 3) identification of "options" or possible different pollution control technologies or combinations of technologies, 5) determination of the "costs" to the industry of using each option, 6) selection of the final option, and 7) promulgation of final numbers which reflect the degree of effluent reduction that could be achieved if the selected option were used by facilities within the subcategory.

b. National or Case-by-Case

In most cases, "technology-based" limits are numbers that have been promulgated by EPA for a category of industrial source, and they apply nationally to all facilities within a specific industry. Where EPA has not promulgated national numbers, the permit writer may develop individual case-by-case limits based on the permit writers "best professional judgment." These are called "BPJ" limits.

In the 1970's, industry argued that EPA did not have the authority to set national effluent limitations. They argued that EPA could only establish general guidelines for setting BPT and BAT under section 304, and that these guidelines were then to be used in setting limits, on a case-by-case basis, in each NPDES permit. Among other things, this approach would have given industry a chance to challenge an effluent limit each time it was included in a permit. In *E.I du Pont de Nemours and Co. v. Train*, 430 U.S. 112, 97 S.Ct. 965, 51 L.Ed.2d 204 (1977), the Supreme Court, for various reasons, rejected this argument and held that EPA could establish binding, nationally applicable effluent limitations guidelines. Effluent limitations guidelines can be challenged once when they are first promulgated, but they are not subject to challenge when included in an NPDES permit.

c. Issues in Developing Technology–Based Limits

(1) Role of Costs

In general, EPA is required to consider the costs to industry of meeting proposed effluent limitations guidelines. It is important to remember that EPA generally considers the costs to the industry as a whole and not to individual sources. Thus, EPA will generally not select a BAT limitation that will put substantial numbers of sources within an industry out of business; it may, however, select an option that is too costly for some sources within the industry.

(a) BPT

In setting BPT, EPA is required to "compare" the costs of pollution reduction with the benefits of pollution reduction. **§ 304(b)(1)(B), 33 U.S.C. § 1314(b)(1)(B)**.

(b) BCT

In setting BCT limits (which apply only to conventional pollutants), EPA is required to 1) compare the reasonableness of the relationship of the costs of pollution reduction with the effluent reduction benefits derived and 2) to compare the costs and levels of reduction by industry with the costs and levels of reduction by POTWs. **§ 304(b)(4)(B), 33 U.S.C. § 1314(b)(4)(B)**.

In *American Paper Institute v. United States EPA*, 660 F.2d 954 (4th Cir.1981), the court held that section 304(b)(4)(B) requires EPA to use both a "cost effectiveness test" and a POTW cost comparison test in setting BCT limits.

EPA has now developed two BCT cost tests that are based on the costs to POTWs to remove conventional pollutants. BCT is generally set at the most stringent level between BPT and BAT that is not so costly that it exceeds either of the two cost tests.

(c) BAT

In setting BAT, EPA is merely required to "consider" costs. **§ 304(b)(2)(B), 33 U.S.C. § 1314(b)(2)(B)**.

(d) NSPS

Section 306 requires EPA to "consider" costs in establishing NSPS. **§ 306(b)(1)(B), 42 U.S.C. § 1316(b)(1)(B)**. In general, EPA "considers" costs in setting NSPS in the same way it considers costs in setting BAT. NSPS limitations on conventional pollutants are not subject to the BCT cost tests.

(2) Role of Benefits

EPA does not consider the environmental benefits to specific water bodies when developing effluent limitations guidelines. EPA typically considers benefits simply by calculating, on a national basis, the total pounds of pollutants that will be removed if an effluent limitation is promulgated.

(3) Technology Transfer

In some cases, no sources within an industry are using the most modern or most effective pollution control technology. In that case, EPA may identify technologies used in other, similar industries and "transfer" that technology. EPA is required to explain why that technology will be effective in the industry to which it is transferred.

Similarly, EPA sometimes identifies novel or experimental technologies that it believes could be used. EPA is required to justify its conclusion that these technologies will work. EPA may have more leeway in selecting unproven technologies when developing BAT and NSPS.

(4) Stringency

Although the CWA identifies factors that EPA must consider in developing effluent limitations guidelines, it does not give specific criteria for determining how stringent the limits must be.

As a rule of thumb, EPA has said that BPT is based on the "average of the best" performers within an industry; this means that BPT limitations frequently are being met by the top quarter of a subcategory.

Both BAT and NSPS represent the "best of the best" and typically, they are being achieved by the very best facilities within a subcategory. Although NSPS could be more stringent than BAT, typically it is not.

BCT must fall somewhere between BPT and BAT. Typically it is the most stringent limitation between BPT and BAT that passes both cost consideration tests.

5. Variances

There are several variances available from otherwise applicable technology-based limitations that individual point sources may receive.

a. Fundamentally Different Factors

The national effluent limitations guidelines are based on assumptions about the typical facility in an industrial subcategory. If a source can demonstrate that it is "fundamentally different" from a typical plant it may be eligible for a "fundamental different factors" of "FDF" variance. The facility must demonstrate that it is "different" with respect to factors that were relevant in establishing the effluent guideline originally. For example, if EPA based its national numbers on the use of biological treatment (which requires relatively warm weather) and a facility operates in Alaska, it may be able to argue that it should get an FDF variance because biological treatment will not operate as effectively. If an FDF is granted, the permit writer would develop a site-specific effluent limitation. EPA claims that the FDF is less a variance from effluent guidelines than development of a case-by-case effluent guideline.

It is important to recognize that the FDF variance is not available simply because a facility cannot afford to meet the national effluent limitation guideline.

The FDF variance is available by statute from BAT and BCT limits. **§ 301(n), 33 U.S.C. § 1311(n)**. EPA regulations also extend the variance to BPT. It is not available for new sources.

b. Cost and Water Quality Variances

Under 301(c) a facility may be eligible for a variance from some BAT limits based on a demonstration that the national number is beyond its economic capability. § 301(c), 33 U.S.C. § 1311(c). In other words, a variance may be available based on the individual facility's ability to pay. Under 301(g) a facility may be eligible for a variance from some BAT limits based on a demonstration that less stringent limits will not interfere with certain acceptable water quality conditions. § 301(g), 33 U.S.C. § 1311(g).

These are very limited variances because they only apply to BAT limits for non-toxic, non-conventional pollutants.

c. Variances for Toxic Pollutants

Section 301(*l*) prohibits modification of effluent limits that apply to any of the 65 designated toxic pollutants. § 301(*l*), 33 U.S.C. § 1311(*l*). The only exception is for the FDF variance. In 1985, in *Chemical Manufacturers Ass'n v. NRDC*, 470 U.S. 116, 105 S.Ct. 1102, 84 L.Ed.2d 90 (1985), the Supreme Court held that section 301(*l*) did not prohibit use of the FDF variance (the case actually involved applying the FDF variance to modify pretreatment requirements) to modify limits on toxic pollutants. In 1987, Congress added section 301(n). Section 301(n) codifies the FDF as it applies to BAT and BCT limits and expressly extends the variance to toxic pollutants.

d. Heat

Section 316 authorizes variances from technology-based limits on heat. **§ 316, 33 U.S.C. § 1326**. Note that "heat" is specifically defined as a pollutant under the Clean Water Act. § 502(6), 33 U.S.C. § 1362(6). This is primarily of significance to power plants which discharge heated water used to cool their facilities.

e. POTW Coastal Discharge

Section 301(h) authorizes some POTWs that discharge into the ocean to get a variance from their requirement to use secondary treatment. § 301(h), 33 U.S.C. § 1311(h).

6. Upset Defense

Even facilities using the best pollution control equipment may occasionally violate effluent limits for reasons beyond their control. Several courts have held EPA must provide some legal protection to facilities that violate technology-based limits in these circumstances. The logic is as follows: a) technology-based limits under the CWA can only require what is currently achievable by technology, b) EPA's own data show that some small, but statistically significant, percentage of the time even the best operated equipment will exceed the technology-based limits, and c) therefore, to penalize a facility for not complying 100% of the time violates the CWA.

EPA responded by creating the "upset defense." EPA regulations require that all federally-issued NPDES permits contain a provision that establishes an affirmative defense from prosecution for violating technology-based limits. To assert the defense, the facility must show that it had installed appropriate technology, that the technology was properly operated, that the violation was for reasons beyond its reasonable control and that it notified the government within 24 hours of the upset. The defense is rarely successful.

The "upset defense" is not available for violations of water quality standards-based limits. Also states need not include an upset defense in state issued permits.

7. Summary of Technology–Based Limitations and Compliance Dates

a. BPT—Best Practicable Technology

Pollutants Covered: All

Sources Covered: Existing industrial sources

Variances Available: FDF

Compliance Date: July 1, 1977 (in some cases March 31, 1989)

Statutory Requirement: Section 301(b)(1)(A)

Factors in Developing: Section 304(b)(1)

b. BCT—Best Conventional Technology

Pollutants Covered: Conventional Pollutants

Sources Covered: Existing industrial sources

Variances Available: FDF

Compliance Date: March 31, 1989

Statutory Requirement: Section 301(b)(2)(E)

Factors in Developing: Section 304(b)(4)

c. BAT—Best Available Technology

Pollutants Covered: Toxic Pollutants and Non-toxic, Non-conventional Pollutants

Sources Covered: Existing Industrial Sources

Major Variances:

Toxic Pollutants—FDF

Non-toxic, Non-conventional Pollutants—FDF, 301(c), 301(g)

Compliance Date: March 31, 1989

Statutory Requirement: Sections 301(b)(2)(A),(C),(D),(F)

Factors in Developing: Section 304(b)(2)

d. NSPS—New Source Performance Standard [also known as BADT or Best Available Demonstrated Technology]

Pollutants Covered: All

Sources Covered: New Sources

Major Variances: None

Compliance Date: Immediately upon Promulgation

Statutory Requirement: Section 306

Factors in Developing: Section 306

e. Secondary Treatment

Pollutants Covered: Potentially all but EPA limits only BOD and TSS

Sources Covered: POTWs

Major Variances: 304(h)

Compliance Date: July 1, 1977

Statutory Requirement: Section 301(b)(1)(B)

Factors in Developing: Section 304(d)

D. Water Quality Standards–Based Limits

1. Role of Water Quality Standards

Section 303 of the CWA requires states to develop and periodically revise water quality standards for every body of water in the state. As discussed below, the standards consist of a "designated use" for the water, "criteria" which describe the maximum levels of pollutants that may exist in the water, and an "antidegradation" statement which prohibits water quality or uses from being degraded.

Limitations in NPDES permits must be sufficiently stringent to ensure that state water quality standards are not violated. **§ 301(b)(1)(C), 33 U.S.C. § 1311(b)(1)(C)**. Water quality standards-based limits will be included in a permit only if necessary based on an assessment of the environmental effect of the discharge.

Water quality standards are adopted by states, but they must be reviewed and approved by EPA. **§ 303(c)(3), 33 U.S.C. § 1313(c)(3)**. EPA has established requirements that states must meet when they revise water quality standards.

2. Elements of Water Quality Standards

a. Designated Uses

States must specify the "designated use" of each body of water in the state. **§ 303(c)(2)(A), 33 U.S.C. § 1313(c)(2)(A)**. Designated uses may include such things as "public drinking water supply" or "warm water fishery."

(1) Fishable/Swimmable Wherever Attainable

Although section 303(c) seems to give states discretion to set designated uses, EPA has taken the position that, wherever attainable, states must set water at a level that will protect aquatic life and allow recreation in and on the water. These are so-called "fishable/swimmable" waters. This "fishable/swimmable" goal is contained in section 101(a)(2) of the Act, **§ 101(a)(2), 33 U.S.C. § 1251(a)(2)**, and EPA claims that it may require states to meet this goal.

(2) Downgrading

EPA regulations provide that states can set designated uses at less than "fishable/swimmable" only if the state can demonstrate that the use is not attainable. Reducing a designated use below this level is called "downgrading." To downgrade a designated use a state must demonstrate that the existing designated use is not attainable because of either natural environmental conditions or because imposing water quality standards-based limits beyond BAT will cause "widespread adverse social and economic impacts."

b. Criteria

Water quality standards also contain "criteria." **§ 303(c)(2)(A), 33 U.S.C. § 1313(c)(2)(A).** These are typically lists of the maximum concentrations of pollutants that may exist in the water body while still preserving the designated use. In 1987, Congress amended section 303(c)(2) to require states to adopt criteria for toxic pollutants. **§ 303(c)(2)(B), 33 U.S.C. § 1313(c)(2)(B).**

Criteria can be expressed in three ways:

(1) Numerical

Criteria may be numerical. Such a criterion might state, for example, that there may be no more than 10 micrograms per liter of cyanide in the water. Section 303(c)(2) requires that criteria for toxic pollutants be numerical where possible. **§ 303(c)(2)(B), 33 U.S.C. § 1313(c)(2)(B).**

(2) Bioassay

Criteria may be based on a "bioassay" or a test of the effect of the discharge on aquatic organisms. **§ 303(c)(2)(B), 33 U.S.C. § 1313(c)(2)(B).** A typical bioassay test is the LC_{50} ("Lethal Concentration–50%"). The LC50 identifies the concentration of the discharge that will kill 50% of test organisms within a certain period of time. A bioassay based criteria may state that a discharge may not exceed some fraction of its LC_{50}.

(3) Narrative

A criteria may be narrative. All states have some form of criterion that prohibits "the discharge of toxic pollutants in toxic amounts."

These state narrative criteria can be the legal basis for including specific numerical limitations in a permit.

(4) National Criteria Guidance

For many years EPA has published recommended criteria values for pollutants. **§ 304(a)(1), 33 U.S.C. § 1314(a)(1).** These values have been published in a series of books. The first of these was in a little red book, known as the "red book." EPA does not specifically require states to use its recommended criteria, but it does require states to justify why they are using different values.

c. Antidegradation

EPA for many years has required states to include "antidegradation" provisions in their water quality standards. The antidegradation provision must include a requirement that existing designated uses that are being met must be maintained and that streams having water quality better than "fishable/swimmable" ("high quality waters") may not be degraded unless the state, after public participation, shows economic or social justification. Additionally, the antidegradation provision provides that if a state designates a water as an "outstanding natural resource water" the water quality may not be degraded.

3. Implementation

Once a water quality standard has been adopted, a permit writer must still translate the standard into a specific limit in an NPDES permit. In theory, there are several elements of this process.

a. Lists of Impaired Waters and Total Maximum Daily Loads

The Act requires states to publish list of waters where required effluent limitations are "not stringent enough to implement any water quality standard applicable to such waters," and states are required to calculate "total maximum daily loads" or "TMDLs" for each listed water body. § 303(d)(1), 33 U.S.C. § 1313(d)(1). The TMDL represents the total amount of each pollutant that can be discharged into the water without violating water quality criteria. The 303(d) lists of "impaired waters" and associated TMDLs are subject to review and approval by EPA. § 303(d)(2), § 33 U.S.C. § 1313(d)(2).

In *Pronsolino v. Nastri*, 291 F.3d 1123 (9th Cir. 2002), the Ninth Circuit held that EPA was authorized to require states to prepare TMDLs on waters that failed to meet water quality standards solely as a result of non-point source pollution.

b.   Waste Load Allocations

The state must allocate the total load among dischargers on the water body. This is called the "waste load allocation."

c.   Mixing Zones

EPA allows states to provide for "mixing zones." This is an area around a facility's discharge pipe where criteria may be exceeded before the discharge is diluted by water in the stream. EPA has placed some limits on the size of mixing zones and water quality conditions within the mixing zone.

d.   How Expressed in Permits

A water quality standards-based limitation in an NPDES permit is typically expressed as a limitation on the quantity or concentration of pollutants that can be discharged from the source. If you see a numerical effluent limitation in a permit, it is impossible to tell whether it is water quality-based or technology-based. You would need to look at the administrative record of permit issuance to tell. It may be important to know the basis for the effluent limit since a facility may only assert the "upset defense" for violation of technology-based effluent limitations.

e.   Enforcement of Water Quality Standards

Under the CWA, a facility is subject to an enforcement action for violating conditions in its NPDES permit, not for causing adverse conditions in the water body. It is not a violation of the federal CWA to cause pollutant levels in a stream to exceed state water quality standards; it is a violation to exceed limits in a permit regardless of the effect of the pollution in the environment.

f.   Variances From Water Quality Standards–Based Limits

There are no statutory variances from water quality standards-based NPDES permit limitations. If a facility wants a less stringent permit limitation, the state must "downgrade" or relax the applicable water quality standards themselves.

4.   Toxic Hot Spots

In the 1987 Amendments, Congress required EPA and the states to deal more effectively with water bodies that were not meeting water quality standards for toxic pollutants. These areas are sometimes known as toxic "hot spots."

a.   304(*l*) Lists

Section 304(*l*) requires states to develop a series of lists that identify segments of water bodies that are not meeting water quality standards for toxic pollutants and the dischargers on the segment which are preventing the standards from being met. **§ 304(*l*)(1)(A)–(C), 33 U.S.C. § 1314(*l*)(1)(A)–(C)**.

b. Individual Control Strategies

States must prepare "individual control strategies" (ICS) to ensure that designated segments will meet water quality standards. **§ 304(*l*)(1)(D), 33 U.S.C. § 1314(*l*)(1)(D)**. The ICS basically consists of the NPDES permit for facilities identified on the 304(*l*) list.

5. Interstate Pollution

Discharges in one state may affect water quality in the downstream state. Both the Clean Water Act and state common law may be a source of limitations on this interstate pollution.

a. Clean Water Act

Section 301(b)(1)(C) requires that NPDES permits contain effluent limits necessary to comply with applicable state water quality standards. EPA regulations provide that an NPDES permit may not be issued if it cannot ensure compliance with water quality standards of *all* affected states. In other words, dischargers in one state are subject to more stringent limits if their discharge will cause a violation of the water quality standards of a downstream state.

In *Arkansas v. Oklahoma*, 503 U.S. 91, 112 S.Ct. 1046, 117 L.Ed.2d 239 (1992), the Supreme Court upheld EPA's authority to require that an NPDES permit contain limits necessary to ensure that the water quality standards in a downstream state were not violated.

b. Common Law

Persons in one state who are injured by discharges originating in another state may be able to bring a tort action against the discharger. In a series of decisions, the Supreme Court has clarified the role of the common law in interstate pollution. First, state common law, rather than federal common law, will govern any nuisance action claiming interstate pollution. *Milwaukee v. Illinois*, 451 U.S. 304, 101 S.Ct. 1784, 68 L.Ed.2d 114 (1981) (Milwaukee II) (federal common law of interstate pollution preempted by Clean Water Act). Second, the common law of the state in which the discharge originates, rather than the common law of the affected downstream state, will govern the nuisance action. *International Paper Co. v. Ouellette*, 479 U.S. 481, 107 S.Ct. 805, 93 L.Ed.2d 883 (1987).

E. Pretreatment Program

1. Role of Pretreatment

Industrial facilities that put their wastes in the sewer for treatment by a POTW are not generally considered "direct dischargers" or "point sources." Therefore they are not subject to the NPDES permit program. Rather, these sources are considered "indirect dischargers," and they are subject to the "pretreatment" program found in section 307(b) of the CWA. **§ 307(b), 33 U.S.C. § 1317(b)**.

The CWA treats indirect dischargers differently because Congress thought it was unnecessary to require facilities to fully treat their wastes when the wastes are going to be treated again by the POTW. Consequently, the pretreatment program focuses on situations where the POTW is not adequately treating industrial wastes. These include:

a. Interference and Pass Through

Pretreatment is necessary if the industrial waste will interfere with operation of biological treatment by the POTW. Large amounts of toxic pollutants, for example, may kill the bacteria that are part of the treatment system. In some cases, wastes are not effectively treated and simply pass through the POTW without being controlled.

b. Contamination of Sewage Sludge—Sewage Sludge Guidelines

Biological treatment systems used by POTWs produce large quantities of sewage sludge. Sewage sludge is organic material left after treatment of sewage, and it can be used as a fertilizer unless it is contaminated with toxic materials. Metals from industrial sources may, for example, settle into the sludge and limit the sludge's ability to be used.

EPA has developed criteria, as required by section 405 of the CWA, that define acceptable levels of pollutants in sewage sludge and specifies acceptable uses for sewage sludge. **§ 405, 33 U.S.C. § 1345.** Under the CWA, POTWs, or in some cases industrial sources, will have conditions in their NPDES permit relating to the use of sewage sludge.

2. Types of Pretreatment Limitations

To prevent these problems, there are several types of limitations which may require facilities to "pretreat" their wastes before they are placed into the sewer.

a. Categorical Standards

EPA has developed technology-based pretreatment standards for categories of industrial sources in much the same way that it develops BPT,

BAT, BCT and NSPS. These limitations are intended to reflect the level of pollution control that the facility would achieve if it were meeting BAT, BCT or NSPS but minus the average treatment that a POTW will provide. These "categorical standards" are nationally applicable numerical limits that facilities within given industrial categories must meet before putting wastes in the sewer. There is a program now in place in which facilities can get "credit" for the amount of toxic pollutants removed by their POTW.

b. General Prohibition

All indirect dischargers, regardless of whether categorical standards have been written for their industry, must also satisfy a "general prohibition." This provision prohibits facilities from discharging wastes to POTWs that cause or contribute to the POTW 1) violating its NPDES permit or 2) the POTW sewage sludge violating sewage sludge standards.

c. Local Limits

Local POTWs, to implement the general prohibition and ensure that they will not violate their NPDES permits, may develop local limits applicable to sources that discharge into the sewers. These local limits have been implemented through contracts or other agreements between the POTW and the facility. EPA is requiring that POTWs implement pretreatment requirements for significant indirect dischargers through documents that are very similar to NPDES permits.

F. Judicial Review of Government Action or Inaction

1. Sources of Federal Jurisdiction

a. 509(b)

Section 509(b) of the CWA contains a list of specific actions by EPA that are subject to initial judicial review in the Court of Appeals. § 509(b)(1), 33 U.S.C. § 1369(b)(1). These include, among other things, review of national effluent limitations guidelines promulgated by EPA and the issuance of NPDES permits by EPA. One of the most important elements of this provision is that review may be obtained only if a petition is filed within 120 days of the date of the government's final action.

b. 505

Section 505 of the CWA authorizes "citizen suits" against EPA where EPA is failing to perform "non-discretionary" duties. § 505(a)(2), 33

U.S.C. § 1365(a)(2). Such citizen suits, for example, have been filed to force EPA to issue regulations that are required by the CWA. It is important to understand that a suit under 505 is only available to force EPA to issue the regulation; it does not provide jurisdiction to review EPA's discretionary decisions about the content of a regulation.

Citizens have tried to use section 505(a)(2) to force EPA to bring an enforcement action against facilities violating the CWA. Courts have generally held that the enforcement decision is discretionary, and section 505 cannot be used to force the government to prosecute.

c. Federal Question

There are certain discretionary actions EPA takes for which judicial review is not provided in section 509. In that case, a citizen would rely on general federal question jurisdiction under 28 U.S.C. § 1331 to obtain review in a federal district court. This has primarily been necessary for citizen's seeking review of EPA's decision to approve or disapprove state water quality standards.

2. Judicial Review of State Issued Permits

Most states have been delegated NPDES permit authority and they are the permit issuers. Judicial review of state issued permits is generally in state, rather than federal, court.

G. Review Questions

1. T or F   The discharge of a pollutant that is not subject to an effluent limitation in an NPDES permit violates the Clean Water Act.

2. T or F   The discharge of a pollutant, although in compliance with the effluent limitation in an NPDES permit, is causing levels of the pollutant in the stream to exceed the state water quality criterion. This discharge violates the requirements of the Clean Water Act.

3. T or F   A POTW that directly discharges pollutants into navigable waters is not required under the CWA to obtain an NPDES permit.

4. T or F   Until EPA proposes and thereafter promulgates a national effluent limitation guideline representing NSPS for a class or category of industry, individual facilities within that class or category are not subject to NSPS.

5. T or F   Until EPA proposes and thereafter promulgates a national effluent limitation guideline representing BAT for a class or category of

industry, individual facilities within that class or category are not subject to BAT.

6. T or F New sources, subject to NSPS, are not required to meet technology-based effluent limits on conventional pollutants unless the limits pass both BCT cost tests.

7. T or F A direct discharger that violates a water quality standards-based effluent limit in its NPDES permit may be able to successfully assert the upset defense if the permittee can prove that the violation occurred for reasons beyond the reasonable control of the permittee.

8. T or F. Isolated, intermittent bodies of water will be classified as "navigable waters" under the Clean Water Act if they are used by migratory birds.

9. T or F An indirect discharger subject to the pretreatment requirements of section 307(b) may be subject to "categorical" pretreatment limits if EPA has promulgated technology-based pretreatment limits for its category of industrial facilities.

10. T or F Section 301(*l*) prohibits the grant of an FDF variance from national BAT limits on toxic pollutants.

11. T or F A citizen may obtain judicial review of an EPA issued NPDES permit in an appropriate U.S. Court of Appeals.

12. T or F A citizen may obtain judicial review of the legality of national effluent limitation guidelines that have been placed in an NPDES permit in a challenge to the issuance of the permit.

13. T or F Under EPA regulations, states are free to establish any designated use that they choose as long as they have considered the factors specified in section 303(c)(2)(A).

14. T or F The Clean Water Act prohibits the direct discharge of pollutants in concentrations that exceed state water quality criteria.

15. T or F States are required to develop TMDLs only for waters that fail to meet water quality standards as a result of the discharge of pollutants from point sources.

*

CHAPTER 6

Clean Air Act

■ ANALYSIS

A. Introduction

The Clean Air Act ("CAA") is the primary federal statute regulating the emission of air pollutants. Many environmental law courses devote a considerable amount of time to study of the CAA since it has a wide variety of programs that illustrate most of the major issues in environmental law. For the same reason, the Clean Air Act may be the most confusing of the modern federal environmental statutes.

1. Structure

The Clean Air Act is composed of a number of different programs. Each of these programs may be a separate source for limitations on the emission of air pollutants. These include, among others, Mobile Source requirements, New Source Performance Standards, programs relating to attainment of National Ambient Air Quality Standards (including the Non-attainment Program and Prevention of Significant Deterioration program), National Emission Standards for Hazardous Air Pollutants, and the Sulfur Allowance Trading program.

2. History

The basic structure of the modern Clean Air Act was adopted in the Clean Air Act Amendments of 1970. The 1970 CAA required the federal government to establish air quality goals, and the Act required states to develop implementation plans to achieve those goals. Additionally, the 1970 amendments expanded federal control of automobile emissions, established a program for technology-based controls on new sources of air pollution, and a program for control of hazardous air pollutants.

By 1977, it was clear that the goals of the 1970 Act were not being met throughout the country. In the Clean Air Act Amendments of 1977, Congress, among other things, established special requirements for areas that were not achieving air quality standards. The amendments also contained new requirements for areas that had air quality better than those standards.

Although there were many attempts to amend the Clean Air Act after 1977, it was not until 1990 that major amendments were again enacted. Although the basic structure of the CAA was not altered, the 1990 Amendments made significant changes. Some of the more significant parts of the 1990 amendments include new requirements and compliance deadlines for areas not meeting air quality standards, a new emphasis on use of market forces to control pollution, new programs relating to sulfur emissions and acid rain, new requirements for control of hazardous air pollutants, and a new permit program for most sources of air pollution.

3. Outline of Major Sections of the Clean Air Act

Title I—General Program Requirements

Section 101, 42 U.S.C. § 7401. Statement of Congressional findings and goals.

Section 107, 42 U.S.C. § 7407. Requirements for designation of Air Quality Control Regions.

Section 108, 42 U.S.C. § 7408. Requirement for preparation of air quality criteria describing latest scientific data about health and environmental effects of certain pollutants.

Section 109, 42 U.S.C. § 7409. Requirement for publication of National Ambient Air Quality Standards for pollutants for which air quality criteria have been published.

Section 110, 42 U.S.C. § 7410. General requirements for preparation of State Implementation Plans and EPA approval of State Implementation Plans.

Section 111, 42 U.S.C. § 7411. Requirement for promulgation of federal New Source Performance Standards.

Section 112, 42 U.S.C. § 7412. Requirement for promulgation of federal standards for hazardous air pollutants.

Section 113, 42 U.S.C. § 7413. Provisions relating to federal enforcement of provisions of the CAA.

Section 116, 42 U.S.C. § 7416. Provision authorizing states, with some exceptions, to adopt air pollution control requirements more stringent than federal requirements.

Part C—Prevention of Significant Deterioration

Sections 160–169B, 42 U.S.C. §§ 7470–7492. Provisions relating to Prevention of Significant Deterioration and visibility protection.

Part D—Non-attainment Provisions

Subpart 1—General

Sections 171–179B, 42 U.S.C. §§ 7501–7509a. General provisions relating to non-attainment areas. These provisions include obligations on new or modified major stationary sources including requirements for offsets and achievement of lowest achievable emission rates.

Subpart 2—Additional Provisions for Ozone Nonattainment Areas

Sections 181–185B, 42 U.S.C. §§ 7511–7511f. Provisions relating to classification of ozone non-attainment areas and compliance obligations in the various classes of ozone non-attainment areas.

Subparts 3–5—Additional Provisions for Non-attainment Areas for other Pollutants.

Title II—Requirements for Mobile Sources

Sections 202–250, 42 U.S.C. §§ 7521–7590. Provisions relating to mobile sources including emission standards, fuel controls and clean fleet and alternative fuel programs.

Title III—General Provisions

Section 302, 42 U.S.C. § 7602. Section containing general definitions for the CAA.

Section 304, 42 U.S.C. § 7604. Citizen suit provisions.

Section 307, 42 U.S.C. § 7607. Judicial review provisions.

Title IV—Acid Rain Provisions

Sections 401–416, 42 U.S.C. §§ 7651–7651o. Provisions relating to issuance and marketing of sulfur emission allowances for the control of acid rain.

Title V—Permits

Sections 501–507, 42 U.S.C. § 7661–7661f. Provisions requiring permits for a broad group of sources of air pollution.

Title VI—Stratospheric Ozone

Sections 601–618, 42 U.S.C. §§ 7671–7671q. Provisions relating to control of substances, including chlorofluorocarbons such as freon, that contribute to depletion of stratospheric ozone.

B. Economic Efficiency, New Source Bias and Marketable Pollution Rights

The Clean Air Act has resulted in the expenditure of billions of dollars to control air pollution, and it has been subject to numerous criticisms that it is economically "inefficient." Two aspects of the Clean Air Act raise significant questions about the costs of achieving clean air under the Act. The first, "new source bias," involves the trigger for imposition of mandatory federal controls under the Clean Air Act. The second, "marketable pollution rights," involves the mechanisms used to induce facilities to control their air emissions. Both of these issues are a major focus of debate over the future of the Clean Air Act.

1. New Source Bias

Many of the most stringent requirements of the CAA, including new source performance standards and New Source Review requirements under the Non-attainment and PSD programs, are imposed on "new" or "modified" sources. Thus, newly constructed facilities or existing facilities that "modify" their equipment in certain ways may be subject to federally mandated pollution control requirements that do not apply to existing sources. This focus on new or modified sources, it is claimed, has discouraged construction of new, more efficient sources or the modernization of older sources.

Some of the more confusing parts of the Clean Air Act arise from efforts to minimize this new source bias. The complex definitions of "modification" that apply to NSPS and NSR determine what types of changes a source may make without triggering the requirements applicable to modified sources. The "bubble" rule allows facilities to avoid requirements if the "net" effect of changes within a facility does not result in more than de minimis increases in pollutants. The NSPS, Non-attainment, and PSD programs are discussed below.

It is important to note, however, that these provisions generally minimize the "new source" bias, not by employing more efficient pollution controls, but by reducing the number of sources that are subject to more stringent federally mandate controls.

2. Marketable Pollution Rights and "Cap and Trade" Programs

Many of the requirements of the Clean Air Act rely on "command and control" provisions in which the government specifies the amount of pollutants that individual facilities may emit. This approach has been criticized as inefficient, and much of the current focus in air pollution policy is on the use of programs, such as "marketable pollution rights" and "cap and trade programs," that allow facilities to buy or sell the right to pollute. The use of marketable pollution rights, it is claimed, allows a given level of pollution control to be achieved more cheaply than if the government set the requirements for each facility.

a. Rationale for Marketable Pollution Rights

Marketable pollution rights programs rely on the fact that different sources have differing "marginal costs" to control pollution. In other words, different sources have different costs for removing a given amount of pollution. One facility may be able to reduce its emission of a ton of a pollutant at a small cost simply by substituting a raw ingredient. Another facility may have to install expensive pollution control equipment to achieve the same reduction.

Marketable pollution rights provide an incentive for the sources with the cheapest marginal cost of control to undertake the most reductions by allowing them to sell the right to pollute to facilities with higher marginal costs. Marketable pollution rights programs rely on individual economic decisions by polluters, rather than commands from the government, to determine which sources will actually reduce their emissions.

Example: Consider two sources that each emit 300 tons of a pollutant. The two sources have differing "marginal costs" of pollution control: Source One can reduce its emissions at $100 per ton while Source Two can reduce emissions at a cost of $500 per ton.

If the government wants a 20 ton reduction of pollutants, it could require each source to reduce its emissions by 10 tons each. The cost of achieving that 20 ton reduction would be $6,000 [$1,000 from Source One (10 tons x $100 per ton)] + $5,000 from Source Two (10 tons x $500 per ton)].

If, however, the government gave each source the right to emit 290 tons each but allowed the sources to buy and sell those rights, the result might be different. Source One could choose to reduce its emissions by the full 20 tons, and sell the right to emit the extra 10 tons to Source Two. Source One would then emit 280 tons and Source Two would continue to emit 300 tons. The combined reduction by the two sources would, however, be the 20 tons the government intended.

Why would Source One reduce more than was required and why would Source Two being will to pay for the right to pollute?

Since it costs Source One $100 per ton to reduce its pollution, it would be willing to reduce its pollution if it could sell the extra right to pollute at more than $100 per ton. Since it costs Source Two $500 per ton to reduce pollution, it would be willing to pay up to $500 per ton for the right to pollute. Market forces create an incentive for Sources One and Two to strike a deal under which Source One would reduce its emissions by an extra ten tons and sell the right to emit those 10 tons to Source Two.

How much would the pollution reduction cost if pollution rights were marketable? Source Two would pay Source One somewhere between $100 and $500 per ton for this right to pollute. The total cost of achieving the same total 20 ton reduction in this case would therefore be between $2,000 and $6000 depending on the price the sources negotiated. It would almost certainly be cheaper, and possibly substantially cheaper, to achieve the 20 ton reduction if the parties are allowed to buy and sell their pollution requirements than if the government commanded each source to reduce its emissions by 10 tons.

The Clean Air Act currently employs several examples of marketable pollution rights. The "offset" requirements in Non-attainment Areas may be satisfied by a new source purchasing the right to pollute from existing sources. These requirements are discussed below in 7.G. Additionally, the Sulfur Trading program is a well established program for control of sulfur emissions from power plants that relies on a cap and trade program. These requirements are discussed at 7.J.

The existing Kyoto Protocol for the control of greenhouse gas emissions has provisions that allow developed countries to meet their required greenhouse gas reduction requirements by "buying" reductions in less developed nations. Virtually all U.S. proposals to address global warming involve some form of marketable pollution rights system for the control of greenhouse gas emissions.

b. Elements of a Cap and Trade Program

"Cap and trade" programs employ marketable pollution rights, and there are several common elements of these programs. First, the government must establish a "cap" on the total amount of a pollutant that the government will allow to be emitted. Second, the government must allocate "credits" or "allowances" that give a source the right to emit a certain amount of the pollutant. The total number of allocated credits should not exceed the cap. Third, sources are allowed to buy or sell credits. A source that can cheaply reduce its pollutants may reduce its pollution and sell the resulting credits to sources that would have higher costs of control. Fourth, the trade must be documented and the sources limited to their authorized emissions after the trade. Fifth, the government must enforce the allocated emissions limits.

c.   Issues in Implementing Cap and Trade Programs

Any cap and trade program must address a number of issues.

(1)   Same Pollutant

Trades must be of the same pollutant. The program does not work properly if one plant reduces its emissions of particulates, while another plant increases it emissions of a toxic pollutant.

(2)   Same Area

If reductions in a pollutant from one source are traded for increases by another source, both sources must be in the same area affected by that pollutant. Additionally, if all of the increases occur in one industrial area, while offsetting reductions are located in various distant areas, the industrial area can become a pollution "hot spot."

(3)   Actual Reductions

In most cases, sources which plan to reduce emissions for sale will commit to an enforceable emission limit below their existing legal limit. This creates a problem if the source was already operating below its legal limit or otherwise planned to make the changes resulting in the reduction. Consider, for example, a plant that is legally authorized to emit 400 tons of pollutants but actually emits only 300 tons. If the plant is allowed to reduce its enforceable limits to 300 tons and sell the 100 ton "reduction," the objectives of the trading program are not achieved. These types of trades are called "paper" trades, and there have been criticisms that many of the trades under the offset program have been of this type.

(4)   Marketability

Efficient trading of any commodity requires a "market" which allows willing buyers and sellers to get together cheaply. There have been a number of novel proposals to address this problem. Pollution "banks," for example, have been established in which facilities that reduce their pollution can "deposit" the reduction as credits; sources seeking to buy a right to pollute can simply go to the bank to buy these rights.

(5) Initial Allocation

Emissions trading generally works by allowing source to sell their pre-existing legal authorization to emit pollutants. The existing regulatory scheme, in effect, allocates a valuable commodity among sources. Some have proposed that no source have an initial allocation, and that all sources bid at an auction for the right to emit a given level of pollutants. The government would control the level of pollution by establishing the amount of pollution rights it will auction.

(6) Uncertainty of Future Requirements

A significant problem in any scheme to trade pollution rights arises from sources' uncertainty about future government environmental requirements. Companies may be unwilling to sell their existing rights to pollute if they fear that the government will impose new requirements in the future.

(7) Ethical Concerns

In theory, marketable pollution rights will help achieve a given level of pollution for the cheapest amount. Many people, however, have raised ethical concerns with the sale of the "right to pollute."

C. Mobile Sources

"Mobile sources," including automobiles, trucks, and buses, are major contributors to air pollution. Federal legislation to regulate automobile emissions existed prior to 1970, but the 1970 CAA established the basic structure of mobile source controls. The 1990 CAA Amendments have expanded the scope of the 1970 requirements.

1. Emission Limits

The CAA establishes federal limits on the emission of certain pollutants from mobile sources. **§ 202, 42 U.S.C. § 7521**. With the exception of the California standards discussed below, the CAA preempts states from establishing their own mobile source emission limits. **§ 209, 42 U.S.C. § 7543**. Thus the Act protects automobile manufacturers from having to manufacture cars meeting varying emission limits in different states.

These limits are pure "technology-forcing" requirements. Congress required automobile manufactures to meet limits that could not be met by technology existing at the time the limits were imposed.

a. Federal Standards

The Clean Air Act imposes limits on emissions from various classes of automobiles, trucks, and buses. Conventional cars are generally known as "light duty vehicles." In the 1970 CAA, Congress required a 90% reduction of emissions of hydrocarbons ("HCs") and carbon monoxide ("CO") by 1975 and nitrogen oxides ("NOx") by 1976. The original statutory deadlines were extended by a combination of Congressional amendments and administrative waivers granted by EPA. The original requirements on HCs and CO have been met, but, in 1977, Congress relaxed the requirements for NOx.

In the 1990 CAA Amendments, Congress added new limits on emissions of Non-methane hydrocarbons ("NMHC"), CO, NOx and particulate matter ("PM"). The limits are to be phased in beginning with the 1994 model year, and automakers must sell an increasing percentage of cars that meet the new limits. By the 1996 model year, all cars sold must meet these limits. **§ 202(g), 42 U.S.C. § 7521(g)**. EPA is required to conduct a study to determine if more stringent standards are necessary after the statutory limits are met. **§ 202(i), 42 U.S.C. § 7521(i)**.

Under § 211(a), EPA can also regulate the emissions from mobile sources of any "air pollutant" that in the Administrator's judgment, may "cause or contribute to air pollution which may reasonably be anticipated to endanger public health or welfare." In *Massachsuetts v. EPA*, 549 U.S. 497, 127 S.Ct. 1438, 167 L.Ed.2d 248 (2007), the Supreme Court held that carbon dioxide, a greenhouse gas that may contributes to global warming, is an "air pollutant" as defined in § 302(g) and that EPA has the authority to regulate the emissions of greenhouse gases from mobile sources if EPA determines that they satisfy the statutory standard by endangering public health or welfare.

In addition to specific emission limits, the CAA establishes requirements on automobile manufacturers to provide warranties on the effectiveness of emission control equipment. EPA is also authorized to recall vehicles that do not comply with standards.

The 1990 CAA Amendments also establish new requirements for emission limits on other mobile sources including urban buses, trucks and off-road vehicles.

b. California Standards

Although the statute establishes uniform, national limits for most cars sold in the U.S., the 1970 CAA allowed California to establish its own, more stringent limits on cars sold in the State. **§ 209(b), 42 U.S.C. § 7543(b).** The CAA now allows other states to require compliance with the more stringent California standards. **§ 177, 42 U.S.C. § 7507.**

2. Regulation of Automobile Fuels

The composition of automobile fuels is an important element in meeting the statutory emission limits, and section 211 of the CAA contains broad provisions authorizing EPA to regulate the composition of fuels. **§ 211, 42 U.S.C. § 7545.**

a. Lead

Lead, which was added to gasoline as an "anti-knock" ingredient, can destroy the effectiveness of catalytic converters (a type of automobile emission control technology) and can be a significant health threat. EPA, under the authority of the 1970 CAA, established requirements for the sale of lead free gasoline and the gradual phase-out of lead from all gasoline. The 1990 CAA Amendments prohibit gasoline from containing lead or lead additives after 1995. **§ 211(n), 42 U.S.C. § 7545(n).**

b. Reformulated Fuels

The 1990 CAA Amendments require the use of "reformulated" gasoline in certain areas of the country that are not meeting national ambient air quality standards for ozone. EPA is establishing standards for the content of this reformulated gasoline that are intended to reduce the emission of ozone forming volatile organic compounds and toxic air emissions. **§ 211(k), 42 U.S.C. § 7545(k).** The statute specifies certain areas that must use reformulated gasoline, but other areas may petition to "opt in" to the reformulated gasoline program.

c. Oxygenated Fuels

Certain areas that do not comply with the national ambient air quality standard for carbon monoxide ("CO") must also use "oxygenated" fuels that reduce the emission of CO. **§ 211(m), 42 U.S.C. § 7545(m).**

3. Alternative Fuels and Clean–Fuel Fleet Program

The 1990 CAA Amendments establish new programs to promote the use of "alternative fuels" that pollute less than gasoline. These alternative fuels include such things as ethanol, natural gas, and electricity. Subpart C of Title

II establishes requirements to encourage the development and use of "clean-fuel vehicles" that can use these alternative fuels.

In certain non-attainment areas that are designated as extreme, severe or serious for ozone and certain non-attainment areas for carbon monoxide, "fleets" of automobiles and certain other mobile sources must meet stringent standards for clean-fuel vehicles. **See § 182(c)(4), 42 U.S.C. § 7511a(c)(4)**. A "fleet" is defined as any group of 10 or more vehicles used by a single operator and capable of being fueled from a central location. **§ 241(5), 42 U.S.C. § 7581(5)**. Most of the areas subject to Clean Fleet program elected to "opt-out" as authorized by the Act.

D.   New Source Performance Standards

Section 111 of the CAA requires that certain sources meet "new source performance standards" ("NSPS"). NSPS apply to "new" or "modified" sources. Existing sources which do not change their production processes or modernize their equipment may avoid imposition of these requirements.

1.   National Technology–Based Emission Limits

NSPS are technology-based emission limits that place restrictions on the quantities or concentrations of air pollutants that a source may emit. Section 111(a)(1) defines NSPS as an emission standard which reflects the "best system of emission reduction," that EPA determines has been "adequately demonstrated." **§ 111(a)(1), 42 U.S.C. § 7411(a)(1)**. Among other things, EPA must consider factors such as cost and achievability in determining what constitutes NSPS. NSPS developed under section 111 are roughly comparable to the technology-based standards applicable to new sources developed under section 306 of the Clean Water Act.

EPA promulgates NSPS for categories of industrial sources, and they are nationally applicable. Thus, NSPS require new sources to meet technology-based emission limits regardless of whether the area in which the source is located meets or exceeds National Ambient Air Quality Standards.

2.   Applicability

NSPS apply to "new sources." Section 111(a)(2) defines a new source as a *stationary source* that is either *constructed* or *modified* after the date of proposal of regulations establishing applicable new source performance standards. **§ 111(a)(2), 42 U.S.C. § 7411(a)(2)**.

a.   Newly Constructed Sources

At its simplest, any facility that is newly constructed after NSPS have been proposed are subject to NSPS requirements. A newly constructed facility will not be subject to NSPS, however, if 1) EPA has not proposed an NSPS or 2) it "commenced" construction before EPA proposed an applicable NSPS.

b. Modified Sources and New Source Bubbles

Existing "stationary sources" that are "modified" are subject to any applicable NSPS. Section 111(a)(3) defines "stationary source" as any "building, structure, facility, or installation which emits or may emit any air pollutant." **§ 111(a)(3), 42 U.S.C. § 7411(a)(3)**. Section 111(a)(4) defines "modification" as a "physical change or change in method of operation" which results in an increase in the amount of any air pollutant previously emitted by the source or the emission of any pollutant not previously emitted. **§ 111(a)(4), 42 U.S.C. § 7411(a)(4)**.

The definition of stationary source raises the critical "bubble" issue—should a stationary source be defined as the entire plant or as each individual source within the plant? The bubble issue is discussed in section 7.G below.

EPA generally applies a "dual" definition in its NSPS. This means that a facility is subject to NSPS if either individually defined sources within a facility have an increase in pollutants or if the facility as a whole has an increase in the emission of pollutants.

3. NSPS and Existing Sources

Although NSPS apply to "new sources,"(remember that a "new source" is defined to include existing sources that undergo a "modification") section 111(d) requires states to develop programs to apply NSPS to existing sources within the industrial categories to which NSPS apply. **§ 111(d), 42 U.S.C. § 7411(d)**. Section 111(d) only requires that these existing sources meet NSPS for pollutants that are *not* subject to NAAQS. NAAQS pollutants are presumably adequately regulated through the SIP requirements in section 110. Section 111(d) has not, however, been used in many cases to impose requirements on existing sources. The major exception is that EPA has used § 111(d) to require states to impose emission limits on waste incinerators. Note also that § 112 allows EPA to set emission limits on sources emitting "hazardous air pollutants."

E. National Ambient Air Quality Standards

1. Primary and Secondary NAAQS

National Ambient Air Quality Standards ("NAAQS") specify the concentrations of pollutants that may be present in the ambient air outside of buildings. There are two types of NAAQS. Primary standards specify the concentrations of pollutants which, if met, are "requisite to protect the public health." **§ 109(b)(1), 42 U.S.C. § 7409(b)(1)**. Primary standards are set specifically to protect human health. Secondary standards specify concentrations that are "requisite to protect the public welfare." **§ 109(b)(2), 42 U.S.C. § 7409(b)(2)**. Effects on public welfare include a variety of environmental effects, effects on agriculture, economic effects of air pollution and effects on human comfort and well being. Public welfare is also defined to include effects on climate. **§ 302(h), 42 U.S.C. § 7602(h)**.

At the moment there are six pollutants for which EPA has established NAAQS. These are Sulfur Dioxide ("SO_2"), Particulate Matter ("PM–10, PM–2.5") (applicable to particulates with a size less than 10 and 2.5 microns in diameter), Carbon Monoxide ("CO"), Ozone ("O_3"), Nitrogen Dioxide ("NO_2") and Lead ("Pb").

2. Obligation to Develop NAAQS

NAAQS must be established for each pollutant for which EPA has issued air quality criteria under section 108. **§ 109(a), 42 U.S.C. § 7409(a)**. Air quality criteria are documents which, among other things, contain the latest scientific information about the public health and environmental effects of an air pollutant.

Under section 108(a)(1), EPA must issue criteria for a pollutant if 1) emissions of the pollutant, in the judgment of the Administrator of EPA, "will cause or contribute to air pollution which may reasonably be anticipated to endanger public health or welfare," 2) the presence of the pollutant in the air comes from "numerous and diverse mobile or stationary sources," and 3) air quality criteria were not issued before December 31, 1970 but which the Administrator plans to issue air quality criteria. **§ 108(a)(1), 42 U.S.C. § 7408(a)(1)**.

Criteria for five pollutants had been issued prior to adoption of the Clean Air Act, and EPA subsequently added nitrogen oxides and removed hydrocarbons from the list. In *NRDC v. Train*, 545 F.2d 320 (2d Cir.1976), the court ordered EPA to issue criteria for lead. This decision was in large part based on the fact that EPA had previously made specific findings that lead met the factors listed in section 108(a)(1) and that, prior to passage of the 1970 Clean Air Act, lead had been included among a list of pollutants for which criteria were already planned. Since *NRDC v. Train*, no court has required EPA to designate another pollutant under § 108(a).

The addition of a new criteria pollutant, and therefore the promulgation of a new NAAQS, has very significant consequences. Once a primary NAAQS is established, states are required to develop implementation plans that will assure attainment of that NAAQS within a specific period of time. **§ 110(a)(1), 42 U.S.C. § 7410(a)(1)**.

3. Setting NAAQS

Primary NAAQS must be set at a level which, based on criteria and "allowing an adequate margin of safety," are "requisite to protect the public health." **§ 109(b)(1), 42 U.S.C. § 7409(b)(1)**. Secondary NAAQS must be set at a level which, based on criteria, are "requisite to protect public welfare." **§ 109(b)(2), 42 U.S.C. § 7409(b)(2).** A number of issues are raised when EPA establishes or revises an NAAQS. Many of these issues were addressed by the court in *Lead Industries Ass'n v. EPA*, 647 F.2d 1130 (D.C.Cir.1980) in a challenge to EPA's NAAQS for lead.

a. Cost

The court in *Lead Industries* held that EPA cannot consider the cost of achieving an NAAQS when it establishes a standard. The court indicated that the level of the NAAQS was a scientific judgment and that economic and technological concerns were to be addressed, if at all, under other provisions of the Act. The Supreme Court confirmed this position in *Whitman v. American Trucking Ass'ns*, 531 U.S. 457, 121 S.Ct. 903, 149 L.Ed.2d 1 (2001).

b. Who Is to Be Protected

The legislative history of the 1970 CAA indicates that the NAAQS are to be set at a level that will protect sensitive subpopulations within the U.S. Thus, the NAAQS need not be set to protect the "average" person, but may be set to protect those people most at risk. This might include people with respiratory diseases or children.

c. Margin of Safety

Primary (but not secondary) NAAQS must allow an "adequate margin of safety." EPA has considerable discretion in determining how to incorporate a margin of safety in the final NAAQS. In establishing the primary NAAQS for lead, for example, EPA, at many points in its calculations, used "conservative" estimates that tended to increase the stringency of the final standards. The court in *Lead Industries* held that EPA has substantial discretion in determining how to implement the "margin of safety" requirement.

4. Obligation to Modify NAAQS

At least once every five years, EPA is required to review each NAAQS, and EPA may revise the NAAQS as "appropriate." **§ 109(d)(1), 42 U.S.C. § 7409(d)(1)**.

F. State Implementation Plans

1. General Requirements

The State Implementation Plan ("SIP") is the primary mechanism for achieving the goals of the CAA. Section 110(a) of the statute requires that every state prepare a SIP that provides for the "implementation, maintenance, and enforcement" of each NAAQS. **§ 110(a)(1), 42 U.S.C. § 7410(a)(1).** The CAA specifies applicable deadlines by which NAAQS must be met.

Through its SIP, each state determines the emissions limitations and other pollution control requirements that it will impose to assure that air quality meets the federally mandated NAAQS. Although there are federally required SIP provisions for areas that violate NAAQS (the non-attainment program) or areas that are cleaner than the NAAQS (prevention of significant deterioration program), the basic concept of the SIP is that states are free to choose what restrictions they will impose and on whom they will impose them.

a. What Constitutes the Applicable SIP?

(1) State Requirements

The SIP is composed of the variety of state laws and regulations, municipal or county ordinances and other legally enforceable requirements adopted by the state or a political subdivision. The state designates the state or local requirements that are included as part of its SIP.

(2) Federal Review and Approval

After a state designates the elements of its SIP, the plan must be submitted for EPA's review and approval. **§ 110(a)(1), 42 U.S.C. § 7410(a)(1).** After reviewing the submission, EPA proposes either to approve, disapprove or conditionally approve the submission. **§ 110(k), 42 U.S.C. § 7410(k).**

If EPA approves the SIP, the elements of the submission become the applicable SIP for purposes of the CAA. If EPA disapproves the SIP, the state must submit a revised SIP. EPA has several sanctions available if a state does not submit an adequate SIP. If EPA conditionally approves a SIP, designated portions of the plan are approved, and the state is given up to one year to correct identified deficiencies.

If EPA approves or conditionally approves the SIP, EPA will formally promulgate the approved elements of the SIP. This gives the SIP the status of federal regulations, and they are enforceable as federal law. Additionally, if a state changes an element of its SIP, the changes must be approved, and promulgated, by EPA. This means that any changes of an approved SIP must be made both by the state and EPA.

b. Process of SIP Development

SIPS must contain sufficient limits on emission of air pollutants to ensure that an NAAQS is achieved or, in the case of clean air areas discussed below, that there is no significant deterioration of that clean air. The process of developing the SIP has a number of steps leading to the imposition of emission limits that will meet the NAAQS.

(1) Air Quality Control Regions

A determination must be made as whether the existing air quality is better or worse (and how much better or worse) than the NAAQS requires. Section 107 of the CAA requires that these determinations be made for "air quality control regions" ("AQCRs"). **§ 107, 42 U.S.C. § 7407**. AQCRs are now classified as "nonattainment," "attainment," or "unclassifiable." You should note that an area may be classified as non-attainment for one pollutant but not for another.

(2) Inventory

EPA regulations require that a state develop an inventory of existing sources of air pollution.

(3) Emission Limits

Once existing air quality and the existing sources of pollution are determined, the state can develop restrictions on emissions necessary to achieve the NAAQS. As discussed below, emission limits may take any of a number of different forms ranging from specific numerical emission limits on pollutants to requirements that piles of coal be wetted to prevent particulates from blowing in the wind.

(4) Modeling

States must make a determination whether their proposed emission limits will, when implemented, assure that air quality meets the NAAQS. This is done by estimating or "modeling" what air quality will be if the restrictions are imposed. Accurately predicting the effect that a reduction of air pollutants will have on air quality is extremely complicated. Air quality is affected by a variety of factors including weather conditions, location of the source of pollutants, and the reaction of pollutants in the atmosphere. Nonetheless, states must estimate whether their proposed SIP will meet NAAQS.

There are a number of different computer models that are used. Courts have generally deferred to EPA on complex modeling issues, but courts have required that the use of a model be adequately explained.

(5) Monitoring

After a SIP is developed and emissions limits imposed, states are required to monitor air quality to determine whether NAAQS are actually achieved.

c. Content of SIPs

Section 110(a)(2) lists the elements that must be included in a SIP. **§ 110(a)(2), 42 U.S.C. § 7410(a)(2)**. These include, among others:

(1) Enforceable Emission Limitations

(a) Emission Reductions

States may include a wide variety of restrictions that result in a reduction of the emission of pollutants. These may be specific restrictions on the concentrations or amount of pollutants that may be emitted, requirements for use of a specific technology, or prohibitions on use of certain ingredients or materials. The main requirement imposed by the CAA is that these reductions result in achievement of the NAAQS by applicable deadlines.

(b) Dispersion Techniques

Rather than reducing the amount of pollutants being emitted, an NAAQS could theoretically be met by "dispersion" techniques. Such techniques might include intermittent controls in which the source reduces the amount of pollutants emitted during times of bad air quality or adverse weather conditions and increases pollution at other times. Additionally, they might include emitting the air pollutants from very tall smoke stacks that minimize the effect of the pollutants on local air quality.

The use of dispersion techniques is not favored in the CAA. The CAA now requires that certain stationary sources of pollution use pollution control devices that continually remove pollutants. **See § 110(j), 42 U.S.C. § 7410(j) and § 302(k)–(m), 42 U.S.C. § 7602(k)–(m).**

Additionally, the effect of a source on local air pollution may not be based on the use of extremely tall smoke stacks. Although such "tall stacks" may be built, air quality will be calculated based only on the height of a stack that represents "good engineering practice." **§ 123, 42 U.S.C. § 7423.**

(2) New Source Review

States SIPs must include provisions to meet the Non-attainment and PSD program requirements of the Act. § 110(a)(2)(I)–(J), 42 U.S.C. § 7410(a)(2)(I)–(J). The requirement for preconstruction review of new or modified major stationary sources under the Non-attainment and PSD programs is known as the New Source Review or NSR program. It is a major and controversial part of the Clean Air Act. The requirements for the Non-attainment program are discussed below at 7.G. The requirements for the PSD program are discussed below at 7.H.

(3) Interstate Pollution

The SIP is required to contain provisions that will prohibit a source from emitting pollutants that will "contribute significantly" to another State being unable to meet or maintain an NAAQS. **§ 110(a)(2)(D), 42 U.S.C. § 7410(a)(2)(D).**

(4) Adequate State Resources

States must also demonstrate that they have adequate enforcement authority and that adequate state resources, such as personnel and funding, exist to assure that the SIP is properly implemented.

d. Role of Cost and Feasibility

A major issue under the CAA is whether, and when, a source may challenge a SIP provision because it is either economically or technologically infeasible. There are various stages in the development and implementation of SIP requirements that this issue arises.

(1) EPA Approval of State SIP

In *Union Electric Co. v. EPA*, 427 U.S. 246, 96 S.Ct. 2518, 49 L.Ed.2d 474 (1976), a company sought to challenge EPA's approval of the

Missouri SIP on the grounds that the SIP requirements applicable to the company were not technologically or economically achievable. The Supreme Court held that EPA does not have authority to reject a state SIP on these grounds. In part, this decision was based on legislative history which showed that Congress contemplated that some sources would be forced to close in order for a state to achieve the NAAQS. In part, this decision was based on section 116 of the CAA which authorizes states, with some exceptions, to adopt more stringent air control provisions than are required by the CAA. **§ 116, 42 U.S.C. § 7416**. Thus, the Court held that states are not prohibited by the CAA from adopting stringent and costly requirements.

(2) State Development of the SIP Provisions

States have considerable flexibility to develop SIP provisions, and during this stage, sources may argue that the state should not impose costly or infeasible restrictions. As long as the combination of restrictions in a SIP assures attainment of the NAAQS, the state may consider costs and feasibility issues in developing its SIP. Note, however, that this is essentially a political issue, and there is nothing in the CAA which requires states to consider these factors.

(3) Challenges to the SIP Under State Law

Although nothing in the CAA prohibits states from adopting costly or technologically infeasible requirements, some states have statutes which may limit the ability of state agencies to adopt such restrictions. Where such statutes exist, a challenge to a SIP on cost or feasibility grounds would be brought in state court alleging violation of state law.

(4) Variances

Some states have adopted variance provisions which allow an individual source to seek relief from stringent SIP provisions on the grounds that a SIP requirement is costly or infeasible. Note that the grant of a variance is normally a revision to the SIP, and EPA approval may be necessary before a state issued variance protects a source from enforcement for violation of the CAA.

(5) Delayed Compliance Orders

EPA has the authority, under section 113(a) of the CAA, to issue "delayed compliance orders" to sources not meeting SIP requirements. **§ 113(a), 42 U.S.C. § 7413(a)**. Such orders may specify a time for a source to come into compliance with its applicable SIP requirements at a date later than specified in the SIP, and EPA may consider such factors as cost and feasibility in issuing a delayed compliance order. At the time the *Union Electric* case was decided, the CAA specified that the Administrator, in a compliance order, could require sources to come into compliance within a "reasonable" time. In 1990, however, Congress amended the CAA to limit the Administrator's discretion. Section 113(a)(4) now provides that a compliance order may not authorize an extension for more than one year after the date the order was issued. **§ 113(a)(4), 42 U.S.C. § 7413(a)(4)**.

(6) Court Ordered Compliance Dates

Courts have the authority, under sections 113(b) (government enforcement), **§ 113(b), 42 U.S.C. § 7413(b)**, and section 304(a) (citizen suits), **§ 304(a), 42 U.S.C. § 7604(a)**, to issue injunctions requiring compliance by sources. Although EPA has limited authority to grant extensions through delayed compliance orders, the same may not be true for courts. Courts may have the discretion to grant sources more than one year to come into compliance based on cost and feasibility factors.

Some courts have held that sources may raise cost and feasibility issues as a defense in civil enforcement proceedings. Most courts, however, have held that such factors are appropriate only in fashioning injunctive relief.

e. Sanctions for Failure to Adopt an Approvable SIP

Once a state has submitted a complete SIP, the Administrator of EPA is required to determine whether the SIP meets the requirements of the CAA.

If the Administrator determines that the plan is inadequate to meet these requirements, the Administrator may give the state up to eighteen months to correct the problems identified by EPA. If the state then fails to adopt an approvable SIP, EPA has several sanctions available.

(1) Federal Implementation Plans

Under section 110(c), the Administrator must adopt federal requirements necessary to ensure that the requirements of the CAA are met. **§ 110(c)(1), 42 U.S.C. § 7410(c)(1)**. Such a federal plan is known as a "Federal Implementation Plan" ("FIP"). EPA has been very reluctant to exercise its authority to adopt FIPs since the control measures necessary to meet the NAAQS may require stringent and politically unpopular limitations. The federal plans which have been adopted have largely been the result of court orders requiring EPA to adopt a FIP in regions that are not meeting the NAAQS.

(2) Highway Sanctions

Under section 179(b)(1), EPA has the authority, in nonattainment areas, to prohibit the grant of federal highway funding. **§ 179(b)(1), 42 U.S.C. § 7509(b)(1)**. This sanction does not apply to highway funds used for certain safety related projects or highway projects, such as mass transit, related to achieving compliance with the NAAQS.

(3) Increased Offset Ratio

Under 179(b)(2), EPA has the authority to change the "offset ratio" applicable to new or modified major sources in non-attainment areas to 2 to 1. **§ 179(b)(2), 42 U.S.C. § 7509(b)(2)**. This means, as discussed below, that a new or modified major source that wishes to operate in a non-attainment area must reduce existing sources of emissions by 2 pounds for every 1 pound of new emissions. This is an extremely stringent requirement, and places a substantial limitation on the ability of new plants to begin operations or existing plants to modify their operations in non-attainment areas.

(4) SIP Calls

Under section 110(k)(5), EPA has the authority after approval of a state SIP to require subsequent revisions if the approved SIP is inadequate to meet the requirements of the Act. A specific requirement by EPA to a state to revise the SIP is known as a "SIP Call." EPA has used the SIP Call process to direct groups of states to address problems of interstate pollution. The treatment of interstate pollution in the Clean Air Act is discussed below at 6.L.

G. Non–Attainment Program

1. Background

When adopted in 1970, the CAA did not expressly deal with the issue of areas that did not attain NAAQS by the statutory deadline. The statute was based on the assumption that states would adopt the restrictions necessary to achieve the NAAQS by 1977. In fact, many areas of the country did not meet the NAAQS by the statutory compliance date, and EPA was faced with the dilemma of what action to take.

The problem was difficult for at least two reasons. First, any approach would affect the ability of new sources to locate in non-attainment areas. To address this problem, EPA developed a regulatory program which allowed new sources to be located in non-attainment areas if, among other things, they met stringent emission limits and "offset" any new emissions they produced by greater reductions from existing sources of emissions.

The second difficulty arose from the fact that states had already imposed the cheap and easy requirements; necessary emission limitations would undoubtedly involve politically controversial restrictions. EPA had, for example, attempted to require states to adopt "transportation control measures" which addressed emissions from the use of cars. Transportation control measures attempted to indirectly reduce auto emissions by such devices as parking surcharges that increased the costs to motorists of using cars. EPA backed down on its attempt to require these controls due to the political controversy they created and some adverse legal decisions relating to EPA's authority.

In the 1977 amendments to the CAA, Congress expressly addressed the non-attainment problem. Areas that did not meet NAAQS were now required to be classified as non-attainment. EPA's policy on new sources in non-attainment areas was essentially codified by Congress, and new or modified major stationary sources were, among other things, required to meet stringent emission limits and "offset" their new emissions by reduction of emission from other sources. Additionally, Congress extended the latest compliance date for non-attainment areas to 1987. Congress, however, limited EPA's ability to require transportation control measures.

Once again, many areas failed to attain the NAAQS by the required date, and, in 1990, Congress amended the CAA to impose new, and more complex, requirements in non-attainment areas. The 1990 amendments continue, with slight modifications, the general non-attainment provisions of the 1977 amendments. Congress has, however, adopted specific new program requirements for areas that are non-attainment for ozone and certain other pollutants.

2. General Program Requirements

Section 172 contains the general SIP requirements for non-attainment areas. **§ 172, 42 U.S.C. § 7502.** This section requires that all states must impose the following requirements in areas that are designated as non-attainment.

a. Attainment Deadlines

Section 172 generally requires that all new non-attainment areas must achieve compliance with primary NAAQS for non-attainment pollutants "as expeditiously as practicable," but no later than 5 years from the date that they are designated as non-attainment. **§ 172(a)(2)(A), 42 U.S.C. § 7502(a)(2)(A).** The Administrator has the discretion to extend the deadline to 10 years (and grant up to two 1 year extensions from that date). Secondary NAAQS must be met "as expeditiously as practicable." **§ 172(a)(2)(B), 42 U.S.C. § 7502(a)(2)(B).**

The sections of the CAA which address non-attainment for specific pollutants, however, have their own compliance deadlines.

b. Reasonable Further Progress

In addition to establishing a final compliance date, section 172(c)(2) generally requires that states make "reasonable further progress" ("RFP"), toward achieving compliance with the NAAQS. **§ 172(c)(2), 42 U.S.C. § 7502(c)(2).** This term is defined in section 171, and it generally requires states to ensure "annual incremental reductions" in emissions until attainment of the NAAQS. **§ 171(1), 42 U.S.C. § 7501(1).** Thus, states cannot adopt SIPs which impose all of their requirements just prior to the final compliance date.

c. RACM/RACT

Section 172(c)(1) requires that all SIPs implement all "reasonably available control measures" ("RACM"), including emissions reductions from existing sources that are achievable through adoption of "reasonably available control technology" ("RACT"), in non-attainment areas. **§ 172(c)(1), 42 U.S.C. § 7502(c)(1).** Neither of these terms is defined in the CAA. States are reguired to undertake a RACM analysis in developing non-attainment SIPs. RACT has generally been interpreted as a technology-based standard that is applicable to existing stationary sources. It is less clear what RACM requires, but is generally directed at emissions from non-stationary sources such as transportation related emissions.

There are no uniform, national RACT standards for industrial sources, and states have some flexibility in determining what constitutes RACT in their SIPs. EPA does issue guidance documents, called "Control Technique Guidance" ("CTGs"), which are used by states and EPA to determine RACT requirements.

The RACT requirement in non-attainment areas is one of the few provisions of the CAA which impose some mandatory technology-based controls on existing sources.

d. Nonattainment Permit Program

Perhaps the most significant element of the non-attainment program is the requirement that all "new or modified major stationary sources" obtain a permit and satisfy stringent conditions prior to operation. Section 173 defines the conditions that a source must meet in order to obtain a non-attainment permit. **§ 173, 42 U.S.C. § 7503**. This is part of the "New Source Review" provisions of the Clean Air Act.

(1) Scope

Section 172(c)(5) provides that "new or modified major stationary sources" must obtain non-attainment permits. **§ 172(c)(5), 42 U.S.C. § 7502(c)(5)**. Definitions relating to this term are found in three different sections of the Act. Section 302(j) defines a "major stationary source" as a source which emits, or has the potential to emit, 100 tons per year of any pollutant. **§ 302(j), 42 U.S.C. § 7602(j)**. Section 171 defines "modified" by cross-reference to the definitions in section 111 which deals with new source performance standards. **§ 171(4), 42 U.S.C. § 7501(4)**. Section 111(a)(4) defines modification as any physical change, or change in process which increases the amount of a pollutant emitted by a source or results in the emission of a pollutant not previously emitted.

Given these definitions, the following sources are subject to the non-attainment permit program.

(a) Newly Constructed Major Sources

Any newly constructed facility which has the potential to emit over 100 tons per year of any single pollutant of any type is subject to the program. The source's "potential to emit" pollutants is generally measured with all applicable pollution control devices in place. Thus, if a new stationary source would emit 500 tons of a pollutant without pollution control equipment, but only 50 tons with such equipment, it is not a major stationary source and is not subject to the permit program.

(b) Modified Major Sources and the Non-attainment "Bubble" Rule

If an existing "major stationary source" (one that has the potential to emit more than 100 tons of any pollutant per year) is "modified," as defined in section 111(a)(4), it is subject to the permit program. EPA has adopted a "bubble" rule under the non-attainment program, and a source is considered to be modified only if there is a net increase in pollutants from the entire facility.

A "bubble" rule is one which defines an entire industrial facility as a stationary source, rather than defining each individual source of emissions within the facility as separate stationary sources. It is called a "bubble" rule because all of the individual sources within a plant are viewed as if they were contained within one big bubble with only one emission outlet.

Use of a "bubble" rule can significantly affect the scope of a program that regulates "modified" sources. Suppose operations at a plant are changed so that a production process located at one part of the plant emits an additional 10 tons per year of a pollutant, but there is a decrease in emissions of that same pollutant by 11 tons per year at another part of the plant. Has a stationary source been modified? If the production process is treated as the source, there has been an increase in the emission of a pollutant, and the process is now regulated as a modified source. If, however, the facility as a whole is treated as the source, there has been no "net" increase in the emission of pollutants, and the facility is not subject to regulation. Using the bubble rule to avoid new restrictions in this way is called "netting out."

In *Chevron, U.S.A. v. NRDC*, 467 U.S. 837, 104 S.Ct. 2778, 81 L.Ed.2d 694 (1984), the Supreme Court upheld an EPA regulation which allowed the use of a "bubble" rule in the non-attainment permit program. This regulation was based on an interpretation of the term "stationary source" as defined in section 111(a)(3). *Chevron* is important because it establishes a very strong presumption that an agency's interpretation of a statute it administers is correct. *Chevron* suggests that EPA could, if it chose, adopt a bubble policy for NSPS, non-attainment and PSD programs.

Determination of what other actions constitute a "modification" of an existing source is one of the most controversial issues under the Act. Among other things, there are complex and controversial provisions to calculate whether a change to a source has produced a net increase in pollutants. This involves difficult issues of identification of the "baseline" of pre-existing emissions and projection of emissions after a change. EPA regulations have also stated that "routine maintenance" does not constitute a modification, but distinguishing between routine maintenance and activities that result in an improvement or expansion of a facility has been difficult.

EPA has also adopted a "de minimis" policy which exempts major stationary sources from the non-attainment permit program if they only have certain small net increases in pollutants. EPA regulations define the "de minimis" levels for specific pollutants.

Note that an existing source which does not have the potential to emit 100 tons per year of any pollutant is *not* subject to the permit program even if it increases its emissions by more than a de minimis amount.

(2) Offsets

No source that is subject to the non-attainment permit program may be modified or commence operations unless it has obtained "offsets" for its new emissions. **§ 173(a)(1), 42 U.S.C. § 7503(a)(1)**. This requires new or modified sources to reduce existing emissions by more than the amount of its new emissions. Thus, the effect of construction or modification of a major stationary source is a net reduction of pollutants in a non-attainment areas. To meet this requirement, sources may, for example, attempt to pay an existing source to reduce its emissions below its otherwise applicable legal requirements. The non-attainment offset program employs a form of marketable pollution rights. *See* 6.B.2.

(3) LAER

Sources subject to the permit program must also meet a stringent technology-based level of control called "lowest achievable emission rate" ("LAER"). **§ 173(a)(2), 42 U.S.C. § 7503(a)(2)**. Section 171(3) defines LAER as the more stringent of two limits. **§ 171(3), 42 U.S.C. § 7501(3)**. First, LAER may be the lowest emission limit for a class of sources found in *any* state SIP unless the source can demonstrate that the limit is not achievable. That means that a source in Texas may be subject to a stringent limit in a California SIP unless the Texas source can demonstrate the California limit is not achievable. Second, LAER may the most stringent limit that in practice is achieved by the sources of the same type as the proposed source. LAER must, at a minimum, be as stringent as any applicable New Source Performance Standard.

(4) Other Requirements

Section 173(a) contains several other requirements. **§ 173(a)(3)–(5), 42 U.S.C. § 7503(a)(3)–(5).** First, it prohibits issuance of a non-attainment permit if the person seeking the permit is violating the CAA at any other source in the state that is owned or operated by that person. Second, it prohibits issuance of a permit if EPA has determined that the state is not adequately implementing its SIP for the non-attainment area. Third, the permit writer is required to assess whether the benefits from construction of the new or modified source significantly outweighs the environmental and social costs.

3. Ozone Non–Attainment Program

Sections 181–185B of the CAA establish a complex set of requirements for areas that have not attained the NAAQS for ozone. Ozone is a reactive form of oxygen that contributes to respiratory problems and is related to the development of smog. Ozone is formed from certain automobile emissions and emissions of "volatile organic compounds" ("VOCs") from stationary sources. Thus a main focus of the statute is reduction of automobile emissions and emissions of VOCs.

a. Classifications

The key element of the ozone non-attainment program is the creation of new classes of non-attainment areas. Non-attainment areas for ozone have now been classified as either "marginal," "moderate," "serious," "severe" or "extreme." **§ 181, 42 U.S.C. § 7511.** Under the statute, the worse the air quality the "higher" the classification. Thus, marginal is the lowest classification and extreme is the highest.

b. Program Requirements

The statute establishes specific requirements, including new compliance deadlines, for each of the non-attainment classifications. **§ 182, 42 U.S.C. § 7511a.** Each area is subject to the requirements applicable to the lower classifications plus the additional requirements specified for its classification.

The statute imposes requirements addressing a number of significant issues:

(1) Reasonable Further Progress

Some of the classifications are required to assure specific incremental reductions prior to meeting the final NAAQS. In "serious" areas, for example, states must demonstrate that the SIP will reduce VOC emissions by 3% per year.

(2) Scope of the Permit Program

The higher the non-attainment classification, the smaller the size of major sources subject to the non-attainment permit program. In "moderate" areas, sources emitting over 50 tons of VOCs may be subject to permit requirements. In "severe" areas, sources emitting over 10 tons of VOCs may be covered.

(3) Offsets

The higher the non-attainment classification, the greater the size of the offsets that sources subject to the non-attainment permit program must obtain in order to be allowed to operate. In "moderate" areas, for example, a source must offset each new 1 pound of VOCs by reducing 1.15 pounds from existing sources of VOCs. In "serious" areas, a source must offset each new 1 pound of VOCs by reducing 1.2 pounds of VOCs from existing sources.

(4) Inspection and Maintenance

The statute requires states to adopt "inspection and maintenance" programs to test whether vehicles comply with applicable automobile emission limits.

(5) Transportation Control Plans

In serious, severe and extreme areas, the statute requires states to begin imposing plans to reduce emissions from automobiles. These plans may include such things as improved mass transit or requirements that encourage car pooling.

(6) Clean–Fuel Vehicle Program

In severe and extreme areas, the statute requires the increased use of cleaner vehicles that use fuels other than gasoline. This will encourage the use of such things as electric cars or cars powered by natural gas or hydrogen.

c. **Summary of Significant Requirements in Ozone Non-attainment Areas**

(1) Marginal Areas

Compliance Deadline: November 15, 1993.

RACT: Impose RACT requirements that existed on November 15, 1990.

Inspection and Maintenance: Impose I & M requirements that existed on November 15, 1990.

Offsets: Require offsets from sources subject to the permit program of at least 1.1:1.

(2) Moderate Areas

All of the requirements applicable to "marginal" areas plus:

Compliance Deadline: November 15, 1996.

Reasonable Further Progress: Reduce emissions of VOCs by 15% from defined "baseline" emissions within 6 years and annual reductions of VOCs and oxides of nitrogen necessary to meet the NAAQS by the compliance deadline.

RACT: Impose new RACT requirements on categories of VOC sources for which the Administrator issues "control technique guidance" and on all major stationary sources of VOCs.

Automobile Vapor Recovery: Require larger gas stations to install vapor recovery systems on gas pumps (unless EPA has required cars to have "on-board" vapor recovery).

Offsets: Require offsets from sources subject to the permit program of at least 1.15:1.

(3) Serious Areas

All of the requirements applicable to "moderate" areas plus:

Compliance Deadline: November 15, 1999.

Scope of Permit Program: "Major Stationary Sources" include sources with the potential to emit 50 or more tons per year of VOCs.

Reasonable Further Progress: Reduction of at least 3 percent per year of VOC emissions.

Inspection and Maintenance: Require "enhanced" I & M including denial of vehicle registration to cars that fail the test.

Clean-fuel Vehicle Program: Require a clean-fuel vehicle program which requires companies operating more than 10 vehicles to begin to switch to alternative fuel vehicles (i.e. electricity, natural gas), that meet stringent emission limits.

Offsets: Require offsets from sources subject to the permit program of at least 1.2:1.

(4) Severe Areas
All of the requirements applicable to "serious" areas plus:

Compliance Deadline: November 15, 2005.

Scope of Permit Program: "Major Stationary Sources" include sources with the potential to emit 25 or more tons per year of VOCs.

Transportation Control Plans: Adopt an enforceable plan to limit the growth of emissions from vehicles. This must include a requirement for employers of more than 100 people to develop car pooling or other plans to reduce auto emissions.

Offsets: Require offsets from sources subject to the permit program of at least 1.3:1. If the state requires all major existing sources in the area to use "best available control technology" then the offset ratio may remain at 1.2:1.

Nonattainment Penalty: Upon failure to meet the NAAQS by the compliance deadline, each stationary source must pay a penalty of $5000 per ton of VOCs in excess of 80% of the lower of their actual or allowable emissions.

(5) Extreme Areas
All of the requirements applicable to "severe" areas plus:

Compliance Deadline: November 15, 2010.

Scope of Permit Program: "Major Stationary Sources" include sources with the potential to emit 10 or more tons per year of VOCs.

Modifications: The CAA limits the "bubble" rule, and provides that the modification of any "discrete operation, unit, or other polluting activity" at the source is a modification for purposes of the non-attainment permit program unless the source offsets those increases by reductions at the source in a ratio of 1.3:1.

4. Programs For Other Specific Pollutants

The statute contains special programs for areas that are non-attainment for carbon monoxide and particulates. It also contains additional requirements for areas that are non-attainment for sulfur oxides, nitrogen dioxide and lead. None of these programs are as detailed or complex as the ozone non-attainment program.

H.   Prevention of Significant Deterioration

1.   Background

Prior to the 1977 Amendments, the Clean Air Act had no specific requirement to preserve the quality of areas that had air quality better than the NAAQS. The "purpose" section of the Act did, however, state that the Act was intended to "protect and enhance" the quality of the Nation's air. **§ 101(b)(1), 42 U.S.C. § 7401(b)(1)**. Based in part on this provision, a court, in *Sierra Club v. Ruckelshaus*, 344 F.Supp. 253 (D.D.C.1972), enjoined EPA from approving state SIPs that allowed areas with air quality better than NAAQS levels to "deteriorate" to the level of the NAAQSs.

In response to this opinion, EPA developed a new regulatory program to prevent "significant" deterioration of air quality. This program was largely adopted by Congress in the 1977 Amendments, and it remains in the current CAA as the "Prevention of Significant Deterioration" ("PSD") program found in Part C, sections 160–169A.

The PSD program essentially "zones" clean air areas into three different classes, and varying amounts of "degradation" are allowed in each class. Additionally, major new sources are required to employ the "best available control technology." The purpose of the PSD program is to allow some growth in clean air areas while still ensuring maintenance of high quality air.

2.   Area Classifications and Increments

An area is classified as a PSD area if it meets the NAAQS for a pollutant or if it is "unclassifiable" due to a lack of information to determine whether the area meets the NAAQS. **§ 162(b), 42 U.S.C. § 7472(b)**. You should note that area classifications are made on a pollutant-by-pollutant basis, and the same area may be a PSD area because it meets the NAAQS for particulates and non-attainment because it exceeds the NAAQS for ozone.

Under the PSD program, areas are divided into 3 different classes. Depending upon the classification, area quality may be degraded by various "increments" up to a maximum of degradation to NAAQS levels.

a. Classifications

Section 162 established the initial classifications of clean air areas. Class I areas include such places as national parks. **§ 162(a), 42 U.S.C. § 7472(a)**. Class II areas were all other areas that had previously been designated as attainment or unclassifiable. **§ 162(b), 42 U.S.C. § 7472(b)**. States, however, have the authority to reclassify most areas as Class III except for certain large national parks and wildlife areas that must maintain their initial classification as Class I or Class II areas. **§ 164, 42 U.S.C. § 7474**.

b. Increments for Particulates and Sulfur Dioxide

Section 163 specifies that each class can be degraded by varying "increments" from its "baseline" air quality conditions:

Class I areas, for example, may have an increase, on an annual basis of 2 micrograms per cubic meter of air of sulfur dioxide. The Act also specifies maximums over shorter periods of time. **§ 163(b)(1), 42 U.S.C. § 7473(b)(1)**.

Class II areas may have an increase on an annual basis of 20 micrograms per cubic meter of air of sulfur dioxide. **§ 163(b)(2), 42 U.S.C. § 7473(b)(2)**.

Class III areas may have an increase on an annual basis of 40 micrograms per cubic meter of air of sulfur dioxide. **§ 163(b)(3), 42 U.S.C. § 7473(b)(3)**.

EPA has promulgated increments for "PM–10" (particulate matter with a diameter of 10 microns or less) that replace the statutory increments for particulate matter.

In no case, may the air quality in a PSD area be allowed to exceed either the primary or secondary NAAQS. **§ 163(b)(4), 42 U.S.C. § 7473(b)(4)**.

c. Increments for Other Pollutants

The CAA establishes specific increments only for particulates and sulfur dioxide. Section 166 authorizes EPA to develop a PSD program to deal with other NAAQS pollutants. **§ 166, 42 U.S.C. § 7476**. To date, EPA has promulgated regulations dealing only with nitrogen dioxide.

3. New Source Review Program

In addition to limiting the maximum amount of degradation in clean air areas, the CAA also requires that all "major emitting facilities" that are "constructed" undergo preconstruction review and that all such facilities employ a stringent technology-based level of control called "best available control technology" ("BACT"). **§ 165, 42 U.S.C. § 7475**. Section 169 contains definitions applicable to the PSD program that help define the scope of the program.

a. Scope of the Program

The PSD preconstruction review program applies to "major emitting facilities." Section 169(1) defines a "major emitting facility" as

1) any stationary source within a specific list of 28 categories of sources (including such sources as fossil-fuel fired power plants, certain cement plants, and certain metal smelters) that emit or have the "potential to emit" 100 tons per year or more "of any air pollutant," and

2) any other stationary source that emits or has the "potential to emit" more than 250 tons per year of any air pollutant. **§ 169(1), 42 U.S.C. § 7479(1)**.

The preconstruction review program applies to the construction or modification of these sources. The definitions cross-reference the definition of modification in section 111(a)(4) which governs NSPS.

In *Alabama Power Co. v. Costle*, 636 F.2d 323 (D.C.Cir.1979), the court reviewed EPA's regulations implementing the PSD program and resolved a number of issues relating to the scope of the PSD program.

(1) Potential to Emit

The amount of pollutants that a facility has the "potential to emit" is determined based on the facility's maximum productive capacity after taking into account the anticipated functioning of air pollution control equipment designed into the facility.

(2) Location of Sources

The preconstruction review requirement applies only to sources actually located within a PSD area; it does not apply to sources outside such areas even if emissions from that "outside" source contribute to the increase of pollutants within the PSD area.

(3) Covered Pollutants

BACT requirements apply to "each pollutant subject to regulation" under the Act, and large numbers of pollutants meet this criterion.

The court rejected EPA's argument that only pollutants emitted in excess of the 100 or 250 ton threshold must be regulated, and it also rejected industry arguments that only sulfur dioxide and particulates must be regulated.

(4) De Minimis Exemptions

The court in *Alabama Power* authorized, and EPA has adopted, "de minimis" thresholds for regulation of certain pollutants. Only modifications of existing "major emitting facilities" that increase levels of pollutants by more than the de minimis amounts will subject the facility to the PSD program.

(5) Bubbles

EPA has adopted a "bubble" rule for the PSD program that defines the term "facility" to include an entire plant and not each individual source of pollutants within the plant.

b. **BACT**

Sources that are subject to the preconstruction review program must employ a stringent level of technology known as BACT. BACT is developed on a case-by-case basis at each facility, and EPA does not promulgate national BACT for classes or categories of sources the way that it promulgates NSPS. BACT must at least be as stringent as NSPS.

The 1990 amendments require EPA to establish a RACT/BACT/LAER clearinghouse which contains examples of past BACT determinations. The clearinghouse provides information for use in developing BACT.

4. Visibility Protection

Section 169A establishes a special program for the protection of visibility in Class I areas. **§ 169A, 42 U.S.C. § 7491**. This program is intended to protect scenic views in Class I areas such as national parks and wilderness areas.

EPA regulations require states to revise their SIPs to implement a visibility impairment program. EPA regulations require that SIPs deal only with emissions traceable to a single or a small number of sources; they do not address visibility problems that result from large numbers of sources in a region.

I. National Emission Standards for Hazardous Air Pollutants

1. Background

a. NESHAPs Prior to the 1990 Amendments

When originally adopted in 1970, section 112 gave EPA the authority to develop nationally applicable, environmental-quality based limitations on the emission of "hazardous air pollutants." EPA was required to promulgate a list of pollutants that met the statutory definition of "hazardous air pollutants" and to develop "National Emission Standards for Hazardous Air Pollutants" ("NESHAPs") that would provide "an ample margin of safety to protect the public health."

EPA had a very difficult time implementing the NESHAP requirements. Between 1970 and 1990, EPA only promulgated NESHAPs for seven pollutants: asbestos, benzene, beryllium, mercury, vinyl chloride, coke oven emissions, inorganic arsenic and some radionuclides.

A major part of the problem arose from the difficulty in determining what constituted an "ample margin of safety" for emissions of carcinogenic air pollutants. EPA, as well as most regulatory agencies, have acted on the assumption that the only completely safe level of exposure to carcinogens is zero. Imposition of a standard of zero emissions would have had tremendous economic consequences, and EPA was reluctant to interpret the statute to require imposition of these costs with uncertain health benefits.

In *NRDC v. United States EPA*, 824 F.2d 1146 (D.C.Cir.1987), the D.C. Circuit interpreted section 112 to require EPA to make an initial determination of a "safe" level of emissions. In the court's view, "safe" did not mean risk-free. EPA was given discretion to define a level of emissions that constituted an "acceptable" risk to health. The court was explicit that EPA was not to consider costs when defining this safe level. The court held that, after EPA had defined the "safe" level, the Agency could further tighten the standard to reflect an "ample margin" of safety. At this stage, EPA could consider costs and technological feasibility.

The court gave EPA little guidance in determining what constituted an "acceptable" risk, and EPA struggled to define this politically sensitive issue.

b. NESHAPs After the 1990 Amendments

In the 1990 Amendments, Congress completely changed the approach to establishing NESHAPs under section 112. NESHAPs are now to be established as technology-based standards based on "maximum achievable control technology" ("MACT"). "Major sources" must meet MACT limitations. Additionally, section 112 authorizes EPA to establish additional requirements after 1998 to control any "residual risk" that exists after application of MACT.

Section 112 also establishes a number of other requirements. Among other things, section 112 requires development of a program to control the emission of hazardous air pollutants from "area sources." Area sources are defined to include all sources that are not "major sources." Section 112 also establishes a program to require certain sources to develop plans to prevent the accidental release of HAPs.

2. Scope of the Program

a. Hazardous Air Pollutants

Section 112(b) establishes a list of 189 pollutants that are designated as "hazardous air pollutants" ("HAPs"). **§ 112(b), 42 U.S.C. § 7412(b)**. EPA has authority to add or delete pollutants from this list.

b. Major Sources

Section 112 requires that "major sources" meet emission limits based on MACT. Section 112(a)(1) defines a major source as a stationary source or group of sources that emits or has the potential to emit after installation of pollution control devices 10 tons per year of any hazardous air pollutant or 25 tons per year or more of any combination of HAPs. **§ 112(a)(1), 42 U.S.C. § 7412(a)(1)**.

MACT applies to both new and existing major sources. Applicable requirements may, however, vary depending on whether the source is a "new" or "existing" source. **§ 112(d)(3), 42 U.S.C. § 7412(d)(3)**. A "new source" is defined as a stationary source which is constructed or "reconstructed" after the date of proposal of applicable emission standards. **§ 112(a)(4), 42 U.S.C. § 7412(a)(4)**.

c. Area Sources

"Area sources" are subject to a distinct regulatory program under section 112. Area sources are defined in section 112(a)(2) as any stationary source of HAPs that is not a major source. **§ 112(a)(2), 42 U.S.C. § 7412(a)(2)**. Cars and other motor vehicles are excluded from the definition of area sources.

3. MACT Standards

Section 112(d) requires EPA to promulgate technology-based MACT standards that limit the emission of HAPs. **§ 112(d)(1), 42 U.S.C. § 7412(d)(1)**. These standards, like NSPS, are promulgated by EPA and are national standards that apply to categories of industrial sources.

a. Technology–Based Limitations

In developing MACT standards, EPA must establish limitations on the emission of HAPs that require the "maximum degree of reduction" that EPA determines is "achievable." **§ 112(d)(2), 42 U.S.C. § 7412(d)(2).** As with other technology-based standards, EPA may consider such factors as cost and availability of control technology. EPA is required to develop lists of industrial categories for which it will promulgate MACT, **§ 112(c), 42 U.S.C. § 7412(c)**, and the standards may vary among categories, or subcategories, of industrial sources.

The MACT standards may also differ for new and existing sources within a category. For new sources, the standard must be based on the "best controlled similar source." **§ 112(d)(3), 42 U.S.C. § 7412(d)(3).** For existing sources, the standard must be based on the emission limits achieved by the best performing 12 percent of the existing sources within the category or, for categories with fewer than thirty sources, the emission limits achieved by the best performing five sources. **§ 112(d)(3), 42 U.S.C. § 7412(d)(3).**

b. Compliance Requirements

Section 112(i), in most cases, requires new or reconstructed major sources to comply with applicable MACT regulations before they begin operation. **§ 112(i), 42 U.S.C. § 7412(i).** Existing major stationary sources must comply with applicable MACT requirements by the date specified in the regulation, which may not be later than three years from their date of promulgation.

Additionally, section 112(j) provides that if EPA has not promulgated an MACT requirement for a listed category after a state adopts a permit program, permit writers must develop case-by-case MACT requirements to be included in the permit. **§ 112(j)(5), 42 U.S.C. § 7412(j)(5).** These limitations must be met immediately by new or reconstructed sources, and no later than three years from issuance of the permit for existing sources.

Finally, section 112(g)(2) provides that, after the effective date of a CAA permit program in a state, major sources may not be "modified," or major sources may not be "constructed" or "reconstructed" until EPA or the state determines that the applicable MACT standard will be met. The determination will be made on a "case-by-case" basis if the MACT standard has not yet been promulgated by EPA. **§ 112(g)(2), 42 U.S.C. § 7412(g)(2).**

c. Early Reduction Compliance Extension

Section 112(i)(5) provides that an existing source that reduces its emission of HAPs by 90% or more (95% for particulates) prior to proposal of an applicable MACT may be given an extra six years to comply with final MACT. **§ 112(i)(5), 42 U.S.C. § 7412(i)(5).** To be eligible for this compliance extension, the source must have an enforceable obligation to maintain its reduced level of emissions.

4. Residual Risk Standards

All major sources are required to meet the technology-based MACT standards, but the 1990 CAA amendments also provide for additional restrictions on the emission of HAPs. **§ 112(f), 42 U.S.C. § 7412(f).** EPA is required to prepare a series of reports relating to the risk remaining after implementation of MACT requirements. Unless Congress acts, EPA is required to develop additional post-MACT emission limits if necessary to provide an ample margin of safety to protect public health or prevent an adverse environmental effect. These additional limitations are to be promulgated within 8 years after promulgation of the applicable MACT limitation. These second-tier emission standards are known as "residual risk" standards.

As discussed above, EPA had a difficult time prior to the 1990 Amendments in defining what level of risk constituted an "ample margin of safety." The 1990 Amendments address this problem; section 112(f)(2)(A) specifically provides that EPA must promulgate a residual risk standard for a carcinogenic HAP if the MACT standards for an industrial category do not reduce "lifetime excess cancer risks" to a "maximally exposed individual" to less than a one-in-a-million. **§ 112(f)(2)(A), 42 U.S.C. § 7412(f)(2)(A).**

5. Area Source Program

Although the MACT program deals with emission of HAPs from large stationary sources, it does not deal with problem of hazardous air pollutants emitted by large numbers of small sources. These small sources are called "area sources" in section 112. EPA is required in section 112(k) to study the problem and, by November 1995, develop a "comprehensive strategy to control emissions of hazardous air pollutants from area sources in urban areas." **§ 112(k), 42 U.S.C. § 7412(k).** EPA must assure that sources are in compliance with the requirements of this strategy by November 1999.

J.   Acid Rain and Sulfur Trading Provisions

1.   Background

a.   The Acid Rain Problem

When emissions of sulfur dioxide and nitrous oxides mix with moisture in the atmosphere they produce acidic precipitation—"acid rain." Acid rain has been attributed to sulfur and nitrogen emissions from large, coal-fired power plants. Although the sources and effects of acid rain are controversial, it has been widely believed that acid rain has adversely affected forests and lakes in the Northeastern states in the U.S. and parts of Canada.

In 1980, Congress established the National Acid Precipitation Assessment Program which took ten years and spent half a billion dollars to reach ambiguous, and controversial, conclusions that suggested that the acid rain problem was less significant than had been thought. The results from this study came out during the last stages of the debate over the 1990 CAA amendments and did not affect the contents of the current CAA acid rain requirements.

b.   Pre–1990 Provisions of the CAA

Under the 1970 CAA, there were no specific provisions dealing with the control of acid rain. In the 1977 Amendments, Congress adopted a controversial change to the NSPS provisions affecting coal burning power plants. The NSPS were required to limit both the total amount of sulfur emissions, which was cheaper to meet by use of coal with a lower sulfur content, and also require a percentage reduction of sulfur regardless of the original sulfur content of the coal. This provision was widely seen as a political compromise between low sulfur coal producing western states and high sulfur coal producing eastern states. In *Sierra Club v. Costle*, 657 F.2d 298 (D.C.Cir.1981), the court, in one of the longest court opinions ever written, upheld the NSPS that EPA had adopted for coal fired power plants.

c.   The 1990 Amendments

In the 1990 Amendments, Congress adopted a new approach to control of acid rain. These provisions are found in Title IV, sections 401 to 416. The CAA now requires that sulfur emissions be reduced by 10 million tons from 1980 levels. By the year 2000, the total annual emissions of sulfur dioxide may not exceed 8.9 million tons. **§ 403(a)(1), 42 U.S.C. § 7651b(a)(1)**. The Act also provides for the reduction of nitrogen emissions by about 2 million tons.

The main focus of the 1990 acid rain program is the creation of a novel system of marketable sulfur allowances. Through the use of these marketable allowances, Congress hopes that market forces will help to achieve the 10 million ton sulfur reduction in the cheapest manner possible. This program is an example of a "cap and trade" form of marketable pollution rights discussed at 6.B.2.

2. Sulfur Allowance Program

a. Sulfur Allowances

Reductions in sulfur emissions are to be accomplished by the issuance of a limited number of "sulfur allowances." Each allowance authorizes the holder to emit one ton of sulfur dioxide each year, and affected facilities may only emit as much sulfur dioxide as they have allowances for.

The CAA implements the sulfur allowance program in two phases. In Phase I, the Act provided for the allocation of sulfur allowances to 111 fossil fuel fired power plants that are specifically listed in the statute. **§ 404, 42 U.S.C. § 7451c.** Phase I became effective on January 1, 1995, and, after that date, the covered facilities could not emit sulfur dioxide unless they had either been allocated or they had purchased a sufficient number of sulfur allowances.

In Phase II, which became effective on January 1, 2000, a reduced number of sulfur allowances were allocated to the Phase I facilities and a larger number of smaller facilities. **§ 405, 42 U.S.C. § 7651d.**

Facilities that are subject to the requirements of the acid rain program are defined as "affected sources." **§ 402(1)–(2), 42 U.S.C. § 7651a(1)–(2).**

b. Trading of Sulfur Allowances

The Act provides that sulfur allowances may be freely bought and sold. **§ 403(b), 42 U.S.C. § 7651b(b).** Facilities that reduce their emissions below their allocation may sell their excess allowances. Other facilities may find it cheaper to purchase allowances rather than reduce their emissions. It remains to be seen how well the market in sulfur allowances will operate. The Chicago Board of Trade has proposed to trade "sulfur allowances" in much the same way hog bellies or other commodities are traded.

To ensure that new and existing sources will be able to purchase sulfur allowances, the CAA establishes a program for the sale or auction of sulfur allowances. § 416, 42 U.S.C. § 7651o. The act requires EPA to withhold 2.8% of sulfur allowances. EPA will sell these allowances in several ways. First, a portion of the allowances may be directly sold at $1,500 per allowance. Second, EPA will conduct an auction to sell a portion of the allowances. This auction will ensure that some allowances will be available at a price dictated by the market. Facilities from which the allowances were withheld will get a pro rata share of the proceeds. The act also allows parties to submit allowances to EPA for sale in the auction.

c. Election for Other Sources

The CAA provides that sources that are not otherwise subject to the sulfur trading program may elect to participate. § 410, 42 U.S.C. § 7651i. If such a source reduces its sulfur emissions below its baseline, it may receive sulfur allowances which can then be sold.

3. Nitrogen Oxide Program

Section 407 establishes requirements for the reduction of nitrogen oxide emissions by sources that are subject to the sulfur allowance program. § 407, 42 U.S.C. § 7651f. EPA is required to promulgate "annual allowable emission limitations" for nitrogen oxides for certain types of utility boilers. EPA is also required to revise NSPS for coal-fired power plants to reflect improved means of control of nitrogen oxides.

4. Permit Program

Facilities subject to the sulfur trading program must obtain an operating permit. § 408, 42 U.S.C. § 7651g. This permit must, among other things, prohibit the emission of sulfur dioxide in excess of the number of allowances held by the facility, prohibit the use of an allowance prior to the year in which it is allocated, and establish otherwise applicable emission rates. Affected facilities requiring a permit must also submit a compliance plan which identifies how they will meet their applicable requirements. The acid rain permit program will be integrated with the general Title V permit program.

K. Permits

1. Background

Prior to the 1990 Amendments, the CAA did not contain a general permit requirement. The Act did contain some requirements that were similar to a permit program. New or modified major stationary sources located in non-attainment areas and major emitting facilities in PSD areas were required to have permits, and new sources subject to NSPS had to undergo pre-construction review. Additionally, a large number of states adopted their own permit requirements. But there was no general federal requirement that sources emitting air pollutants were required to have a permit. This was in contrast to the Clean Water Act which requires that every point source have an "NPDES" permit.

The absence of a permit requirement created problems. Since no one document contained its air pollution requirements, it was difficult for a source to know what its applicable requirements were. Enforcement, both by citizens and the government, was hindered by this lack of specifically identified obligations. There was also no permit application process in which sources submitted information about their operations, and this made case-by-case review of facility operations more difficult.

In the 1990 Amendments, Congress adopted a permit program modeled after the NPDES permit program. These permit requirements are now contained in Title V, sections 501 to 507.

2. Scope of the Title V Permit Program

Section 502(a) provides that it is unlawful for certain types of sources to operate without a permit or violate any requirements of a permit. **§ 502(a), 42 U.S.C. § 7661a(a)**. The sources to which this requirement applies include:

- an "affected source" which means a source subject to the sulfur trading program;

- a "major source" as defined in the NESHAP provisions of section 112 (a stationary source which emits or has the potential to emit 10 tons per year of any single HAP or 25 tons per year or more of any combination of HAPs);

- a "major stationary source" as defined in section 302(j) (a stationary source which emits or has the potential to emit 100 tons per year of any pollutant);

- a "major stationary source" as defined under the non-attainment permit program (a stationary source which emits or has the potential to emit from 100 to 10 tons per year of any air pollutant depending upon the ozone non-attainment classification);

- any other source subject to regulation under sections 111 or 112 (including new sources subject to NSPS, existing sources subject to NSPS under section 111(d), and area sources that are regulated under section 112(k));

- any other source required to have a permit under the PSD or non-attainment programs;

- any other source in a category designated by EPA.

3. State Permit Programs

Under the Clean Air Act, states are required to develop a permit program and issue the permits. **§ 502(d), 42 U.S.C. § 7661a(d)**. EPA becomes the permit issuer only in certain cases where the state fails to develop an approved permit program. **§ 502(i)(4), 42 U.S.C. § 7661a(i)(4)**. This is in contrast to the Clean Water Act, in which EPA issues NPDES permits unless a state requests, and receives, delegation of the permit program.

a. Minimum Program Elements

EPA is required to adopt regulations establishing the requirements for a state permit program. **§ 502(b), 42 U.S.C. § 7661a(b)**. The statute specifies certain minimum elements including, among others:

- standard permit application forms;

- collection of "permit fees" from permittees in an amount sufficient to pay the administrative expenses of the state in implementing and enforcing the permit program. The statute provides that the minimum amount of the fee, unless varied by EPA, is $25 per ton of regulated pollutant;

- certain minimum permit conditions including a maximum duration of five years;

- procedures for public participation in the permit process and judicial review of final permit actions in State court;

- provisions for public access to permit applications, permits, monitoring and compliance reports;

- provisions to allow changes within a permitted facility without requiring a revision of the permit, subject to a requirement that the facility provide advanced written notification to EPA and the state of the proposed changes.

b. Review and Approval of State Permit Programs

States are required to develop programs for the issuance of CAA permits, and they are required to submit their programs for review by EPA. **§ 502(d)(1), 42 U.S.C. § 7661a(d)(1)**. If the state program does not meet the permit program requirements developed by EPA, EPA may disapprove the state program and impose the sanctions contained in section 179(b) (withholding certain highway funds and, in some cases, altering the "offset" requirements in non-attainment areas). **§ 502(d)(2), 42 U.S.C. § 7661a(d)(2)**. Additionally, in some cases, if the state fails to submit an approved program, EPA may adopt and administer a permit program in that state.

4. Permit Conditions

a. Minimum Requirements

Section 504 establishes certain minimum requirements for inclusion in permits. **§ 504, 42 U.S.C. § 7661c**. Permits must, among other things, include enforceable emission limits, monitoring requirements, and provisions relating to inspection and monitoring of the facility.

Additionally, as discussed above, section 502 requires that state permit programs ensure that permits be limited to a term of no more than five years and allow facilities to change their operations without obtaining a modification of their permit.

b. Permit Shield

Section 504(f) establishes a "permit shield." **§ 504(f), 42 U.S.C. § 7661c(f)**. This section provides that if a source is complying with its permit conditions it cannot be prosecuted for operating without a permit or for violating its permit. Section 504(f) further provides that compliance with a permit will also protect a source from prosecution for violation of other requirements of the CAA but only if 1) the permit includes the applicable requirements or 2) the permit writer specifically makes a determination that other provisions are not applicable. This means that if a permit fails to include an applicable requirement (and the permit writer has not specifically determined that the requirement is not applicable) a source may still be subject to prosecution even if it is in compliance with its permit.

5. EPA Review of State Issued Permits

Under section 505, states are required to submit permit applications and proposed permits to EPA for its review. **§ 505, 42 U.S.C. § 7661d**. EPA may object to a proposed permit if EPA determines that the permit does not meet the requirements of the Act. If after EPA objects, the state fails to revise the permit, EPA must issue or deny the permit. EPA's action in issuing or denying the permit (but not objecting to the permit) is subject to judicial review.

If EPA does not object to a permit, any person may petition EPA to request that EPA object to the permit. If EPA denies the petition, the person may seek judicial review of EPA's action. This means that federal judicial review under the CAA is always available for permits issued by states.

L. Interstate Pollution Problems

Interstate pollution—pollution problems in one state caused by emissions in another state—has been a difficult problem under the Clean Air. Under the original 1970 CAA, EPA merely required states to exchange information about interstate pollution. In 1977, Congress amended section 110(a)(2)(D) and required state SIPs to control emissions in their state that would "prevent attainment or maintenance" of NAAQS in neighboring states. Additionally, Congress added section 126 which allowed states to petition EPA for a finding that a major source was violating the requirements of section what is now section 110(a)(2)(D). If EPA made such a finding, it could prohibit the construction of a proposed new or modified major source or the operation of a major existing source. Neither of these provisions were effective in part because of the problems of defining the level of pollution from neighboring states that would "prevent attainment or maintenance" and modeling the effects of interstate pollution.

The 1990 Amendments, however, added several provisions addressing interstate problems. First, the Amendments added the significant sulfur trading program to address regional problems of acid rain. This program is addressed in Section J above. Second, the Amendments established a new standard for SIP provisions dealing with interstate pollution. Section 110(a)(2)(D) now requires SIPs to control sources that "contribute significantly" with non-attainment of an NAAQS or "interfere with maintenance" of an NAAQS in another state. **§ 110(a)(2)(D), 42 U.S.C. § 7410(a)(2)(D)**. This change presumably clarifies the CAA standards for assessing the impact of interstate pollution. Third, Congress amended section 126 to apply not only to individual major sources but to "groups of stationary sources." **§ 126(b), 42 U.S.C. § 7426(b)**. The 1990 Amendments also adopt, in sections 176A and 184, special requirements for "interstate transport regions" where emissions from one or more states "significantly contribute" to violations of an NAAQS.

M. International Pollution Problems

The CAA now contains several provisions dealing with problems of the transportation of pollutants between countries.

1. General Provisions

Section 115 specifically addresses the issue of international air pollution. **§ 115, 42 U.S.C. § 7415.** Under section 115, EPA may determine, based on reports from a "duly constituted international agency," that emissions from U.S. sources were causing or contributing to serious pollution problems in another country. EPA must then require the state in which the sources are located to modify its SIP to control those sources. EPA must also take such action if requested by the Secretary of State. This section only applies if the foreign country has reciprocal provisions to protect U.S. air quality.

2. Protection of Stratospheric Ozone and the Montreal Protocols

One of the most important international air pollution problems involves the emission of pollutants, primarily chlorofluorocarbons, that are destroying ozone in the upper atmosphere. This "ozone layer" protects the earth's surface from high levels of ultraviolet radiation from the sun.

In the Montreal Protocols, the U.S. entered an international agreement to limit the production and use of ozone destroying chemicals. The 1990 Amendments to the CAA added Title VI which contains special provisions to implement the Montreal Protocols and that take additional steps to control chlorofluorocarbons. Among other things, the Montreal Protocols and Title VI require the phase out of the use of numerous ozone destroying chemicals, including such common chemicals as freon that is widely used in refrigeration equipment.

N. Judicial Review of Government Action and Inaction

Under section 307(b), any action of the Administrator under the CAA is subject to judicial review in a federal Court of Appeals. **§ 307(b)(1), 42 U.S.C. § 7607(b)(1).** Review of certain enumerated actions and promulgation of any nationally applicable regulation is in the Court of Appeals for the District of Columbia. Other actions, such as approval of state SIPs, and any other action that is "locally or regionally applicable" is in the Court of Appeals for the appropriate circuit. Petitions for review of EPA actions must be brought within 60 days of publication of notice of the action, unless the petition is based on new information arising after 60 days.

Additionally, section 304 authorizes citizens to bring an action against the Administrator of EPA for failure to perform a non-discretionary duty. § 304(a)(2), 42 U.S.C. § 7604(a)(2).

O. Review Questions

1. T or F   States may establish automobile emission standards that are more stringent than federal standards established under section 202 if the more stringent state standards are necessary to meet an NAAQS.

2. T or F   Once a state SIP is approved and promulgated by EPA, the provisions of the SIP remain federally enforceable until changed both by the state and EPA.

3. T or F   MACT limits on the emission of hazardous air pollutants are set at a level that ensures that a "maximally exposed individual" will incur less than a one in a million increased risk of cancer.

4. T or F   EPA has the authority to promulgate a "Federal Implementation Plan" if a state fails to submit an approvable SIP.

5. T or F   The non-attainment permit program applies to all "major stationary sources" located in non-attainment areas.

6. T or F   If a "major stationary source" constructed prior to proposal of a new source performance standard is later modified it may be subject to the NSPS limitations.

7. T or F   For purposes of satisfying their obligations under section 110, state SIPS can ensure attainment of NAAQS by allowing facilities to build tall smoke stacks which widely disperse pollutants.

8. T or F   Under the Clean Air Act, all industrial sources of air pollution are required to obtain an enforceable Title V permit.

9. T or F   Under the "permit shield" provision in section 504(f), a facility that complies with the requirements contained in its permit will be deemed to be in compliance with all of its requirements under the Clean Air Act.

10. T or F   EPA must set a primary NAAQS at a level necessary to assure, with an ample margin of safety, that no person will suffer a material

health impairment from exposure to the pollutant.

11. T or F   When setting a primary NAAQS, EPA must consider the economic impact of compliance with the standard, and EPA may not establish a primary NAAQS at a level that is not economically or technologically "feasible."

12. T or F   A "major emitting facility" that is newly constructed in an area subject to the PSD program is subject to BACT limitations for all pollutants subject to regulation under the Clean Air Act.

13. T or F   EPA may not approve those portions of a state SIP that establish requirements that are not economically or technologically "feasible."

14. T or F   EPA has promulgated enforceable, nationally applicable RACT limitations that must be met by all existing sources located in a non-attainment area.

15. T or F   The owner of a "major stationary source" located in a moderate ozone non-attainment area is planning to modify the source in a way which will increase its emissions of VOCS by 10 tons per year. The facility will satisfy its "offset" requirement if other sources located within the non-attainment area adopt enforceable reductions of emissions of VOCS by 10 tons per year.

*

CHAPTER 7

Resource Conservation and Recovery Act

■ ANALYSIS

A. **BACKGROUND**
  1. Structure of RCRA
     a. Hazardous Wastes—Subtitle C
     b. Non-hazardous, Solid Wastes—Subtitle D
     c. Underground Storage Tanks—Subtitle I
     d. Used Oil—§ 3014
  2. History
  3. Outline of Major Statutory Provisions
B. **HAZARDOUS WASTES—SUBTITLE C**
  1. Basic Structure
     a. Manifest Requirement
     b. TSDF Permit Requirements
  2. Definition of Hazardous Waste
     a. Definition of Solid Waste

        (5)   Corrective Action

   6. Land Ban

      a.   No Migration Petitions

      b.   Pretreatment to BDAT Levels

          (1)   Technology–Based Standards

          (2)   Treatment to Levels Below Characteristic Levels

   7. Export of Hazardous Wastes

C.   NON–HAZARDOUS SOLID WASTES—SUBTITLE D

   1. Sanitary Landfill Criteria

   2. Open Dumping Prohibition

D.   JUDICIAL REVIEW

   1. Review of Regulations and Permits

   2. Failure to Perform Non-discretionary Duties

E.   IMMINENT AND SUBSTANTIAL ENDANGERMENT

   1. Government

   2. Private Parties

F.   REVIEW QUESTIONS

A. Background

The Resource Conservation and Recovery Act (RCRA) is the primary federal statute dealing with the disposal of solid and hazardous wastes.

1. Structure of RCRA

The statute has separate programs that deal with hazardous wastes, non-hazardous solid wastes, underground storage tanks, used oil, and citizen suits to compel the cleanup of solid waste.

a. Hazardous Wastes—Subtitle C

The main focus of the statute has been on "Subtitle C" which contains the statutory provisions that regulate disposal of hazardous wastes. Subtitle C sets up a so-called "cradle to grave" system which regulates hazardous waste from the point at which it is generated to the point of its disposal.

b. Non-hazardous, Solid Wastes—Subtitle D

Subtitle D of RCRA has a limited regulatory program that applies to non-hazardous solid waste. Under subtitle D, the disposal of non-hazardous solid waste is legal only if done in "sanitary landfills." EPA has promulgated criteria defining "sanitary landfills." Disposal of non-hazardous waste at facilities that do not meet the sanitary landfill criteria is the prohibited act of "open dumping."

c. Underground Storage Tanks—Subtitle I

RCRA contains a separate program for regulating the storage of materials in underground storage tanks ("USTs"). The program applies to storage of a variety of wastes (other than hazardous wastes) and products (including gasoline) in underground storage tanks. The UST program requires, among other things, that owners and operators of underground storage tanks register their tanks with the government, upgrade their tanks to meet minimum technology requirements, and close their tanks properly when they remove them from service. Additionally, Subtitle I contains provisions relating to the cleanup of contamination from leaking USTs.

d. Used Oil—§ 3014

Used oil, even if it is not a hazardous waste, is subject to regulation under RCRA. § 3014, 42 U.S.C. § 6935. EPA has promulgated a complex set of regulations that apply to the recycling of used oil, including the burning of used oil as a fuel. The regulations impose requirements on the generators, transporters, sellers and recyclers of used oil.

e. Imminent and Substantial Endangerment—§ 7002(a)(1)(B)

Under the citizen suit provisions of § 7002(a)(1)(B), citizens may sue a variety of persons who have contributed to an "imminent and substantial endangerment" from a solid or hazardous waste. § 7002(a)(1)(B), 42 U.S.C. § 6872(a)(1)(B). Only injunctive relief, such as an order compelling the cleanup of the waste, is available under § 7002(a)(1)(B).

2. History

RCRA was adopted in 1976 as an amendment to the Solid Waste Disposal Act. It is universally known as RCRA.

Congress adopted major amendments to RCRA in 1984. These were the Hazardous and Solid Waste Amendments or HSWA, and you may see reference to the separate provisions established by HSWA. These include, among others, the "land ban," "corrective action," and minimum technology requirements for hazardous waste disposal facilities. Congress also adopted Subtitle I, the Underground Storage Tank program, in HSWA.

In 1980, Congress adopted the Used Oil Recycling Act which requires EPA to regulate used oil. These provisions, including subsequent amendments, are found in § 3014 of RCRA.

3. Outline of Major Statutory Provisions

Subtitle A, Subchapter I—General Provisions

Section 1004, 42 U.S.C. § 6903. Definitions.

Subtitle C, Subchapter III—Hazardous Wastes

Section 3001, 42 U.S.C. § 6921. Provisions relating to identification and listing of hazardous wastes and special provisions for small quantity generators.

Section 3002, 42 U.S.C. § 6922. Provisions applicable to generators of hazardous waste.

Section 3003, 42 U.S.C. § 6923. Provisions applicable to transporters of hazardous waste.

Section 3004, 42 U.S.C. § 6924. Provisions applicable to treatment, storage and disposal facilities and provisions relating to the land ban and corrective action.

Section 3005, 42 U.S.C. § 6925. Provisions relating to permitting of treatment, storage and disposal facilities.

Section 3006, 42 U.S.C. § 6926. Provisions relating to delegation of permitting authority to states.

Section 3008, 42 U.S.C. § 6928. Provisions relating to federal enforcement.

Section 3009, 42 U.S.C. § 6929. Provisions authorizing states to adopt requirements more stringent than those established by RCRA.

Section 3014, 42 U.S.C. § 6935. Provisions relating to regulation of the recycling of used oil.

Section 3017, 42 U.S.C. § 6938. Provisions relating to the export of hazardous wastes.

Subtitle D, Subchapter IV—Solid Wastes

Section 4004, 42 U.S.C. § 6944. Provisions relating to criteria for sanitary landfills.

Section 4005, 42 U.S.C. § 6945. Provisions relating to prohibition on open dumping.

Subtitle G, Subchapter VII—Miscellaneous Provisions

Section 7002, 42 U.S.C. § 6972. Provisions relating to citizen suits for violation of RCRA and for contributing to an imminent and substantial endangerment.

Section 7003, 42 U.S.C. § 6973. Provisions relating to government actions against persons contributing to an imminent and substantial endangerment.

Section 7006, 42 U.S.C. § 6975. Provisions relating to judicial review of final regulations promulgated under RCRA.

Subtitle I, Subchapter IX—Underground Storage Tanks

Sections 9001–9010, 42 U.S.C. § 6991–6991i. Provisions relating to Underground Storage Tanks.

B.   Hazardous Wastes—Subtitle C

1.   Basic Structure

Subtitle C of RCRA contains most of the provisions that regulate the management and disposal of hazardous waste. RCRA is frequently described as being a "cradle to grave" system for regulating hazardous waste, and it imposes requirements on the generator and transporter of hazardous wastes and requirements on the "treatment, storage, and disposal facility" (TSDF) that receives the wastes.

RCRA has two elements that are central to its cradle to grave system.

a. Manifest Requirement

RCRA requires that a manifest accompany most shipments of hazardous waste. **§ 3002(a)(5), 42 U.S.C. § 6922(a)(5).** The manifest is signed by the generator, carried and signed by the transporter, and signed after receipt by an authorized TSDF. After receipt of the waste, the TSDF must return a signed copy of the manifest to the original generator. If the generator does not receive the copy within a designated period of time, the generator is required to notify the government. This system is intended to ensure that wastes are actually received by an authorized disposal facility and not illegally dumped by the transporter.

b. TSDF Permit Requirements

Under RCRA, neither generators nor transporters are required to have permits, but TSDFs are required to obtain federally mandated permits. **§ 3005(a), 42 U.S.C. § 6925(a).** These permits contain a variety of conditions including in most cases, groundwater or air monitoring, minimum technology, and requirements to plan and finance closing of the facility when it ceases to operate.

2. Definition of Hazardous Waste

The requirements of Subtitle C apply to "hazardous wastes." Section 1004(5) of RCRA defines a "hazardous waste" to mean a "solid waste" that causes certain adverse human health or environmental affects if improperly managed. **§ 1004(5), 42 U.S.C. § 9603(5).** Therefore, in determining whether a material is a hazardous waste, it is necessary to 1) identify if the material is a "solid waste," and 2) to then determine if that waste meets the criteria for classification as a hazardous waste.

a. Definition of Solid Waste

Relevant definitions of "solid waste" are found in two places. First, section 1004(27) contains the statutory definition of the term. **§ 1004(27), 42 U.S.C. § 6903(27).** Second, EPA has promulgated a regulation, 40 C.F.R. § 261.2, which defines "solid wastes" for purposes of the Subtitle C program.

(1) Solid Waste Need Not Be Solid

A waste can be a solid waste even if it is not solid. The statutory and regulatory definitions of solid waste include material that is solid, semi-solid, liquid, or a contained gas.

(2) It Must Be a Discarded Material

Under the statute and regulation, a material is a solid waste if it has been "discarded." A material will be classified as discarded if it meets one of EPA regulatory criteria. These criteria are found in the regulatory definition of solid waste at 40 C.F.R. § 261.2(a).

(a) Abandoned

If a material has been abandoned it is a solid waste. This includes simply throwing material away.

(b) Recycled

EPA claims that materials that are recycled are subject to regulation as hazardous waste under RCRA. This is perhaps the most complex and controversial part of EPA's regulatory definition. Under this definition, a material is classified as a solid waste depending on the type of material it is and the way it is to be recycled.

To determine if a recycled material is initially classified as a solid waste, a generator must go through a series of steps.

First, the generator must determine if the material is one of a specified group of secondary materials. These secondary materials include spent materials, sludges, byproducts, discarded commercial chemical products, and scrap metal.

Second, the generator must determine if the materials are going to be recycled in one of four specified ways. These include recycling by a "use constituting disposal" (applying the material to the ground), burning it as a fuel, reclaiming the material, or speculatively accumulating the material. The regulations contain definitions of these terms.

Third, the generator must consult a chart or matrix found at 40 C.F.R. § 261.2 and see if the combination of waste material and recycling method results in the material being classified as a solid waste.

A recycled material is generally not defined as a solid waste if, without first being reclaimed, it is used or reused as an ingredient to make a product, as a substitute for a product, or, in some cases, returned for reuse in the original process from which it was generated.

In a number of decisions, the D.C. Circuit has attempted to define the limits of EPA's regulatory authority over materials that are part of an on-going industrial process. Beginning in 1987, the court in *American Mining Congress v. United States EPA*, 824 F.2d 1177 (D.C.Cir.1987), invalidated EPA's definition of solid waste as it applied to certain mining and petroleum refining wastes that were "recycled" on-site by being reinserted into on-going mining and petroleum refining operations. The court, among other things, reasoned that materials were not "solid wastes" if they were "destined for beneficial reuse or recycling in a continuous process by the generating industry itself." The scope of the court's opinion was unclear, and in subsequent opinions, the court upheld EPA's ability to define materials as wastes if, among other things, they had "become part of the waste disposal problem." In *Association of Battery Recyclers, Inc. v. United States EPA*, 208 F.3d 1047 (D.C.Cir.2000), the court reasserted limits of the scope of RCRA by rejecting EPA's attempt to define certain mining materials as solid waste if they were stored on bare land prior to further processing. The court again stated that the definition of solid waste did not extend to materials that were part of a continuous process within the generating industry.

Although the scope of EPA's authority to regulate materials that are recycled within an industry remains uncertain, other types of recycling, such as sending materials for reclamation at a facility in a different industry, remain subject to control as solid wastes under RCRA.

It may be useful to think of *American Mining Congress* and *Association of Battery Recyclers* as dealing with the issue of when a material in an industrial process can first be classified as a waste. Once a material has become a waste, courts have generally held that EPA has the authority to regulate the material as a hazardous waste even if it is subsequently recycled.

(c) Inherently Waste Like

EPA has also published a short list of certain materials that it has determined are solid wastes because they are "inherently waste like." Any of this short list of "inherently waste like" materials are solid wastes regardless of how they are recycled.

(d) Military Munitions

EPA has separate provisions that define and regulate the disposal of military munitions such as unexploded ordinance or munitions fragments.

(3) Exclusions

The statute and EPA regulations specifically exclude a variety of materials from classification as solid waste. Two of the more important exclusions include:

(a) Domestic Sewage

Wastes that go down a sewer to a municipal sewage treatment plant regulated under the Clean Water Act are not classified as solid wastes for purposes of RCRA. This includes industrial wastes placed in a sewer if they mix with domestic wastes. This exclusion is extremely important because it means that hazardous materials placed into the sewer are not regulated under RCRA. Rather they are regulated under the "pretreatment" program of the Clean Water Act.

(b) NPDES Point Source Discharges

Industrial discharges that are point sources "subject to" regulation under the NPDES permit program in the Clean Water Act are not classified as solid wastes under RCRA. Note that this exclusion applies to the discharge itself. Wastes generated as part of treatment of wastewater prior to discharge may be regulated under RCRA.

b. Definition of Hazardous Waste

The relevant statutory provisions relating to the definition of "hazardous waste" are found in § 1004(5) and 3001(a)–(b) of RCRA. **§ 1004(5), 42 U.S.C. § 6903(5) and § 3001(a)–(b), 42 U.S.C. § 6921(a)–(b)**. EPA regulations defining hazardous waste are found at 40 C.F.R. § 261.3.

If a material is a solid waste, it may then be classified as a hazardous waste in one of two ways.

(1) Listed Wastes

EPA has published several "lists" of hazardous wastes. These lists include wastes from specific industries (such as certain sludges from petroleum refineries), certain types of wastes regardless of the industry which produces them (such as halogenated spent solvents), and certain discarded commercial chemical products. A generator does not need to test the waste to see if it is hazardous; if it is on the list it is classified as a hazardous waste. EPA's lists of hazardous waste are found at 40 C.F.R. §§ 261.31–.33.

Generators may petition to have their particular wastes "delisted" by EPA, but this is time consuming and costly.

(2) Characteristic Wastes

Even if a solid waste is not specifically listed, it may still be a hazardous waste if that particular waste, when tested, exhibits any of four hazard "characteristics." Each of these characteristics is defined by specific test methods. EPA regulations governing "characteristic" hazardous waste are found at 40 C.F.R. § 261.20–.24.

(a) Ignitability

Ignitability refers to the tendency of a material to catch fire. Spent paint wastes may, for example, test as ignitable.

(b) Corrosivity

Corrosivity refers to the acidity or alkalinity (pH) of the waste. Spent acids may, for example, test as corrosive.

(c) Reactivity

Reactivity refers to the tendency of a material to explode. Certain wastes containing sodium, for example, may be reactive.

(d) Toxicity Characteristic or TC Rule

A solid waste may be classified as hazardous if it contains any one of 40 metals or organic constituents above levels set by EPA. This is called the toxicity characteristic or TC.

To determine if a solid waste contains these constituents above the regulatory levels, a liquid extract of the solid must first be obtained. This is done by using the "toxicity characteristic leachate procedure" or TCLP.

A solid waste exhibits the Toxicity Characteristic only if the extract of the waste contains one of the specified constituents above EPA's specified regulatory level.

Example: A waste exhibits the Toxicity Characteristic for lead, for example, only if a TCLP derived extract contains lead at a concentration of 5.0 mg/l or above.

(3) Mixture, Derived-from and Contained-in Rules

Under existing EPA rules, certain mixtures of hazardous and non-hazardous wastes or the residues derived from treatment of hazardous waste are classified as hazardous waste.

(a) Mixture Rule

The "mixture rule" basically provides that if a "listed" hazardous waste is mixed with a non-hazardous solid waste, the entire resulting mixture is treated as a hazardous waste. If, however, a "characteristic" hazardous waste (hazardous because it exhibits one of the four hazard characteristics) is mixed with a non-hazardous waste, the resulting mixture is only a hazardous waste if the mixture itself exhibits the characteristic.

(b) Derived–From Rule

The "derived-from rule" provides that any wastes derived from a listed hazardous waste are themselves a hazardous waste. Wastes derived from a characteristic hazardous waste are only hazardous if they exhibit a characteristic. Therefore, if a listed hazardous waste is incinerated, the ash remaining after the incineration is treated as a hazardous waste. Similarly, any sludge produced from the treatment of a listed hazardous waste is itself a hazardous waste.

(c) Contained-In Interpretation

Additionally, EPA has adopted a "contained-in" interpretation which generally provides that any waste "containing" a listed hazardous waste is itself treated as a hazardous waste. The contained-in rule has been applied to contaminated soil and groundwater generated as part of the cleanup of a hazardous waste site.

Example: Soil that has been contaminated with a listed hazardous waste is excavated. The soil, once it has been excavated and is now handled as a waste, might be treated as a hazardous waste under the contained-in interpretation.

(4) Exclusions

RCRA and EPA regulations contain a number of exclusions from classification as a hazardous waste. Note that these excluded materials may still be solid wastes; they are simply not classified as hazardous waste for purposes of the Subtitle C program. Two of the most important exclusions are:

(a) Household Hazardous Waste

Household wastes are not classed as hazardous waste even though they may contain hazardous material such as old pesticide containers. This means, among other things, that neither homeowners nor in most cases the municipality that picks up household waste are regulated under Subtitle C.

The household waste exclusion was originally adopted by EPA regulation, but in 1984 Congress adopted a cryptic reference to the household waste exclusion in a provision exempting certain municipal incinerators burning household wastes from regulation as treatment, storage or disposal facilities. **§ 3001(i), 42 U.S.C. § 6921(i)**. The Supreme Court has held, however, that section 3001(i) does not exempt ash generated at municipal incinerators from classification as a hazardous waste.

(b) Mining Wastes and Oil and Gas Exploration and Production Wastes

Section 3001(b)(2) and (3) of RCRA contain a specific statutory exclusion for most mining wastes and most wastes associated with the exploration and production of oil and gas. **§ 3001(b)(2)– (3), 42 U.S.C. § 6921(b)(2)–(3)**. There is not, however, an exclusion for petroleum under RCRA, and used oils may be classified as hazardous waste.

(5) Contingent Management

Perhaps the most significant development in RCRA over the last decade has been EPA's use of the concept of "contingent management." Through this approach, EPA has established regulations that state that a material is *not* a hazardous waste if it is managed in certain ways. Through the use of contingent management, EPA can assert regulatory controls over wastes without imposing the statutorily required controls that apply to hazardous waste and without having to label the materials as a hazardous waste.

3. Generator Requirements

Facilities that generate hazardous waste are not required to obtain a federal permit under RCRA. RCRA does, however, impose certain limited requirements on generators. Most of the statutory provisions governing generator requirements are found in § 3002 of RCRA, **§ 3002, 42 U.S.C. § 6922**. Most of the regulatory requirements relating to generators are found in 40 C.F.R. Part 263.

a. Obtaining an EPA I.D. Number

Generators must obtain an EPA Identification number that is used on all hazardous waste manifests and reports.

b. Hazardous Waste Determination

Generators are required to determine whether they have produced hazardous waste. They do this by determining whether a waste is listed or whether it exhibits a characteristic. A generator is not obligated to run laboratory analysis to determine if its waste is hazardous. To determine if a waste is a "listed" waste, the generator needs to check the regulatory lists. To determine if a waste is a "characteristic" waste, the generator may rely on its "knowledge of process" to determine if the waste exhibits a hazard characteristic. If the generator improperly concludes that the waste is not hazardous, the generator may be in violation of RCRA.

For purposes of the land ban, discussed below, generators must determine each of the different ways in which their wastes may be classified as hazardous.

c. Manifest

Hazardous waste sent for off-site treatment, storage or disposal must be accompanied by a manifest that, among other things, identifies the type of waste being transported, and the permitted facility to which it is being sent. If the generator does not receive, within 45 days, a copy of the manifest signed by the TSDF, the generator must notify the appropriate government agency.

d. On–Site Accumulation

Generators are allowed to store and treat wastes on-site for up to ninety days. There are restrictions on how wastes must be managed during that period. If wastes are stored for more than ninety days or if the facility wishes permanently to dispose of wastes on-site, the facility must obtain a TSDF permit. Small quantity generators, those generators that produce between 100 and 1000 kilograms per month of hazardous waste, may accumulate wastes on-site for up to 180 days. Do not confuse "small quantity generators" with "conditionally exempt small quantity generators," ("CESQGs") discussed below. Small quantity generators are generally fully regulated under RCRA; CESQGs are largely exempt from regulation.

e.   Conditionally Exempt Small Quantity Generators

Facilities that generate 100 kilograms per month (about one 55 gallon drum) or less of hazardous waste are largely exempt from regulation under the Subtitle C program. **§ 3001(d)(4), 42 U.S.C. § 6921(d)(4)**. Hazardous wastes generated at such facilities may, for example, be disposed of at municipal landfills without using manifests. Regulatory provisions relating to these "Conditionally Exempt Small Quantity Generators" ("CESQGs") are found at 40 C.F.R. § 261.5.

4.   Transporter Requirements

Hazardous waste transporters are not required under RCRA to obtain a permit, but they are subject to a limited set of requirements. They must, among other things, obtain an EPA Identification number, transport wastes only if the wastes are accompanied by a manifest, and deliver the wastes only to another transporter or permitted TSDF facility. EPA and the Department of Transportation have established requirements for packaging and labeling hazardous wastes in transit.

Most of the transporter requirements are found in § 3003 of RCRA, **§ 3003, 42 U.S.C. § 6923**, and 40 C.F.R. Part 264.

5.   Treatment, Storage and Disposal Facilities

Facilities that treat, store, or dispose of hazardous waste are subject to the most stringent requirements under RCRA. TSDFs include, among others, landfills and incinerators.

a.   Obligation to Have Permit

All facilities that treat, store, or dispose of hazardous wastes must obtain a TSDF hazardous waste permit. **§ 3005(a), 42 U.S.C. § 6925(a)**.

(1) Federal or State Issuance

EPA initially issued all TSDF permits. States may, however, be delegated authority to issue these permits if they have adopted hazardous waste permit programs that are substantially equivalent to the federal program. **§ 3006, 42 U.S.C. § 6926**. Since the 1984 HSWA amendments, some states may have received delegation to issue permits covering some parts of the program while EPA continues to impose conditions relating to HSWA requirements. Once states adopt programs covering HSWA requirements they may receive delegation to manage that portion of the program.

(2) Final and Interim Status

To avoid eliminating needed disposal facilities, RCRA authorized existing facilities to obtain "interim status." **§ 3005(e), 42 U.S.C. § 6925(e)**. Interim status facilities must have submitted an application for a final permit, and they must meet certain minimum requirements including groundwater monitoring and financial assurance. Facilities can operate under interim status until their permits are processed by EPA or the state.

New facilities may operate only after they have received a final permit.

b. Permit Conditions

TSDF permits must meet a series of requirements. General requirements are found in § 3004(a). **§ 3004(a), 42 U.S.C. § 6924(a)**.

(1) Technical Requirements

Facilities are subject to minimum technological requirements for operation of the facility. **§ 3004(o), 42 U.S.C. § 6924(o)**. For landfills, this includes requirements for proper liners to ensure that hazardous wastes do not leach into the groundwater. For incinerators, this includes requirements that the incinerator can, for most pollutants, destroy 99.99% of the pollutants that are fed into the incinerator.

(2) Closure and Post Closure Plans

Facilities must at the time of permit issuance have prepared plans for closing the facility and for properly maintaining and monitoring the facility for a period of thirty years after closure.

(3) Financial Responsibility

Facilities at the time of permit issuance must provide assurance, through bonds or other financial devices, that they have sufficient money to pay for personal or financial damages that occur while the facility is being operated and that they have sufficient money to implement closure and post-closure plans.

(4) Monitoring

Facilities are required to establish monitoring programs to detect releases of hazardous substances. Landfills are required to establish groundwater monitoring programs which include a series of groundwater monitoring wells. Incinerators are required to monitor gases being emitted from the incinerator.

(5) Corrective Action

Under RCRA, TSDFs may be required to take "corrective action" to remove not only hazardous waste but also solid wastes that are found at the facility. These corrective action requirements are applicable to permitted TSDFs and facilities that were at any time eligible for interim status. These requirements may be included in the facility's TSDF permit, **§ 3004(u), 42 U.S.C. § 6924(u)**, or they may be imposed through a separate corrective action order issued by EPA. **§ 3008(h), 42 U.S.C. § 6928(h)**.

6. Land Ban

In 1984, Congress adopted a general prohibition on the disposal of hazardous waste in landfills or by underground injection into wells. **§ 3004(d)–(k), 42 U.S.C. § 6924(d)–(k)**. This is known as the "land ban." The land ban was implemented in phases, and EPA issued five different land ban rules which addressed various classes of pollutants.

The land ban is not an absolute prohibition, and hazardous wastes may be land disposed *if* 1) the land disposal facility has been granted a "no migration" variance, **§ 3004(d), 42 U.S.C. § 6924(d)**, or 2) the wastes have first been treated to levels representing "best demonstrated available technology" or "BDAT." **§ 3004(m), 42 U.S.C. § 6924(m)**.

a. No Migration Petitions

A facility may petition for a variance from the land ban if it can demonstrate that there will be "no migration" of hazardous constituents from the disposal unit or injection zone as long as the wastes remain hazardous. **§ 3004(d)(1), 42 U.S.C. § 6924(d)(1)**.

b. Pretreatment to BDAT Levels

Hazardous wastes may generally be land disposed if they are first "pretreated" to levels achievable by use of "best demonstrated available technology." **§ 3004(m), 42 U.S.C. § 6924(m)**. The statute requires EPA to promulgate these pretreatment standards as "levels or methods of treatment" that "minimize" threats to the environment. Several significant issues arise in developing BDAT levels for purpose of the land ban.

(1) Technology–Based Standards

EPA has promulgated BDAT requirements that specify either the type of pretreatment technology that must be used or final levels of hazardous constituents in waste that must be achieved. These are "technology-based standards" which are based on EPA's assessment of the "best" technology that is available to reduce the toxicity of each type of listed or characteristic waste.

In *Hazardous Waste Treatment Council v. United States EPA*, 886 F.2d 355 (D.C.Cir.1989), the court upheld EPA's "technology-based" approach. The court concluded that EPA's construction of the statute, even thought it might require treatment below levels necessary to protect the environment, was not unreasonable given the uncertainties associated with risk assessment. It further concluded that requiring use of the best technology was consistent with the statute's requirement to "minimize" threats from hazardous constituents.

(2) Treatment to Levels Below Characteristic Levels

When EPA promulgated BDAT requirements for characteristic hazardous waste, it set the levels for some, but not all, wastes at levels below the hazard characteristic levels.

In *Chemical Waste Management v. United States EPA*, 976 F.2d 2 (D.C.Cir.1992), the court upheld EPA's authority to require treatment of characteristic wastes below the level at which the wastes are hazardous. The court, however, invalidated portions of EPA's rules that did not require treatment below characteristic levels. The court required EPA to justify BDAT levels as the lowest levels possible to minimize the threat from hazardous constituents in wastes.

The land ban levels for Toxicity Characteristic wastes may be below TC levels, and the land ban may therefore require treatment of wastes that no longer exhibit the Toxicity Characteristic. *In other words, this means that the land ban can apply to materials that are no longer hazardous waste if they were, at one point, classified as hazardous wastes.*

7. Export of Hazardous Wastes

RCRA does not prohibit the export of hazardous wastes. It does, however, require "informed consent" prior to the export of the wastes. **§ 3017, 42 U.S.C. § 6938.** Persons seeking to export the wastes must notify EPA. EPA is then required to notify the government of the country receiving the wastes and the countries through which the waste will be transported. If the receiving country provides written statement that it does not object to receipt of the wastes, they may be exported.

Exports to countries with which the U.S. has bilateral agreements concerning the export of wastes, such as Canada, are subject to the requirements of the treaty rather than RCRA. The "Basel Convention" is the major multinational treaty dealing with the export of hazardous waste. Although more stringent in some respects than RCRA, it relies on informed consent much as does RCRA.

C. Non–Hazardous Solid Wastes—Subtitle D

Subtitle D of RCRA establishes a limited regulatory program for the disposal of non-hazardous solid waste. The Subtitle D program has two key elements.

1. Sanitary Landfill Criteria

EPA has promulgated criteria for landfills receiving non-hazardous solid waste. **§ 4004, 42 U.S.C. § 6944.** Facilities meeting these criteria are known as "sanitary landfills."

In addition to criteria generally applicable to facilities receiving non-hazardous wastes, EPA has also promulgated specific, more detailed requirements applicable to Municipal Solid Waste Landfills ("MSWLFs"). These criteria contain requirements similar to those imposed on hazardous waste treatment, storage and disposal facilities. Remember that household hazardous waste is exempt from Subtitle C requirements and hazardous wastes generated by CESQGs may be disposed of in municipal landfills. Therefore a considerable amount of hazardous waste may under RCRA be legally disposed of in MSWLFs.

2. Open Dumping Prohibition

RCRA contains a prohibition on the "open dumping" of non-hazardous solid waste. **§ 4005(a), 42 U.S.C. § 6945(a).** Open dumping includes disposal of solid waste anywhere other than at a sanitary landfill.

D. Judicial Review

1. Review of Regulations and Permits

Judicial review of EPA action is authorized by section 7006 of RCRA. **§ 7006, 42 U.S.C. § 6976**. Judicial review of regulations issued under RCRA is in the Court of Appeals for the District of Columbia. Review of EPA's issuance or denial of a TSDF permit or EPA's actions relating to delegation to a state of permit issuing authority is in the appropriate Court of Appeals. All petitions must be filed within ninety days of the final action that is being challenged.

2. Failure to Perform Non–Discretionary Duties

Section 7002(a)(2) authorizes citizens to sue the Administrator for failure to perform a "non-discretionary" duty required by the Act. **§ 7002(a), 42 U.S.C. § 6972(a)**.

E. Imminent and Substantial Endangerment

1. Government

Section 7003 authorizes the government to issue an order to past or present generators, transporters and owners/operators of TSDFs who "cause or contribute" to an "imminent and substantial endangerment" from the management of solid or hazardous waste. **§ 7003(a), 42 U.S.C. § 6973(a)**. This order may require any of these persons to cleanup the solid or hazardous waste. An order may be issued under section 7003 even if the handling of the wastes does not violate the regulatory requirements of RCRA. EPA has similar authority to compel the cleanup of hazardous substances under CERCLA.

2. Private Parties

Under section 7002(a)(1)(B), citizens may bring a civil action in federal district court against any person who has caused or is contributing to an "imminent and substantial endangerment" from the management of solid or hazardous waste. **§ 7002(a)(1)(B), 42 U.S.C. § 6972(a)(1)(B)**. This section authorizes citizens to seek a court order compelling persons to cleanup releases of solid or hazardous waste. Section 7002(a)(1)(B) applies even if there has been no violation of the requirements of RCRA. Since CERCLA contains no authority for citizens to compel the cleanup of hazardous substances, section 7002(a)(1)(B) is an important source of authority for citizens seeking the cleanup of hazardous wastes and hazardous substances.

The statute requires that citizens provide notice ninety days before bringing the suit. **§ 7002(b), 42 U.S.C. § 6972(b)**. However, the action can be commenced immediately after notice is supplied if the action involves a violation of Subtitle C. An action under section 7002(a)(1)(B) may not be brought if the government is "diligently prosecuting" an action under RCRA or the Comprehensive Environmental Response Compensation and Liability Act ("CERCLA") to require appropriate persons to respond to the problem or the government is itself cleaning up the problem under CERCLA. § 7002(b)(2)(B), 42 U.S.C. § 6972(b)(2)(B).

F. Review Questions

1. T or F   An industrial facility must obtain a permit before it may legally generate or store hazardous waste.

2. T or F   After the generator has shipped hazardous waste for disposal at an off-site permitted TSDF, the generator has no continuing obligation under RCRA.

3. T or F   Solid waste will be classified as a hazardous waste under RCRA if it is either a "listed" waste or exhibits any of the hazard characteristics.

4. T or F   Mixtures of listed hazardous waste and non-hazardous waste are not classified as a hazardous waste if the mixture does not exhibit a hazard characteristic.

5. T or F   Soil contaminated with a listed hazardous waste is removed for disposal as part of a cleanup of property. The soil would be classified as a hazardous waste under EPA's mixture rule.

6. T or F   EPA does not claim the legal authority under Subtitle C of RCRA to regulate any materials that are recycled since they are treated as products rather than wastes.

7. T or F   A generator may legally send any hazardous waste for disposal in a landfill that has received a TSDF permit.

8. T or F   If a solid waste is not classified as a hazardous waste, it is not subject to any restrictions under RCRA.

9. T or F   Wastewater produced at an industrial facility is discharged from a pipe into a stream. The facility has an NPDES permit issued under the Clean Water Act, and the discharge is in compliance with the

permit. If the wastewater exhibits a hazard characteristic, it is a hazardous waste subject to the requirements of Subtitle C of RCRA.

10. T or F An industrial facility discharges wastes into a sewer connected to a municipal sewage treatment system (known as a publicly owned treatment works under the Clean Water Act). If the waste exhibits a hazard characteristic, it is a hazardous waste subject to the requirements of Subtitle C of RCRA.

11. T or F A generator must perform laboratory analyses of its wastes in order to determine whether the wastes are properly classified as a hazardous waste.

12. T or F Under RCRA, EPA is required to issue all permits to TSDFS.

13. T or F Only hazardous wastes are subject to regulation in a permit issued to a TSDF under Subtitle C.

CHAPTER 8

Comprehensive Environmental Response, Compensation and Liability Act

■ ANALYSIS

c. Federally Permitted Release

d. Indemnification Agreements

e. Waiver of Liability Among Private Parties

f. Bankruptcy

6. Recoverable Damages

a. Response Costs

b. Attorney's Fees

c. Natural Resource Damages

7. Elements of a Cost Recovery Claim

a. Release or Threat of Release

b. Defendant Is a Potentially Responsible Party

c. Incurred Response Costs

d. Consistency With the National Contingency Plan

F. **EXTENT OF CLEANUP—HOW CLEAN IS CLEAN**

1. Background

a. National Contingency Plan

b. Removal and Remedial Actions

(1) Removal Actions

(2) Remedial Actions

c. National Priorities List

2. Cleanup Standards

a. Long–Term, Permanent, On–Site

b. ARARs

c. State Laws

3. Administrative Process

a. RI/FS and RODs

b. Public Participation

c. Alternatives

G. **SETTLEMENT OF CERCLA CLAIMS**

1. Releases From Liability

2. Contribution Protection

3. De Minimis Settlements

4. Judicial Review

H. **BROWNFIELDS**

I. **CITIZENS SUITS**

J. **REVIEW QUESTIONS**

The Comprehensive Environmental, Response, Compensation, and Liability Act (CERCLA or Superfund) is the primary Federal statute dealing with the cleanup of hazardous substances.

A. Introduction

1. Name of Statute

The Comprehensive Environmental Response, Compensation and Liability Act is known as CERCLA. It is also sometimes referred to as Superfund because part of the statute establishes a trust fund, known as the Superfund, to be used by the government to finance cleanups of hazardous substances.

2. Structure of CERCLA

Unlike most of the other statutes you study in Environmental Law, CERCLA imposes few direct regulatory obligations. Other than an obligation to report certain releases of hazardous substances, CERCLA itself does not require that anyone do anything. Rather, CERCLA gives the government the power to compel persons to cleanup hazardous substances, and it gives the government and private parties a cause of action to recover costs of cleanups which they incur. It is thus important in forcing cleanups and in allocating the cost of cleanup.

3. History

CERCLA was adopted late in 1980 just before President Carter left office. Courts frequently complain about the confusing provisions of CERCLA and the lack of legislative history that accompanied the statute.

Major amendments to CERCLA were adopted in 1986. These were contained in the Superfund Amendment and Reauthorization Act or SARA. SARA included a number of significant provisions which, among other things, clarified the level of cleanup that was necessary for sites addressed under CERCLA, facilitated settlement with the government and expressly established a right of contribution among liable parties.

In January 2002, the Small Business Liability Relief and Brownfields Revitalization Act was signed into law, and this Act made a number of significant amendments to the liability provisions of CERCLA. Among other things, the Act provides an exemption from liability for "bona fide prospective purchasers" of contaminated property who purchased contaminated property after January 2002. Unlike the innocent landowner defense, a bona fide prospective purchaser generally has no CERCLA liability even if it bought with knowledge of existing contamination. The Act also establishes a variety of other exemptions from liability and provides incentives for state cleanup programs.

4. Delegation of Presidential Authority to EPA

Unlike most environmental statutes, CERCLA specifically provides that the President, rather than the Administrator of EPA, is authorized to take certain actions to respond to releases of hazardous substances. By Executive Order, the President has delegated to EPA the authority to implement the activities that in CERCLA are subject to Presidential control.

5. Retroactive Effect

Although CERCLA was adopted in 1980, courts have held that it applies retroactively, and the government can compel the cleanup of hazardous substances that were released prior to 1980. This means that persons who legally disposed of waste in the past can be held liable for the cost of cleaning up the sites today.

One of the more interesting and controversial issues you should be considering is the rationale and fairness of the retroactive effect of CERCLA. Many have advocated that the cost of cleanups required by past, legal disposal practices should be born generally by the public through use of general tax money. Others argue that past generators obtained the benefit of low cost and inadequate disposal practices, and they should rightly bear the costs of remedying a situation from which they received a past benefit.

6. Outline of Major Statutory Provisions

Section 101, 42 U.S.C. § 9601. Definitions.

Section 102, 42 U.S.C. § 9602. Provisions relating to designation of hazardous substances and reportable quantities.

Section 103, 42 U.S.C. § 9603. Provisions relating to reporting of releases of hazardous substances.

Section 104, 42 U.S.C. § 9604. Provisions relating to government funded removal and remedial actions.

Section 105, 42 U.S.C. § 9605. Provisions relating to the establishment of the National Contingency Plan and National Priorities List.

Section 106, 42 U.S.C. § 9606. Provisions relating to issuance of orders to compel cleanup of hazardous substances.

Section 107, 42 U.S.C. § 9607. Provisions defining class of potentially responsible parties and defenses.

Section 109, 42 U.S.C. § 9609. Provisions relating to civil penalties.

Section 111, 42 U.S.C. § 9611. Provisions relating to use of the Hazardous Substances Superfund.

Section 112, 42 U.S.C. § 9612. Provisions relating to certain claims against the Superfund.

Section 113, 42 U.S.C. § 9613. Provisions relating to civil proceedings under CERCLA including timing of judicial review, standard of judicial review and right of contribution.

Section 120, 42 U.S.C. § 9620. Provisions relating to the application of CERCLA to federal facilities.

Section 121, 42 U.S.C. § 9621. Provisions relating to cleanup standards.

Section 122, 42 U.S.C. § 9622. Provisions relating to settlement agreements.

Section 310, 42 U.S.C. § 9659. Provisions relating to citizen suits.

B. Applicability to Hazardous Substances

The notification and cost recovery provisions of CERCLA in most cases apply only to the release of "hazardous substances." It is important to recognize that the reach of CERCLA is not limited to hazardous wastes as defined under the Resource Conservation and Recovery Act ("RCRA"). Rather, EPA has published a list of specific chemicals or wastes that constitute hazardous substances for purposes of CERCLA.

1. Designated Hazardous Substances

CERCLA, in section 101(14), defines "hazardous substances" by cross reference to other environmental statutes. **§ 101(14), 42 U.S.C. § 9601(14)**. At a minimum, hazardous substances include all materials that are 1) hazardous substances designated under section 311 of the Clean Water Act, 2) hazardous wastes under RCRA, 3) toxic pollutants under section 307(a) of the Clean Water Act, 4) hazardous air pollutants under section 112 the Clean Air Act, and 5) certain imminently hazardous chemicals substances or mixtures under the Toxic Substances Control Act. Additionally, EPA can designate additional substances as hazardous substances. **§ 102(a), 42 U.S.C. § 9602(a)**.

2. Petroleum Exclusion

CERCLA excludes "petroleum" (including oil, gasoline and natural gas) from the definition of hazardous substances. This means that oil spills are not covered under the notification or cleanup provisions of CERCLA. **§ 101(14), 42 U.S.C. § 9601(14)**.

The petroleum exclusion does not apply to substances that have been separately designated as hazardous substances under CERCLA. Thus, certain petroleum wastes that are "listed" hazardous wastes under RCRA are also hazardous substances under CERCLA.

If petroleum is contaminated with other hazardous substances, the contaminated petroleum may be treated as a hazardous substance. EPA and the courts have, however, concluded that petroleum will not be treated as a hazardous substance solely because it contains either 1) hazardous substances, such as benzene, that are normally found as constituents of petroleum and are present at normal concentrations or 2) hazardous substances, such as lead, that are added as part of normal petroleum refining processes. Waste oil contaminated with hazardous substances that are not a normal constituent of petroleum or were not part of the refining process is not subject to the petroleum exclusion.

The petroleum exclusion means that most leaks of oil or gasoline from underground storage tanks (USTs) are not covered by CERCLA. The UST program of RCRA does, however, contain requirements for responding to releases of petroleum from underground tanks, **RCRA § 9003, 42 U.S.C. § 6991b**, but the UST program does not provide a private cost recovery action or right of contribution by persons required to respond to petroleum leaks from USTs.

3. RCRA Special Wastes

The definition of hazardous substances in section 101(14)(C) provides that all RCRA hazardous wastes are hazardous substances except "any waste the regulation of which under [RCRA] has been suspended by Act of Congress." **§ 101(14)(C), 42 U.S.C. § 9601(14)(C)**. Under RCRA, these suspended wastes, known as special wastes, include certain wastes associated with the exploration and production of oil and gas and certain wastes from the mining industry. **RCRA § 3001(b)(2)–(3), 42 U.S.C. § 6921(b)–(c)**.

Oil and gas and mining interests have argued that the exclusion in section 101(14)(C) of RCRA special wastes acts to exempt all RCRA special wastes from classification as hazardous substances under CERCLA. Courts that have considered this issue have rejected this argument and concluded that RCRA special wastes may be treated as hazardous substances if they contain hazardous substances listed under any other subsection of section 101(14). Thus, if a special waste contains a toxic pollutant under Clean Water Act or a hazardous air pollutant under the Clean Air Act it may be treated as a hazardous substance. Since most oil and gas and mining wastes contain such substances, they have been subject to CERCLA.

C. Notification of Release of Hazardous Substances

CERCLA does impose one direct and important regulatory requirement. Under section 103(a), any person who "knows" of the release of a "reportable quantity" of a hazardous substance must report the release to the National Response Center. **§ 103(a), 42 U.S.C. § 9603(a)**. This can be reached twenty-four hours a day by calling a national "800" number.

Under CERCLA the basic "reportable quantity" is the release of one pound of the substance within a twenty-four hour period. **§ 102(b), 42 U.S.C. § 9602(b)**. EPA has adjusted the reportable quantities for many of the specific hazardous substance.

CERCLA authorizes the imposition of substantial penalties for failure to report a release as required by section 103(a). **§ 109, 42 U.S.C. § 9609**.

D. Options for Cleaning Up Hazardous Substances

CERCLA provides mechanisms to both the government and private parties to promote the cleanup of property that is contaminated with hazardous substances.

1. Government Options

EPA basically has two options to deal with the release or threat of release of a hazardous substance.

a. Clean up the Site and Institute Cost Recovery

Under the provisions of section 104, EPA has the authority to go in and clean up a site itself. **§ 104(a), 42 U.S.C. § 9604(a)**. As discussed more fully below, EPA's ability to spend money may depend on how much risk the site poses and how long the cleanup will take.

EPA's money to finance cleanups comes from the Hazardous Substances Superfund, also known as Superfund. The Superfund is financed primarily through taxes on the petrochemical industry.

EPA is authorized, under section 107(a)(4)(A), to institute an action against a defined group of "Potentially Responsible Parties ('PRPs')". In a government cost recovery action, the government may recover costs that it incurs in a manner that is "not inconsistent with the National Contingency Plan ('NCP')." **§ 107(a)(4)(A), 42 U.S.C. § 9607(a)(4)(A)**. The elements of a cost recovery action are discussed below.

b. Issue a Cleanup Order

EPA also has the authority under section 106(a) to issue an order to compel persons to cleanup the site. **§ 106(a), 42 U.S.C. § 9606(a)**. Since this option does not require EPA to spend money, it is frequently employed. Section 106 also authorizes EPA to go to federal district court to obtain a court order to compel persons to cleanup a site. Since section 106 allows EPA to issue an order without going to court, EPA rarely seeks a court order.

Although section 106 allows EPA to issue an order to "any person," in most cases such orders will only be sent to persons who are classified as PRPs under section 107(a).

(1) Liability for Violation of a 106 Order

Under CERCLA, persons who fail to comply with a 106 Order are potentially subject to penalties of up to $25,000 per day of violation, **§ 106(b)(1), 42 U.S.C. § 9606(b)(1)**, and they may further be required to pay up to treble the final cost of the cleanup. **§ 107(c)(3), 42 U.S.C. § 9607(c)(3)**. These are substantial penalties and provide enormous incentive to comply with the order.

(2) Preenforcement Review

Given the enormity of the penalties for failure to comply with 106 orders, parties would prefer to go to court before they cleanup the site to contest whether they are in fact responsible parties or to contest the scope of the government required cleanup. Section 113 of CERCLA, however, precludes this "pre-enforcement" review. **§ 113(h), 42 U.S.C. § 9613(h)**. Congress concluded that parties must cleanup first and litigate later.

Without pre-enforcement review, parties who wish to contest the cleanup order have two options. First, they may violate the order and attempt to raise their objections as a defense in a government prosecution for violation of the order. Second, they may cleanup a site in compliance with the order and then attempt to recover their money from the Superfund. Section 106 allows private parties who have spent money complying with a 106 order to recover from Superfund if they were not actually PRPs or the government's cleanup was arbitrary and capricious. **§ 106(b)(2), 42 U.S.C. § 9606(b)(2)**.

2. Cost Recovery by Private Parties

Private parties do not have the authority under CERCLA to compel another person to cleanup a site contaminated with hazardous substances. Persons seeking to compel responsible parties to cleanup contaminated property may, however, be able to use the "imminent and substantial endangerment" provisions of section 7002(a)(1)(B) of RCRA. *See* 7.E.2.

CERCLA does, however, establish two different causes of action which allow private parties who have spent money cleaning up a site to sue PRPs to obtain reimbursement for all or part of their cost of cleanup. Section 107(a)(4)(B), adopted as part of the original CERCLA provisions in 1980, allows any person to seek cost recovery from PRPs. A right of contribution in § 113(f) was added to CERCLA in 1984. There was considerable controversy over the relationship and scope of these two provisions, but the Supreme Court issued decisions in 2004 and 2007 that have largely, but not completely, resolved issues relating the scope of these provisions.

a. Private Cost Recovery Actions

Section 107(a)(4)(B) authorizes "private cost recovery actions." Under section 107(a)(4)(B), plaintiffs may recover all or part of their cleanup costs from PRPs if they have cleaned up hazardous substances in a manner "consistent with the National Contingency Plan." **§ 107(a)(4)(B), 42 U.S.C. § 9607(a)(4)(B)**. The elements of a private cost recovery action are discussed below. In *United States v. Atlantic Research*, ___ U.S. ___, 127 S.Ct. 2331, 168 L.Ed.2d 28 (2007), the Supreme Court held that PRPs who voluntarily cleanup their property may sue for cost recovery under Section 107(a)(4)(B).

b. Contribution Actions

Section 113(f) authorizes an action for "contribution." **§ 113(f), 42 U.S.C. § 9613(f)**. Section 113(f)(1) allows a person to seek contribution "during or following" a civil action under § 107 or 106. This means that a PRP who has been sued (or is being sued) for cost recovery by the government or a private party may seek contribution from other PRPs. Section 113(f)(3)(B) allows persons who have entered certain approved CERCLA settlements with the State or federal government to seek contribution from non-settling PRPs for amounts they reimbursed the government as part of the settlement.

In *Cooper Indus. v. Aviall Servs. Inc.,* 543 U.S. 157, 125 S.Ct. 577, 160 L.Ed.2d 548 (2004), the Supreme Court held that PRPs who voluntarily cleaned up property could not seek contribution under § 113(f). In the Court's analysis, a PRP who seeks cost recovery after voluntarily cleaning up their property, is not suing "during or following" a civil action or government settlement, and thus the plain language of § 113 does not provide a right of contribution. In *United States v. Atlantic Research,* discussed above, the Court later clarified that the PRPs could sue for cost recovery under § 107(a)(4)(B).

c. Extent of Private Party Cost Recovery

In most cases, parties who bring a private cost recovery action or an action for contribution will not generally recover all of their cleanup costs. In an action for contribution under by a PRP under § 113(f)(1), the court may allocate costs among the parties based on "equitable factors." If a PRP seeks cost recovery under § 107(a)(4)(B), the defendant can file a counterclaim seeking contribution under § 113(f)(1). In that case, the court is also able to allocate the costs between the parties based on equitable factors.

This ability to recover cleanup costs is a powerful incentive to private parties voluntarily to cleanup a site or to agree, as part of a settlement with the government, to cleanup a site. The availability of a statutory right of cost recovery under CERCLA has also had a major impact on real estate transactions. Most major real estate transactions now include some express contractual provision dealing with liability for cleanup of hazardous substances.

E. Liability Provisions

Under section 107(a), persons who are designated as "potentially responsible parties" may be liable both to the government and to other private parties for their share of the cost of cleaning up hazardous substances. **§ 107(a), 42 U.S.C. § 9607(a).**

1. Reading Section 107(a)

Section 107(a) is awkwardly worded, and complex to parse. It can be parsed (and paraphrased) as follows:

Notwithstanding any other provision or rule of law, and subject only to the defenses set forth in subsection (b)—

(1) the current owner or operator of a facility

(2) the person who, at the time of disposal, was the owner or operator of a facility

(3) the person who "arranged for disposal or treatment" of a hazardous substance at a facility, and

(4) the transporter who transported hazardous substances to a facility which the transporter selected,—

from which there is a release or a threatened release which causes the occurrence of response costs, of a hazardous substance, shall be liable for—

(A) all costs of removal or remedial action incurred by the U.S. government, or a State or Indian tribe not inconsistent with the national contingency plan,

(B) any other necessary costs of response incurred by any other person consistent with the national contingency plan,

(C) damages for injury to, destruction of, or loss of natural resources,

(D) the costs of any health assessment or health affects study carried out under section 104(i).

2. Prerequisites to Liability

Under section 107(a) a person can only be liable if there is a "release or threatened release" from a "facility" of "hazardous substances."

a. Release or Threat of Release

This phrase has been broadly interpreted to apply to almost any act involving the spilling or leaching of hazardous substances. Even corroded drums that have not yet leaked may constitute a threat of release.

The broad definition of "release" in section 101(22) does exclude, however, most releases affecting workers in a workplace where the workers are subject to Occupational Safety and Health Act or worker compensation provisions, emissions from engines of cars and planes, and releases of certain radioactive material subject to the Atomic Energy Act, and the normal application of fertilizer. **§ 101(22), 42 U.S.C. § 9601(22)**.

b. Facility

The definition of "facility" in section 101(9) is very broad and certainly includes most areas from which hazardous substances may be releases. **§ 101(9), 42 U.S.C. § 9601(9)**. The definition excludes, however, any consumer product in consumer use.

c. Hazardous Substance

As discussed above, the definition of hazardous substances in section 101(14) is very broad. Petroleum is the only substance excluded from this definition.

3. Potentially Responsible Parties

There are four classes of persons who may be PRPs.

a. Current Owner/Operators

Under section 107(a)(1), "owner and operators" of facilities are PRPs. **§ 107(a)(1), 42 U.S.C. § 9607(a)(1)**. This includes the current owner of a site containing hazardous substances regardless of whether the owner had an involvement with or responsibility for the release of hazardous substances. Subject to the defenses discussed below, if you own property containing hazardous substances you are a PRP. Additionally, a person may be liable as an "operator" of a site containing hazardous substances even if that person does not own the site. Although the section states that owners and operators are PRPs, courts have held that persons are liable if they are either owners *or* operators.

The scope of liability under this section has been addressed in a number of contexts.

(1) Lender Liability

The definition of "owner/operator" in section 101(20)(A) of CERCLA excludes lenders, such as banks, who "own" the property through such security interests as mortgages. **§ 101(20)(A), 42 U.S.C. § 9601(20)(A)**. The statute, however, excludes lenders only if they have not "participated in management" of the facility.

In amendments to the definition of "owner and operator," Congress clarified and substantially limited the liability of lenders. Lenders are generally protected from liability while they hold a security interest if they do not "actually" participate in the operations or management of a facility. Additionally, lenders are protected from liabilityo after foreclosure if the lender takes certain steps immediately to sell the property. § 101(20)(E)–(F), 42 U.S.C. § 9601(20)(E)–(F).

(2) Parent Company Liability

Many corporations are organized in such a way that they "own" the stock of corporate subsidiaries and, under basic principles of corporate law, such parent companies are not typically liable for the obligations of their subsidiaries. In *U.S. v. Bestfoods*, 524 U.S. 51, 118 S.Ct. 1876, 141 L.Ed.2d 43 (1998), the Supreme Court clarified the two ways in which a parent company may be liable under CERCLA for the liabilities of subsidiaries. First, under traditional principles of corporate law, a court may "pierce the corporate veil" to find the parent company liable for the obligations of the subsidiary. Second, a parent may be directly liable as an owner/operator under CERCLA if it engaged in certain types of direct control of the subsidiary. In *Bestfoods*, the Supreme Court generally narrowed the ability of courts to find a parent company directly liable by requiring that the parent have exercised control over the hazardous waste management activities of the subsidiary. Additionally, the Supreme Court clarified that a parent company would not be liable if it engaged in the types of control typical of a parent company such as supervision of the general practices of the subsidiary or the presence of a person who holds a corporate office in both the parent and subsidiary.

Note that companies are fully liable for the conduct of corporate divisions or other parts of their corporation that are not separately incorporated.

(3) Successor Company Liability

When a company purchases the assets of another company, it does not typically acquire the liabilities of the seller. In some cases, however, courts have held "successor" corporations liable for the acts of the seller if the court concludes that the transaction constitutes a "de facto merger" between seller and purchaser or if the purchaser is continuing the same operations of the seller. The court may reach this conclusion if, after the sale, the purchased assets are run by the same officers and directors, the shareholders are the same, or the name of the company has not changed. No one factor is critical, and it can be difficult for a company to ensure that it will not be liable under CERCLA if it purchases the assets of a company that is liable.

You should note that successor company liability is not typically an issue when the purchaser buys contaminated property. As the new owner of the property, the purchaser may be directly liable under section 107(a)(1).

The issue of successor company liability more typically arises when a company purchases the assets of another company that has incurred CERCLA liability for its offsite disposal of hazardous substances. In such a case, a court might determine that the successor company has also assumed the CERCLA liabilities of the company from which it purchased the assets.

(4) Federal, State and Municipal Governments

Federal, state and municipal governments are included within the definition of owners and operators. This is important since many CERCLA clean ups involve municipal landfills or facilities that have been owned or operated by the federal government. There are some limited exclusions from liability for governments, however, if they acquired the property "involuntarily" through tax delinquency, bankruptcy or eminent domain. Compare **§ 101(20)(D), 42 U.S.C. § 9601(20)(D),** [exclusion for state or local governments] with **§ 101(35)(A)(ii), 42 U.S.C. § 9601(35)(A)(ii)** [defense from liability applicable to federal government].

b. Past Owner/Operators

Under section 107(a)(2), persons who owned or operated a site "at the time of disposal" are PRPs even if they no longer own the site. **§ 107(a)(2), 42 U.S.C. § 9607(a)(2).** Thus, past owners in the chain of title may also be PRPs. In some cases, persons who bought and later sold contaminated property without themselves disposing of hazardous substances may avoid liability. At least some courts, however, have said that former owners are liable even if the disposal of the hazardous substances occurred prior to the time they bought the property. This is based on a theory of "passive" disposal in which the on-going leaching or spreading of contamination constitutes disposal even if the active dumping occurred earlier.

c. Persons Who "Arranged for Disposal"

Under section 107(a)(3), persons who "arranged for disposal" of hazardous substances at another site are liable as PRPs for the cleanup of that site. **§ 107(a)(3), 42 U.S.C. § 9607(a)(3).** Typically, this section involves the liability of generators of hazardous substances who sent their wastes to another site for disposal. At a major cleanup site there may be literally hundreds of generators who are liable as generators under section 107(a)(3).

The need to prove "causation" to impose liability is discussed below, but basically, if a generator sent *a* hazardous substance to a site, they are liable for the cost of cleaning up the entire site if *any* hazardous substance is released from the site. They are liable even if it is a completely different type of hazardous substance that is released.

Persons who sent materials for recycling have been found to be liable as "arrangers" under section 107(a)(3). In 1999, Congress amended CERCLA by adding a new section 127 that largely exempts recyclers of certain types of materials from liability. **§ 127, 42 U.S.C. § 9627.** Recycling facilities at which there is a release are not exempt.

d. Transporters Who Selected the Site

Under section 107(a)(4), transporters who carried the hazardous substances from the generator to the disposal site may also be liable as a PRP, but only if the transporter "selected" the site to which the substances were taken. **§ 107(a)(4), 42 U.S.C. § 9607(a)(4).**

4. Extent of Liability

a. Strict Liability

PRPs are subject to "strict liability." This means that they are liable even if they were not negligent in their management of the hazardous substances. It also means that a PRP can be liable even if their actions were fully in accordance with the law. CERCLA establishes strict liability through its definition of "liable" in § 101(32). **§ 101(32), 42 U.S.C. § 9601(32).** That definition cross-references the standard of strict liability under section 311 of the Clean Water Act.

b. Joint and Several Liability

Liability under CERCLA is "joint and several." This means that a PRP is liable for 100% of the cost of cleanup even if the PRP only contributed a small percentage of the hazardous substances at a site. CERCLA does not expressly provide for "joint and several" liability, but courts have held that CERCLA imposes this liability. This conclusion is based, in part, on legislative history which states that CERCLA is based on "traditional and evolving principles of common law."

c. Allocation of Liability

There are several ways in which a PRP may attempt to allocate liability. First, under common law principles, some courts have indicated that a PRP may be liable only for its share if the harm is "divisible." Although cases suggest this is possible, courts rarely find that liability is divisible. Second, even if a PRP is "jointly and severally" liable for 100% of the cleanup cost, courts may "equitably" apportion cleanup costs among PRPs in an action for contribution.

In most cases, allocation among "generators" who sent waste to a site is based on the percentage of the total volume of waste sent by generators to the site. In rare cases, other factors such as the toxicity of the waste, may be considered in allocating clean up costs.

Example: 1000 gallons of hazardous substances were sent to a disposal site. Generator X sent 10 gallons of hazardous substances to the site, and Generator Y sent 20 tons. Generator X may be allocated 1% of the cost of cleanup and Generator Y may be allocated 2%.

d. Causation Issue

A PRP is liable under CERCLA if 1) there is a release or threat of release of a hazardous substance from a facility, and 2) that PRP sent a hazardous substance to the facility. A PRP is liable for the cost of cleanup even if there is no proof that the particular hazardous substances it sent to the facility has been released. In fact, a PRP is liable if hazardous substances are released even if they are a different type of hazardous substance than the one a PRP sent. Thus, liability can be imposed without any showing of "causation" as that term is used in tort.

Example: Company A sends wastes containing chromium to a dump site. Later, copper is found to be leaching from that site. Company A may be liable under CERCLA for the entire cost of cleaning up the dump site.

If this strikes you as unfair, consider the following. First, a CERCLA cleanup typically involves cleanup of all of the hazardous substances found at a site even if they are not being released. Thus, Company A did, by increasing the amount of material that must be cleaned up, "cause" an increase in cost and level of cleanup. Second, Company A may be able to recover portions of its cost of cleanup from other PRPs at the site either through a private cost recovery action or through an action for contribution.

5. Defenses to Liability

CERCLA contains a limited number of affirmative defenses to liability. Section 107(b) is titled "defenses," but there are a number of other defenses in the statute with which you should be familiar.

a. Act of God

Under section 107(b)(1), it is a defense to liability if a release is caused by an "act of God." **§ 107(b)(1), 42 U.S.C. § 9607(b)(1)**. Section 101(1) defines "act of God" to include unanticipated natural events, "the effects of which could not have been avoided by the exercise of due care or foresight." PRPs have, for example, argued that releases caused by heavy rainfall were acts of God. Since this defense requires that the natural phenomena be unanticipated and the effects unavoidable this defense has rarely been asserted successfully.

b. Act of War

Section 107(b)(2) provides a defense to liability if a release is caused by an "act of war." "Act of War" is not defined in CERCLA, and PRPs have been largely unsuccessful in arguing that releases from facilities operated by the government or under contract with the government to supply materials during World War II and the Vietnam War are eligible for this defense.

c. Third Party Defense

Under section 107(b)(3), a PRP has a a defense to liability if the release of hazardous substances was caused by a "third party." **§ 107(b)(3), 42 U.S.C. § 9607(b)(3)**. This defense is limited, however, since it will not apply if the PRP 1) has a direct or indirect contractual relationship with the third party, 2) failed to exercise "due care" with respect to the hazardous substances, and 3) failed to take precautions against foreseeable acts or omissions of the third party.

d. Landowner Defenses

There are three defenses to liability as "owner/operators" that specifically apply to landowners. In addition to specific elements applicable to these defenses, each require that the landowner satisfy certain common elements including the requirement to conduct "all appropriate inquiry" prior to purchasing the property.

(1) Innocent Landowner Defense

Courts have held that the chain of title is an indirect contractual relationship among landowners. Thus, prior to the 1986 SARA amendments, a current landowner could not successfully assert the third party defense by claiming that a former owner caused the release. In 1986, however, Congress established an "innocent landowner" defense. Note the placement of this defense. It is contained in the definition of "contractual relationship" in section 101(35), and, through this definition, a landowner may assert the third party defense by claiming the release was caused by a former owner. **§ 101(35)(A), 42 U.S.C. § 9601(35)(A)**.

To assert the "innocent landowner" defense, however, the current owner must establish that, at the time the property was purchased, he or she did not know or have reason to know of the existence of hazardous substances at the property and the owner must have undertake "appropriate inquiry" prior to purchasing the property. **§ 101(35)(B), 42 U.S.C. § 9601(35)(B)**. Since this defense is an application of the third party defense in § 107(b)(3), a PRP must also exercise "due care" and take precautions against foreseeable actions of others.

(2) Contiguous Landowner Defense

In 2002, Congress added a new "contiguous owner" defense to liability as "owner/operators" for persons who purchase property without knowledge of contamination and who later discover contamination coming from an adjacent property. To satisfy this defense, the landowner may not have known of the contamination at the time they purchased the property, and, among other things, they must have conducted "all appropriate inquiry" prior to purchase. **§ 107(q), 33 U.S.C. § 9607(q)**.

(3) Bona Fide Prospective Purchaser and Windfall Lien

In 2002, CERCLA was amended to establish a new limitation on liability of purchasers of property. Under the "bona fide prospective purchaser" defense, landowners who purchase property after January 2002 will not be liable as owner/operators even if they purchased the property with knowledge of the contamination. **§ 107(r), 33 U.S.C. § 9607(r).** Such persons would not be entitled to an "innocent landowner" or "contiguous landowner" defense because of this knowledge. To assert the bona fide prospective purchaser defense, the landowner must, among other things, have conducted "all appropriate inquiry" prior to purchase of the property, exercise "due care" with respect to hazardous substances, not impede any subsequent cleanup and comply with any institutional controls (such as deed restrictions on the use of the property) imposed as part of a cleanup. Many of the requirements for this defense are specified in the definition of "bona fide prospective purchaser" contained in § 101(40), 33 U.S.C. § 9601(40).

Although a "bona fide prospective purchaser" will not be liable for the cost of cleanup, if the property is later cleaned up by the federal government, the government can assert a lien on the property equal to the amount by which the cleanup increased the market value of the property above the market value prior to cleanup. This is known as the "windfall lien" provision. **§ 107(r)(2)–(4), 42 U.S.C. § 9607(r)(2)– (4).**

(4) **"All Appropriate Inquiry"**

Each of the three landowner defenses requires that the landowner conduct "all appropriate inquiry" prior to purchasing the property. "All appropriate inquiry" involves an evaluation of the property to assess the possible presence of hazardous substances. This type of environmental review is generally known as a Phase I Environmental Audit, Environmental Site Assessment or Due Diligence Review.

The scope of actions necessary to satisfy the standard of "all appropriate inquiry" has been unclear. In the 2002 amendments to CERCLA, however, Congress required EPA to promulgate federal regulatins that define "all appropriate inquiry." **42 U.S.C. § 9601(35)(B)(ii)– (iv).** The EPA regulations found at 40 C.F.R. Part 312 are applicable to commercial property purchased after November 1, 2006. The regulations require, among other things, that an inquiry include a physical inspection of the property, interviews with the current owner and major tenants, a search of certain government records, a check of the "chain of title" of prior purchasers. The regulations require that the inquiry be conducted by a "qualified environmental professional." "All appropriate inquiry" for reviews conducted prior to November 2006 is subject to different standards.

Note that there is no requirement to undertake any physical sampling or analysis of soil or groundwater as part of "all appropriate inquiry." Further investigation that involves actual sampling and analysis of soil or groundwater is generally referred to as a Phase II Environmental Audit.

e. Federally Permitted Release

Section 107(j) provides that a PRP is not liable under CERCLA for any release of hazardous substances that was a "federally permitted release." **§ 107(j), 42 U.S.C. § 9607(j)**. "Federally permitted release" is defined in section 101(10) and includes certain releases that are authorized under other federal environmental statutes. **§ 101(10), 42 U.S.C. § 9601(10)**. For example, a PRP will not be liable if hazardous substances are discharged in compliance with an NPDES permit issued under the Clean Water Act.

f. Waiver of Liability among Private Parties

Courts have generally upheld agreements in which one party contractually waives any claim it might have under CERCLA. Thus, a purchaser taking a property "as is" might waive any claim under CERCLA it might otherwise have against the seller. Courts have required that such waivers be clear, and they have split over whether a simple "as is" provision is explicit enough to constitute a waiver of a cause of action under CERCLA.

Section 107(e), does not allow private parties contractually to transfer their CERCLA liability to another person. Thus, even if landowners sell property with an "as is" clause, this will not limit their CERCLA liability to third-parties, including the government, who are not party to the contract.

g. Bankruptcy

A continuing controversy involves the extent to which bankruptcy will discharge potential liability under CERCLA. Under the federal Bankruptcy Code, certain "claims" are discharged if they arose prior to the debtor filing bankruptcy. Some courts have held that potential CERCLA actions by PRPs or the government become claims when the release or threat of release occurred. Under this theory, a debtor in bankruptcy could be discharged from liability under CERCLA before the person seeking to assert a CERCLA claim knew that the debtor was a PRP. Other courts have held that the CERCLA action becomes a claim only if the person seeking to assert the claim had reason to know of the potential claim at the time of bankruptcy.

Bankruptcy does not, however, discharge liability for injunctive orders to prevent continuing problems. Thus, a person may be subject to liability under the citizen suit provisions of section 7002 of RCRA even following bankruptcy.

6. Recoverable Damages

a. Response Costs

CERCLA authorizes the recovery of "response" costs; this includes a variety of expenses associated with the cleanup of hazardous substances. CERCLA does *not* provide for the recovery of personal injury damages or damages from loss of property. Those damages are recoverable, if at all, through a tort suit.

The class of eligible response costs includes such items as the actual cleanup expenses, but it may also include costs of investigating the extent of the problem, providing security, such as fences, in a contaminated area and, in some cases, costs of providing alternate drinking water supplies.

b. Attorney's Fees

Additionally, the government is authorized in its cost recovery actions to recover attorney's fees and "indirect costs," such as employee salaries and the costs of rental of office space allocated to responding the release of hazardous substances.

In *Key Tronic Corp. v. United States,* 511 U.S. 809, 114 S.Ct. 1960, 128 L.Ed.2d 797 (1994), the Supreme Court held that private parties could not generally recover attorney's fees under CERCLA. The Court held, however, that certain non-litigation attorney's fees related to a cleanup, such as the costs for identifying other PRPs, may be recoverable.

c. Natural Resource Damages

Section 107(a)(4)(C) authorizes the recovery of "natural resource damages." **§ 107(a)(4)(C), 42 U.S.C. § 9607(a)(4)(C).** Natural resource damages include such things as loss of fish and wildlife and other natural resources on property controlled by the federal, state, or local governments and, in some cases, Indian tribes. Recovery of natural resource damages is somewhat more complex than recovery of response costs. For one thing, an action for recovery of natural resource damages may only be brought by a designated "trustee" for the natural resources.

Additionally, the trustee must show that the damage to natural resources "resulted from" the release of hazardous substances. This requires a stricter showing of "causation" than is required for recovery of response costs. Finally, there are complex and controversial issues associated with calculating the value of the lost resources. Section 107(a)(4)(C) does not authorize recovery of damages to private lands nor does it allow private parties to recover damages as "private attorneys general."

7. Elements of a Cost Recovery Claim

Plaintiffs must plead and prove certain elements when they bring a cost recovery action under section 107(a). The elements, with some exceptions, are the same regardless of whether the action is brought by the government or by private parties.

a. Release or Threat of Release

Plaintiffs, both government and private parties, must establish that there was a release or threat of release of a hazardous substance.

b. Defendant Is a Potentially Responsible Party

Plaintiffs, both government and private parties, must establish that the defendants are within the class of potentially responsible parties specified in section 107(a).

c. Incurred Response Costs

Both government and private parties must have "incurred" response costs prior to bringing a cost recovery action. They need not have completed the cleanup, but they must have spent some money that qualifies as a response cost. Typically, parties will incur some costs and then go to court to obtain a judgment for those costs. They may also obtain a declaratory judgment that the defendant is liable for future response costs. **§ 113(g)(2), 42 U.S.C. 9613(g)(2).** Once a court has determined that parties are liable for response costs, they are typically far more willing to negotiate the payment of cleanup costs.

d. Consistency With the National Contingency Plan

To recover response costs, those costs must be "consistent" with the National Contingency Plan ("NCP"). As discussed below, the NCP is the set of government regulations that define both the procedures that must be followed in a CERCLA cleanup and the necessary stringency of the cleanup. For the government to recover, their costs may not be "inconsistent" with the NCP. For private parties to recover, their costs must be "consistent" with the NCP. Courts have interpreted these provisions to place the burden of proof with regard to consistency on defendants in a government cost recovery action and on plaintiffs in a private cost recovery action.

A major issue in private cost recovery actions involves how strictly private parties must conform to the NCP. The current NCP provides that the actions of private parties must be in "substantial compliance" with the provisions of the NCP. What this means in terms of providing for public participation, consideration of alternatives and other factors is uncertain.

Additionally, the NCP has different requirements depending on whether the cleanup was a "removal" or "remedial" action. The distinction between these two types of response actions is discussed below. Much of the litigation involving the consistency requirement involves classification of the cleanup as a removal or remedial action.

F. Extent of Cleanup—How Clean is Clean

1. Background

In addition to establishing a mechanism for allocating the cost of cleanup, CERCLA also contains substantive and procedural requirements that help establish how stringent a cleanup must be. This issue is known as "how clean is clean." In general, CERCLA requires that a cleanup be sufficient "to protect human health and the environment." In practice, implementing this requirement has proven controversial.

To understand how cleanup levels are established, it is important to understand several key statutory terms that affect the level of cleanup.

a. National Contingency Plan

Section 105 of CERCLA requires EPA to establish procedures for the cleanup of hazardous substances. **§ 105(a), 42 U.S.C. § 9605(a)**. This set of regulations is known as the National Contingency Plan or "NCP." The NCP, among other things, specifies the steps that must be taken to identify the level of cleanup. As described above, both government and private cleanups must be consistent with the NCP in order to recover costs under section 107(a).

b. Removal and Remedial Actions

CERCLA identifies two types of cleanups: removal and remedial actions. Both the procedures that must be followed and the actions that can be taken are affected by the classification of the cleanup.

(1) Removal Actions

Removal actions are generally short term actions necessary to remove the immediate threat. **§ 101(23), 42 U.S.C. § 9601(23).** This includes such actions as studying the site, putting up fencing, and removing drums of hazardous substances. In most cases, removal actions are limited to cleanup actions that take less than twelve months or cost less than $2 million. **§ 104(c)(1), 42 U.S.C. § 9604(c)(1).**

(2) Remedial Actions

Remedial actions are generally long term actions necessary to cleanup sites to meet final cleanup standards. **§ 101(24), 42 U.S.C. § 9601(24).** This may include a variety of actions such as removal or incineration of contaminated soil or other techniques to reduce the threat from the site. There are no statutory limits on the duration or cost of remedial actions.

c. National Priorities List

CERCLA requires that EPA establish a list of the most contaminated sites around the country. **§ 105(a)(8), 42 U.S.C. § 9605(a)(8).** This list is known as the National Priorities List or "NPL." In determining whether to list a site, EPA assesses a variety of factors including the toxicity of the hazardous substances, the threat to drinking water supplies and the number of people living near the site. EPA has established a system for scoring sites known as the "hazard ranking system ('HRS')". **§ 105(c), 42 U.S.C. § 9605(c).**

Listing of a site on the NPL has one main consequence. EPA, through regulation, has limited its ability to spend money from the Superfund for long-term, or remedial, cleanups at sites on the NPL.

2. Cleanup Standards

There are typically a variety of actions that can be taken to reduce the environmental threat at a CERCLA site. These actions range from covering a site with asphalt to minimize leaching, to digging up soil and hauling it to another site, to incinerating the contaminated soil. Selection of the final cleanup technique can drastically affect the final cost and degree of environmental protection at a site.

Selecting the final cleanup technique has been controversial, and, in the 1986 SARA amendments, Congress adopted section 121 of CERCLA which specifies factors that must be considered in selecting a cleanup level. **§ 121, 42 U.S.C. § 9621.**

a. Long–Term, Permanent, On–Site

Section 121 establishes a preference for cleanups that are long-term, permanent and on-site. **§ 121(b)(1), 42 U.S.C. § 9621(b)(1)**. In practice, this discourages cleanups that simply haul the contaminated soil from one site to another and encourages techniques, such as on-site inciner-ation, that permanently reduce the threat from the site.

To facilitate on-site cleanups, CERCLA provides a waiver from permit requirements, such as those under RCRA that would apply if wastes were permanently disposed of on-site. **§ 121(e), § 9621(e)**. If wastes are taken for disposal at another site, RCRA requirements will apply.

b. ARARs

CERCLA does not specify final cleanup standards. Rather, final stan-dards are established in many cases by looking at standards established under other statutes. **§ 121(d), 42 U.S.C. § 9621(d)**. These are known as "Applicable, Relevant and Appropriate Requirements" or "ARARs." "Applicable" standards are those that would be imposed if the cleanup were not conducted under CERCLA. This includes the standards that would be imposed under the RCRA, the federal statute that deals with the permitting of hazardous waste disposal facilities. "Relevant and Appropriate" standards are those that, while not strictly applicable, are relevant to setting final cleanup standards. Relevant and Appropriate standards may include "Maximum Contaminant Levels" ("MCLs") (levels for contaminants in drinking water established under the Safe Drinking Water Act) or "Water Quality Criteria" (levels of pollutants in surface water established under the Clean Water Act).

In addition to determination of ARARs, EPA will undertake a risk assessment, known as a "baseline risk assessment" or "BRA," and establish a final level of cleanup that is necessary to protect public health and the environment. In most cases, the NCP provides that the final risk level for exposure to carcinogens should not exceed a range of one in ten thousand to one in a million increased risk.

c. State Laws

CERCLA also requires that any more stringent state substantive cleanup standards must also be met at the site. **§ 121(d)(2)(C), 42 U.S.C. § 9621(d)(2)(C)**. States are required, however, to help fund the cleanup if their standards are to be met.

3. Administrative Process

The NCP establishes a series of procedural steps that must be followed in CERCLA cleanups.

a. **RI/FS and RODs**

The initial steps in a CERCLA cleanup involve an assessment of the site and a determination of possible cleanup techniques. This process is referred to as a "Remedial Investigation/Feasibility Study" ("RI/FS"). The final cleanup plan is contained in a document called a "Record of Decision" ("ROD").

b. **Public Participation**

The NCP also requires that the public be allowed to review and comment on the cleanup plans. The requirements for public participation include such things as making documents available for public inspection and the right of the public to comment on the proposed final plan.

c. **Alternatives**

In developing a final cleanup plan, the NCP requires that a range of alternatives be considered. At a minimum, all acceptable alternatives must ensure that public health and the environment is protected. The final cleanup technique selected, however, may be based on a consideration of the relative cost of the different options.

G. Settlement of CERCLA Claims

Although the government has enormous power to compel parties to cleanup sites contaminated with hazardous substances, the government generally attempts to reach a "voluntary" agreement with PRPs. In these settlement agreements or consent decrees, PRPs agree to reimburse the government for costs the government has incurred and to undertake cleanup activities at a site. In most cases, the government requires settling PRPs to undertake the entire cleanup or a discrete portion of the cleanup, such as the RI/FS. The government only very rarely will agree to use money from Superfund to split the cost of cleanup with PRPs. Although the group of PRPs who have entered the settlement agreement are responsible for the entire cost of the agreed cleanup, they may sue for contribution from other PRPs who are not parties to the agreement.

In the 1986 SARA amendments, Congress added section 122 which establishes certain conditions for entering settlement agreements. Section 122 also provides for certain procedures to expedite settlement. For example, if government decides to try to reach settlement it will suspended any action at a site for 120 days. **§ 122(e), 42 U.S.C. § 9622(e).**

In exchange for agreeing to undertake cleanups, PRPs may obtain some benefit from entering settlement agreements. Section 122 specifies some of the elements which the government might agree to in exchange for signing the agreements.

1. Releases From Liability

One of the most important protections that PRPs want in a settlement agreement is a release from future liability. They want to know that if they agree to take certain actions, the government will not simply sue them later to require that they do more. Section 122(f) provides that the government may agree to a limited "covenant not to sue." **§ 122(f), 42 U.S.C. § 9622(f)**. Typically, the government will only agree not to sue settling PRPs in the future to remedy problems that have been identified at the time the settlement agreement was entered. Settling parties may remain liable for problems that were not known at the time of settlement.

2. Contribution Protection

Settling parties also want protection from suits by other PRPs. Section 113(f)(2) provides that persons who have entered settlement agreements with the government are not liable for contribution from non-settling parties. **§ 113(f)(2), 42 U.S.C. § 9613(f)(2)**. This provision creates a strong incentive to settle with the government. If you do not settle while others do, they may sue you for contribution, but you cannot sue them.

In *United States v. Atlantic Research*, ___ U.S. ___, 127 S.Ct. 2331, 168 L.Ed.2d 28 (2007), the Supreme Court held that PRPs who voluntarily cleanup property may bring a cost recovery action under § 107(a)(4)(B). In the opinion, the Court indicated that the "contribution protection" provisions of § 113(f)(2) would not protect a settling party from such a cost recovery action. This substantially minimizes the protection provided in a settlement.

3. De Minimis Settlements

At major CERCLA sites there may be a large number of persons who are PRPs because they arranged for disposal of small volumes of hazardous substances to the site. In general, "de minimis" parties are those who contributed less than one or two percent of the hazardous substances found at a site. These "de minimis" parties would like to pay money and completely resolve their liability at the site.

Section 122(g) provides that the government may enter into de minimis settlements with such parties. **§ 122(g), 42 U.S.C. § 9622(g)**. Typically, de minimis parties obtain broader covenants not to sue in which they are released from all future liability at the site. In exchange, the de minimis parties typically pay a premium. This means that they agree to pay their percentage share of the cleanup costs (i.e., 1 or 2 percent of the estimated cost of cleanup) plus an additional amount (up to three times their percentage share). The administrative provisions for approving de minimis settlements are somewhat easier than approval of other settlement agreements. Among other things, the government may enter a de minimis settlement without getting court approval.

4. Judicial Review

Settlement agreements (other than de minimis settlements) must be approved by a court before they become final, and the court may accept or reject the proposed agreement based on the court's assessment of whether it is in the public interest. **§ 122(d), 42 U.S.C. § 9622(d)**. Before the court rules, the proposed settlement agreement must be made available for public comment. **§ 122(d)(2), 42 U.S.C. § 9622(d)(2)**. Review of settlement agreements can be an important stage at which parties can challenge the adequacy of the proposed cleanup.

H. Brownfields

Brownfields generally refer to contaminated industrial property, and a major focus of CERCLA has been to encourage reuse of such sites for industrial purposes. Brownfields related programs include such things as state voluntary cleanup programs, certain tax incentives and grants in CERCLA, **§ 104(k), 33 U.S.C. § 9604(k)**, and liability relief for "bona fide prospective purchasers." **§ 107(r), 33 U.S.C. § 9607(r)**.

I. Citizens Suits

Section 310 of CERCLA contains a "citizen suit" provision that looks much like the citizen suit provisions of the Clean Water Act or RCRA. **§ 310(a), 42 U.S.C. § 9659(a)**. Citizens can sue for violations of the Act or sue the government to require it to perform non-discretionary duties. The citizen suit provision of CERCLA, however, is limited. Release of hazardous substances is not a violation of CERCLA, and citizens cannot sue to compel a party to cleanup a site. They can only sue to ensure that government cleanup orders are complied with or sue if a party has not submitted notification of a release as required by section 103(a).

If citizens wish to sue to compel the cleanup of solid or hazardous wastes, they must do so under the "imminent and substantial endangerment" provisions of section 7002(a)(1)(B) of RCRA discussed at 7.E above.

J. Review Questions

1. T or F   A person in charge of a facility has an obligation to report a spill of a hazardous substance only if he or she has "knowledge" of the

release of a "reportable quantity" of the hazardous substance.

2. T or F   The current owner of property at which there has been a release of hazardous substances is not a "potentially responsible party" under section 107(a)(1) if the person did not cause the release or arrange for disposal of the hazardous substances.

3. T or F   To establish the "innocent landowner" defense, the current owner of property contaminated with hazardous substances need only prove that he or she purchased the property without knowing of the existence of the hazardous substances.

4. T or F   Petroleum can be classified as a hazardous substance, notwithstanding the "petroleum exclusion" in section 101 if it contains any constituents, such as benzene, which are designated as hazardous substances.

5. T or F   Lenders who have a security interest in property at which there has been a release of hazardous substances cannot be "potentially responsible parties" if they do not foreclose on the property.

6. T or F   Persons may bring a "citizen suit" under section 310 to compel PRPs to cleanup property at which there has been a release of a hazardous substance.

7. T or F   If a PRP enters into an approved settlement agreement with the government, other PRPs are barred from seeking contribution from the settling PRP for costs within the scope of the settlement agreement.

8. T or F   Private parties who bring a cost recovery action under section 107(a)(4)(B) have the burden of proving that their cleanup was undertaken in a manner that was "consistent with the national contingency plan."

9. T or F   A generator who arranged for disposal of a hazardous substance at a site is not liable as a PRP under section 107(a)(3) unless the specific hazardous substance sent by the generator is released at the site.

10. T or F   It is a defense to generator liability under section 107(a)(3) if the generator can prove that the disposal complied with all legal obligations existing at the time the generator arranged for disposal.

11. T or F   A person who receives a section 106 order from EPA may immediately go to court and enjoin EPA from enforcing the order if the person can prove that he or she is not a PRP.

12. T or F   Persons who own property at which there has been a release of hazardous substances cease to be PRPs after they sell the property.

13. T or F   A person who purchases property at which there has been a release of hazardous substances can avoid liability under CERCLA if the seller contractually agrees to assume all liability.

14. T or F   A PRP who has voluntarily cleaned up its property in a manner "consistent with the NCP" may seek contribution from other PRPs under § 113(f) to recover an equitable portion of its response costs.

*

Government Enforcement and Citizen Suits

■ **ANALYSIS**

A. **GOVERNMENT ENFORCEMENT**
1. Compliance Order
2. Administrative Penalties
3. Civil Prosecution
4. Criminal Prosecution

B. **CITIZEN SUITS**
1. Constitutional Prerequisites
   a. Standing
   b. Mootness
2. Statutory Prerequisites
   a. Notice and Delay
   b. Diligent Prosecution
   c. Wholly Past Violations

The Clean Air Act, Clean Water Act, and the Resource Conservation and Recovery Act contain provisions authorizing government criminal and civil enforcement. They all also contain provisions authorizing "citizen suits" private enforcement actions brought by one private party against another. The initial provisions for enforcement and citizen suits were contained in the Clean Air Act of 1970 and the provisions of the Clean Air Act, Clean Water Act and the Resource Conservation and Recovery Act are similar.

RCRA also authorizes citizen suits in certain circumstances where there is an "imminent and substantial endangerment" from a solid or hazardous waste. This type of citizen suit is discussed in Ch. 7.E.

A. Government Enforcement

The government has a variety of options when it determines that there has been a violation of the CAA, CWA or RCRA. Note that although the statutes specify specific maximum penalties, Congress in 1996 adopted a requirement that the range of penalties be periodically adjusted to reflect the effect of inflation. EPA has promulgated regulations increasing the maximum penalties under the CAA, CWA and RCRA.

1. Compliance Order

The EPA, under the CAA, CWA and RCRA, may issue a compliance order to a person alleged to be in violation of certain requirements of the statutes. **CAA, § 113(a), 42 U.S.C. § 7413(a); CWA, § 309(a), 33 U.S.C. § 1319(a); RCRA, § 3008(a), 42 U.S.C. § 6928(a).** The compliance order will typically give the person a specified period of time in which to come into compliance. Violation of the order is itself a separate violation of the statute.

2. Administrative Penalties

The CAA, CWA and RCRA also provide mechanisms for imposition of administrative penalties. **CAA, § 113(d), 42 U.S.C. § 7413(d); CWA, § 309(g), 33 U.S.C. § 1319(g); RCRA § 3008(a)–(c), 42 U.S.C. 6928(a)–(c).** This means that the EPA, without going to court, can issue an order requiring payment of a financial penalty for violation of the statute. There are varying procedural requirements for imposition of administrative penalties, and they are subject to judicial review.

EPA has established "penalty policies" that guide its calculation of proposed administrative penalties. In general, the proposed penalty is calculated based on an assessment of the "gravity" of the violation (such as the potential environmental harm created by the violation) and the "economic benefit" that the person received by avoiding or delaying compliance. It is EPA's policy that any penalty should at least require the violator to pay an amount greater than the amount of money the violator saved through non-compliance.

There are several factors that EPA may consider in reducing a proposed administrative penalty. One of these factors is whether the violator is willing to undertake a "supplemental environmental project" or "SEP" in which the violator agrees to undertake some environmentally beneficial project not otherwise required by law.

3.   Civil Prosecution

The CAA, CWA and RCRA all provide for "civil penalties." **CAA, § 113(b), 42 U.S.C. § 7413(b); CWA, § 309(b),(d), 33 U.S.C. § 1319(b),(d); RCRA, § 3008(a),(g), 42 U.S.C. § 6928(a),(g)** This means that the federal government may go to federal court to seek injunctive relief and financial penalties for violation of the requirements of the statutes. These civil enforcement actions are brought by the Department of Justice in federal district court.

4.   Criminal Prosecution

The CAA, CWA and RCRA also provide for criminal prosecution. **CAA, § 113(c), 42 U.S.C. § 7413(c); CWA, 309(c)(1)–(2), 33 U.S.C. § 1319(c)(1)–(2); RCRA, § 3008(d), 42 U.S.C. § 6928(d).** Substantial fines and jail terms can be imposed, in most cases, for willful or knowing violations of the statutes. The CAA and RCRA also contain provisions for more stringent criminal penalties if, under certain circumstances, they place a person in imminent danger of death or serious bodily injury. **CAA, § 113(c)(3)–(4), 42 U.S.C. § 7413(c)(3)–(4), RCRA, § 3008(e), 42 U.S.C. § 6928(e).** CERCLA also contains criminal penalties for failure to report certain releases of hazardous substances. **CERCLA, § 103(b), 42 U.S.C. § 9603(b).**

Most general criminal statutes require some element of "mens rea" or guilty knowledge by the defendant, and the CAA, CWA and RCRA all contain some variation of the requirement that a defendant's violation have been "knowing." This raises the issue of what the government must prove the defendant knew. In general, courts have not required that the government prove that the defendant actually knew that their conduct violated a statute. Rather, consistent with a line of cases involving construction of "public welfare statutes," courts have generally held that the government need only prove that defendants knew they were performing the prohibited acts; knowledge of the actual legal or regulatory requirements is not necessary. Since the issue of "mens rea" may vary depending on the language of the statute, different "knowledge" requirements may apply under different statutes and different sections of the same statute. The CWA, for example, provides for criminal prosecution for "negligent" as well as "knowing" violation of the statute.

B. Citizen Suits

The CAA, CWA and RCRA all contain "citizen suit" provisions that, among other things, allow "any citizen" to bring an action in federal district court against any person alleged to be in violation of certain requirements of the respective statutes. **CAA, § 304(a)(1), 42 U.S.C. § 7604(a)(1); CWA, § 505(a)(1), 33 U.S.C. § 1365(a)(1); RCRA, § 7002(a)(1)(A), 42 U.S.C. § 6972(a)(1)(A).** Under the CWA, a citizen suit can be brought for violation of an "effluent standard or limitation" which is defined to include the discharge of a pollutant without a permit. **CWA, § 505(f), 33 U.S.C. § 1365(f).**

Citizens may only seek civil penalties (which are paid to the federal government) or an injunction. Citizens may *not* recover damages for personal injury or property damage in a citizen suit. Plaintiffs in appropriate cases may use the citizen suit provisions to establish federal jurisdiction and bring state tort claims for personal injury or property damages under principles of ancillary jurisdiction.

The citizen suit provisions authorize the award of attorneys' fees to "prevailing or substantially prevailing" parties.

There are both constitutional and statutory prerequisites to bringing a citizen suit.

1. Constitutional Prerequisites

a. Standing

Article III of the U.S. Constitution provides that federal courts have jurisdiction over "cases and controversies." One application of this constitutional provision is the requirement that parties have "standing" to institute an action in federal court. The issue of whether private parties have standing to bring citizen suits has been the subject of increasing attention by the Supreme Court. The elements of standing are discussed in Chapter 2.B.

b. Mootness

In some cases, federal courts may lose jurisdiction that existed at the time the suit commenced if the case has become moot. In citizen suits, this issue may arise if the defendant has ceased the conduct that led to the violation. In *Friends of the Earth v. Laidlaw Environmental Services (TOC), Inc.*, 528 U.S. 167, 120 S.Ct. 693, 145 L.Ed.2d 610 (2000), the Supreme Court held that defendant's voluntary cessation of the violation will not render a case moot unless it is "absolutely clear" that the challenged conduct cannot reasonably be expected to recur. The burden of proof is on the defendant claiming mootness.

2. Statutory Prerequisites

The citizen suit provisions of the CAA, CWA and RCRA have similar, but not identical, statutory requirements that must be satisfied as a prerequisite to bringing a citizen suit. Unlike standing, these are statutory requirements and could be altered by Congress.

a. Notice and Delay

Each of the statutes requires that plaintiffs provide notice of their intention to commence a citizen suit to the prospective defendant, the federal government and the state in which the alleged violation occurs. Additionally, the statutes have provisions that generally require plaintiffs to wait 60 days after providing notice before they can file their complaint in federal court. **CAA, § 304(b), 42 U.S.C. § 7604(b); CWA, § 505(b), 33 U.S.C. § 1365(b); RCRA, § 7002(b)(1), 42 U.S.C. § 6972(b)(1).**

Citizen suits under the CAA involving an allegation of violation of section 112 and suits under RCRA involving an allegation of violations of the hazardous waste provisions of Subtitle C of RCRA may be filed after notice without delay. This requirement of "notice and delay" is intended in part to give the defendant an opportunity to come into compliance and the government the opportunity to file its own enforcement action prior to the citizen suit.

In *Hallstrom v. Tillamook Cty.*, 493 U.S. 20, 110 S.Ct. 304, 107 L.Ed.2d 237 (1989), the Supreme Court held that the notice and delay requirements of RCRA were "jurisdictional" and must be satisfied to provide federal court jurisdiction.

b. Diligent Prosecution

The CAA, CWA and RCRA all provide that a citizen suit may not be brought if the government has "commenced" and is "diligently prosecuting" an enforcement action prior to the filing of the citizen suit. **CAA, § 304(b), 42 U.S.C. § 7604(b); CWA, § 505(b), 33 U.S.C. § 1365(b); RCRA, § 7002(b)(1), 42 U.S.C. § 6972(b)(1).**

Citizen suits can be barred not only if enforcement actions are commenced in federal court, but also, in some cases, citizens can be barred from recovering civil penalties if the government seeks administrative penalties. Under section 309(g)(6)(A) of the Clean Water Act, citizens may not seek civil penalties if EPA has issued a final order imposing administrative penalties or if a state has imposed final administrative penalties under a "comparable" state law. **§ 309(g)(6)(A), 42 U.S.C. 1319(g)(6)(A)**. There is considerable case law analyzing whether state administrative penalties were issued under comparable laws.

If EPA files an action for administrative penalties under the Clean Water Act (or a state files an action for administrative penalties under a "comparable" state law) after a citizen provides notice, the citizen may still bring the citizen suit if the complaint is filed within 120 days of giving notice. **§ 309(g)(6)(B), 42 U.S.C. § 1319(g)(6)(B)**.

c. Wholly Past Violations

The citizen suit provisions generally allow a plaintiff to bring an action against another party who is "in violation" of the statute. In *Gwaltney of Smithfield Ltd. v. Chesapeake Bay Foundation*, 484 U.S. 49, 108 S.Ct. 376, 98 L.Ed.2d 306 (1987), the Supreme Court held, based on this language in section 505 of the CWA, "supplementary role" that citizen suits play, and certain other reasons, that federal courts have jurisdiction to hear citizen suits only if the alleged violator is currently in violation of the Act at the time the suit is filed. Citizen suits cannot be brought for "wholly past" violations. *Gwaltney* and subsequent case law indicate, however, that a violation may not be wholly past if a violation occurs after the filing of the citizen suit or if there was a series or pattern of past violations that indicate the likelihood that violations will occur in the future. Courts have also held that a court has jurisdiction if the defendant is in violation at the time the citizen suit is filed even if it is not in violation at the time of trial. Principles of "mootness" may apply if a defendant corrects violations after commencement of the citizen suit.

Gwaltney holds that a plaintiff need only make good faith allegations of continuing violations to withstand a motion to dismiss for failure to state a claim. Defendants can challenge the factual accuracy of the plaintiff's allegations through motions for summary judgment.

In 1990, the citizen suit provision of the Clean Air Act was amended to address the *Gwaltney* issue. Under the CAA, a citizen suit may be commenced if the defendant was "alleged to have violated (if there is evidence that the alleged violation has been repeated)." **CAA, 304(a)(1), § 42 U.S.C. 7604(a)(1).**

*

Regulation of Toxic Substances

■ ANALYSIS

E. **TREATMENT OF TOXIC SUBSTANCES UNDER FEDERAL STATUTES**
1. Clean Air Act
2. Clean Water Act
3. Federal Insecticide, Fungicide and Rodenticide Act
   a. Registration
   b. Cancellation, Suspension and Emergency Orders
   c. Indemnification for Canceled Pesticides
   d. Regulation of Pesticides in Food
4. Toxic Substances Control Act
   a. Testing Requirements
   b. Premanufacture Notification
   c. Regulation of Chemical Substances
   d. Reporting and Recordkeeping

A. Introduction

In the 1970's, much of the focus of environmental regulation was on "conventional" pollutants. These were pollutants which had traditionally been the focus of pollution control efforts and that had environmental effects which were thought to be well understood. Increasingly, attention has focused on "toxic pollutants" or "hazardous substances." These substances generally include pollutants that may produce adverse health effects, particularly cancer, when people are exposed at low levels.

Although there is no general definition of toxic pollutant or hazardous substance, it is very important to note that the terms may have a precise meaning under a particular statute. For example, there is a specific list of 65 "toxic pollutants" that are listed under section 307(a)(1) of the Clean Water Act. There are now 189 "hazardous air pollutants" listed under section 112(b) of the Clean Air Act. There is also a specific list of "hazardous substances" under the Comprehensive Environmental Response, Compensation and Liability Act. When dealing with a question about toxic or hazardous substances, it is important to note the statute with which you are dealing.

B. Dealing With Uncertainty

Virtually all of the problems in regulating toxic substances arise from the fact of "uncertainty." For most toxic substances, there are very little data about their effects on human health and the environment. Notwithstanding a lack of data, decisions must be made about whether and how stringently to regulate the substance.

In common law tort actions, a plaintiff typically has the burden of proving, based on a "preponderance of the evidence," that a toxic substance caused a human health effect. A lack of data may mean that a plaintiff cannot recover damages.

Most environmental statutes that deal with toxic substances are preventative; they seek to prevent harm by limiting exposure prior to the occurrence of a harm. The problem of uncertainty deals with the level of information that is necessary to justify the regulation of toxic substances.

Two cases are widely cited for their discussion of the role of uncertainty in decisionmaking under environmental statutes.

1. Reserve Mining Co. v. EPA

In *Reserve Mining Co. v. EPA*, 514 F.2d 492 (8th Cir.1975) (en banc), the plaintiffs sought to enjoin the discharge of mine tailings by the Reserve

Mining Co. The action was brought, among other things, under the Clean Water Act which authorized courts to abate discharges that "endanger" human health. Although the evidence of harm from drinking or breathing the mine tailings was inconclusive, the tailings contained fibers similar to asbestos which were known to cause disease. In an earlier opinion, the court had implied that the government could not meet its burden of proof in establishing that the discharge endangered public health since the effects of the discharge were unproven.

In its en banc opinion, however, the court thoroughly reviewed the evidence of health effects and concluded that, although the data did not indicate that the probability of harm was more likely than not, the evidence did give rise to a reasonable medical concern. The court concluded that the endangerment standard in the statute was intended to be precautionary and that a decision to regulate could be based on a weighing of the probabilities of a health risk and the consequences or magnitude of this risk. In fashioning a remedy, the court balanced this risk against the benefits conferred by the plant's operation. Ultimately, the court concluded that the data required an injunction which forced the plant to phase out the discharge of the mine tailings but which did not require an immediate halt of the discharge.

2. Ethyl Corp. v. EPA

Ethyl Corp. v. EPA, 541 F.2d 1 (D.C.Cir.1976), involved a challenge to EPA's regulation of lead additives in gasoline. Section 211 of the Clean Air Act authorized EPA to regulate additives that "will endanger" public health or welfare. The data were inconclusive on the health effects of exposure to lead from gasoline, and petitioners claimed that EPA had not demonstrated that the lead additives "will endanger" public health.

The court concluded that the statute authorized regulation even when the health effects of an additive were uncertain. Since the Clean Air Act was intended to be "precautionary legislation," the court concluded that EPA could regulate based on data which suggested that lead created a "significant risk of harm." Citing *Reserve Mining*, the court indicated that this included an assessment of the probability and severity of harm.

C. Defining "Safety"

In many cases regulatory agencies are required to determine a "safe" level of exposure of exposure to toxic substances. In some cases, this may require an agency to determine whether an exposure constitutes a "significant risk." In other cases, an agency must identify a level of exposure which, with an "ample margin of safety," will protect human health and the environment.

1. Threshold v. Non–Threshold Pollutants

For some toxic substances, it may be possible to identify a level below which there are no observed health effects. In other words, only exposures at levels above this "threshold" will cause adverse effects. For such pollutants, it is at least conceptually possible to determine a "safe" level of exposure with a margin of safety. The agency can identify the threshold level and then set an acceptable exposure level at some fraction of the threshold.

For carcinogens the problem is different. Many scientists and most regulatory agencies assume that there is no safe level of exposure to carcinogens and that any exposure, regardless of how small, will increase the risk of getting cancer. Carcinogens, in this view, are "non-threshold" pollutants. If any exposure increases the risk of getting cancer, it is impossible objectively to identify a "safe" level. The best that can be done is to identify a level of exposure where the increased risk is so small that it is considered acceptable.

2. Defining a Level of Acceptable Risk

Through the process of "risk assessment," discussed below, it may be possible for an agency to estimate the risks arising from exposure to a toxic substance. An agency, for example, may be able to state that a certain level of exposure to a carcinogen will increase the exposed individual's risk of contracting cancer by 1 in ten thousand (1×10^{-4}) or by 1 in a million (1×10^{-6}). These numbers do not, however, tell what increased level of risk is "safe" or "significant" or "acceptable."

In some limited cases, Congress has given specific guidance on the level of acceptable risk. The "Delaney clause" of the Food, Drug and Cosmetic Act prohibits the use of any food additive that has been shown to be a carcinogen. This has been characterized as a "zero risk" standard. Section 112(f) of the Clean Air Act will require EPA to regulate carcinogenic hazardous air pollutants if they create an increased risk of cancer of greater than one in a million.

In most cases, however, statutes are silent as to the level of risk that is acceptable. Although this issue essentially involves a policy judgment, some have advocated that it be made based on an assessment of the range of risks that are accepted by the public. This means that an agency might compare a risk it is considering regulating with the risks that people accept, for example, in driving a car. Social scientists recognize, however, that people respond to different kinds of risk in different ways, and they have studied how people judge risks and what factors affect their decisions.

Two cases are widely discussed for their analysis of the process of selecting a safe or acceptable level of risk.

a. Industrial Union Dept., AFL–CIO v. American Petroleum Institute, (the benzene decision)

In *Industrial Union Dept., AFL–CIO v. American Petroleum Institute*, (the benzene decision), 448 U.S. 607, 100 S.Ct. 2844, 65 L.Ed.2d 1010 (1980), the Supreme Court held that the Occupational Safety and Health Administration ("OSHA") could not issue an occupational standard that limited the level of benzene in the workplace until it had identified that the existing level of exposure constituted a "significant risk." The court based this conclusion on section 3(8) of the Occupational Safety and Health Act ("OSH Act") which defined an occupational standard as one that was "reasonably necessary or appropriate to provide safe and healthful employment." In his plurality opinion, Justice Stevens stated that the term "reasonably necessary" implies 1) that a workplace must be "unsafe," 2) that unsafe does not mean risk free, and 3) that a showing that a workplace is unsafe requires a showing that significant risks are present.

The court stated that the government had the burden of showing that a significant risk existed, but gave limited guidance on how to make this judgment. Justice Stevens, without citation, stated that a risk of one in ten thousand might be significant while a risk of one in a billion was clearly not significant. Since most risks with which regulatory agencies deal will fall within this range, the opinion does little to help the Agency select a significant risk level.

b. NRDC v. EPA (the Vinyl Chloride case)

In *NRDC v. United States EPA*, 824 F.2d 1146 (D.C.Cir.1987) (en banc), the court reviewed EPA's issuance of an air standard for vinyl chloride under section 112 of the Clean Air Act. At that time, section 112 required EPA to regulate hazardous air pollutants at a level which provides "an ample margin of safety to protect the public health." [Section 112 was substantially modified by the 1990 Clean Air Act Amendments]. Since EPA considered vinyl chloride a carcinogen, it assumed that there was no safe level of exposure. The Agency therefore decided to establish a standard based, among other things, on the cost and feasibility of controlling vinyl chloride emissions.

In its final decision, the D.C. Circuit held that EPA must first determine what is a "safe" level of exposure to vinyl chloride. Citing *Industrial Union* (the benzene case), the court stated that this does not mean risk-free. Rather the court stated that the decision was to be left to the EPA's expert judgment based on such factors as an assessment of the risks that are generally considered acceptable by the public. The court stressed, however, that the determination of "safety" was to be made without considering the cost of regulation. After EPA had identified a "safe" level, it could set its regulatory limit at a lower level to reflect a "margin of safety." In determining this margin of safety, the court stated that EPA could consider factors such as cost and feasibility.

3. Defining a Level of Unreasonable Risk

In some cases, a determination of "safety" might involve some comparison of the costs and benefits of regulation. We might be willing, for example, to spend ten dollars to reduce a risk to one in a million, while we might not be willing to spend ten million dollars to attain that level of safety. The role of cost/benefit analysis varies depending on the statute under which the agency is regulating.

Some statutes require that a regulator determine if a toxic substance constitutes an "unreasonable risk." Such statutes typically allow an agency expressly to balance the risks from the substance with the cost of regulation. For example, the Federal Insecticide, Fungicide and Rodenticide Act ("FIFRA"), discussed below, requires EPA to balance the costs and benefits of a pesticide to determine if its use will have "unreasonable adverse effects."

Other statutes allow or require consideration of costs and benefits in different ways. In *NRDC v. EPA*, (the vinyl chloride case), discussed above, the court held that EPA could consider costs only after it had made a threshold determination of acceptable risk. In *American Textile Manufacturers Institute v. Donovan*, 452 U.S. 490, 101 S.Ct. 2478, 69 L.Ed.2d 185 (1981) (the Cotton Dust case), the Supreme Court held that the OSH Act did not require use of a cost/benefit analysis in setting occupational exposure standards. This opinion was something of a surprise since the Court had recently issued the Benzene decision, discussed above, which held that OSHA could not issue a standard without first demonstrating that existing exposure levels constituted a significant risk.

D. Risk Assessment Methodology

Risk assessment is the process of estimating the risk to human health or the environment arising from exposure to toxic substances. These assessments are prepared by federal agencies for a variety of reasons. They may be used as the basis for establishing specific regulatory levels when a statute requires regulation to protect human health. They may be employed to document whether a toxic substance constitutes a "significant risk" as a basis for taking further regulatory action. They may also be used as a management tool by an agency as the basis for allocation of agency resources in responding to risks.

Many people distinguish risk assessment from risk management. Risk assessment involves the "scientific" analysis of risks from a toxic substance. Risk management involves the "policy" judgments about what steps should be taken in light of the risk assessment. In practice, it is difficult to separate the scientific from the policy issues in this area.

Although there are a variety of methods employed by various agencies in undertaking risk assessments, there seems to be consensus that it involves four basic steps.

1. Hazard Identification

Hazard identification involves a judgment as to whether a substance is a potential carcinogen or toxic substance. Although hazard identification may result in different labels (i.e., probable human carcinogen v. possible human carcinogen), the process basically involves a "yes" or "no" determination as to whether a substance is a carcinogen or toxic substance.

Data used in such an assessment may include epidemiological studies on human populations exposed to the substance, studies based on exposure of animals to the substance, tests of the effect of the substances on bacteria or other cells and "structural activity" relationships which attempt to estimate toxicity by the physical and chemical similarities among substances.

None of these data in themselves may be dispositive on the question of potential human carcinogenicity. Together, based on a scientific assessment of the validity and consistency of the data, they can form the basis for the classification of a substance as a human carcinogen.

2. Dose–Response Assessment

"Dose-response" assessment is the process of quantifying the relationship between the level of exposure and increased risk of adverse affects such as cancer. A risk assessment frequently results in a formula that allows calculation of the statistical increase in risk of getting cancer resulting from a given level of exposure to a carcinogen. Thus, a risk assessment for a carcinogen may include information that exposure to X amount of the carcinogen will increase an individual's risk of getting cancer by 1 in a million ($1 \times 10(-6)$), exposure to Y amount will increase the risk by 1 in a hundred thousand ($1 \times 10(-5)$), and exposure to Z amount will increase the risk by 1 in ten thousand ($1 \times 10(-4)$).

The purpose of a risk assessment is usually to identify the effects on humans from exposure to low levels of carcinogens. This information is difficult to obtain. First, there are usually no actual data documenting the effects on humans of exposure to low doses of carcinogens. Second, it is difficult and expensive to identify carcinogenic effects by exposing laboratory animals to low doses of carcinogens. If animals were exposed to low doses of a not very potent carcinogen, the carcinogenic effect might not be detected unless huge numbers of animals were exposed for a long period of time. Therefore, dose-response analysis usually involves extrapolation from data derived from experiments in which a limited number of laboratory animals have been exposed to high doses of carcinogens.

This process has been criticized on a number of grounds. First, there are reasons to believe that effects which occur when an animal is exposed to high doses of a substance do not occur when the animal is exposed to lower doses. Second, there are reasons to question whether data on the effects on laboratory animals, such as rats, are relevant to the effects on humans. Third, extrapolation of data from high doses to low doses involves the use of a mathematical model. There are a number of different models that could legitimately be used to perform this extrapolation, and they may vary in their low dose estimates by many orders of magnitude.

3. Exposure Assessment

Exposure assessments characterize the extent to which an individual or a population may be exposed to a toxic substance. An exposure assessment may involve such factors as identification and characterization of the population exposed to the substance, quantification of the amount of the substance to which the population is exposed, and quantifying how long the individual or population was exposed. It also may involve an investigation of the route of exposure (breathing it vs. drinking it). An exposure assessment based on a "maximally exposed individual" may, for example, assume that exposure occurs at the highest possible concentrations for a lifetime. Other exposure assessments may be based on other assumptions about the extent and duration of exposure.

4. Risk Characterization

Risk characterization involves the assessment of data derived from the three previous steps to make judgments as to the magnitude of risk to human populations from exposure to the substance.

E. Treatment of Toxic Substances Under Federal Statutes

1. Clean Air Act

Section 112 of the Clean Air Act provides for the promulgation of National Emission Standards for Hazardous Air Pollutants ("NESHAPs"). Prior to 1990, section 112 required EPA to promulgate NESHAPs at a level which provides "an ample margin of safety to protect public health." As illustrated by *NRDC v. EPA*, discussed above, EPA had a very difficult time implementing this standard, and the agency issued only a limited number of NESHAPs.

In the 1990 Clean Air Act Amendments, Congress completely restructured section 112. As discussed in more detail in Chapter 6, section 112 specifically designates 189 pollutants as "hazardous air pollutants". Section 112 now requires EPA to set technology-based standards for these hazardous air pollutants and to later set environmental quality based standards to address any "residual risk."

2. Clean Water Act

Under section 307(a)(1) of the Clean Water Act, EPA has designated 65 pollutants as "toxic pollutants." Designation of a pollutant as a toxic pollutant has several consequences. First, EPA sets BAT effluent limitations guidelines for toxic pollutants, and there are almost no variances available from these limitations. Second, states must set water quality criteria for toxic pollutants. These criteria, as discussed in Chapter 5, may be in the form of specific numbers, bioassay tests or general narrative prohibitions on the discharge of toxic pollutants. Finally, EPA may establish an environmental-quality based "toxic effluent standard" under section 307(a)(2). EPA has issued only six such standards, and none since 1977.

3. Federal Insecticide, Fungicide and Rodenticide Act

The Federal Insecticide, Fungicide, and Rodenticide Act, 7 U.S.C. § 136 et seq., ("FIFRA") is the primary federal statute regulating the use of pesticides.

It was initially adopted in 1947, but was substantially amended by the Federal Environmental Pesticide Control Act in 1972. Since that time there have been several significant amendments to the statute.

FIFRA operates by requiring that all pesticides be registered by EPA, and, in most cases, the sale or use of unregistered pesticides is prohibited. **§ 3(a), 7 U.S.C. § 136a(a)**. EPA may impose conditions on the use of pesticides and may also establish specific labeling requirements. FIFRA authorizes the Agency to cancel or suspend use of a pesticide under certain conditions.

a. Registration

A pesticide may be registered under FIFRA if, among other things, EPA determines that 1) the pesticide's composition warrants its claims of "efficacy," 2) the registrant has complied with labeling and data submission requirements and 3) the pesticide "will not generally cause unreasonable adverse effects on the environment." **§ 3(c)(5), 7 U.S.C. § 136a(c)(5)**. The term "unreasonable adverse effects" is defined under the statute to include "any unreasonable risk to man or the environment taking into account economic, social and environmental costs and benefits of the use of any pesticide." **§ 136(bb)**. Unlike most other environmental statutes, this definition authorizes the use of a something close to a cost/benefit analysis as part of the registration process.

The registration process is lengthy and expensive. Applicants are required to submit extensive information on the health and environmental effects of the pesticide. One issue that has been controversial under FIFRA is the use of this data by later registrants who wish to register similar pesticides. FIFRA allows subsequent registrants to use this prior data, and thus avoids requiring them to perform the same costly tests. FIFRA requires, however, that these later registrants, under certain circumstances, to pay compensation to the first registrant for use of their data. **§ 3(c)(1)(D), 7 U.S.C. § 136a(c)(1)(D)**. In *Ruckelshaus v. Monsanto Co.*, 467 U.S. 986, 104 S.Ct. 2862, 81 L.Ed.2d 815 (1984), the Supreme Court held that the provisions of FIFRA which authorized the later use of a registrant's data did not constitute a "taking" of property under the federal Constitution.

FIFRA now also addresses the problem of pesticides that were previously registered without an adequate review of their health and environmental impacts. In 1988, Congress amended FIFRA to require the re-registration of certain pesticides registered before November, 1984.

§ 4, 7 U.S.C. § 136a–1. This process places the burden on the pesticide registrant to submit the health and safety data necessary to justify re-registration.

b. Cancellation, Suspension and Emergency Orders

FIFRA allows EPA to either cancel or suspend the use of a pesticide. EPA may permanently cancel the use of a pesticide if, among other things, continued use causes unreasonable adverse effects on the environment. § 6(b), 7 U.S.C. § 136d(b). Cancellation generally involves protracted administrative proceedings, and the pesticide may continue to be used during this process. EPA may, however, order an immediate suspension of the use of a pesticide before final cancellation if EPA finds there is an "imminent hazard." FIFRA provides for an expedited hearing following suspension, and the pesticide's registration continues during this expedited hearing. EPA may prohibit use of a pesticide prior to any hearing only in certain circumstances which EPA deems an emergency. § 6(c)(3), 7 U.S.C. § 136d(c)(3).

c. Indemnification for Canceled Pesticides

Prior to 1988, FIFRA required EPA to indemnify producers, distributors and others who suffered economic loss from the cancellation or suspension of a pesticide. This was seen as discouraging EPA from exercising its authority under FIFRA. In 1988 Amendments to FIFRA, Congress limited the class of persons who could receive indemnification and transferred liability for payment of indemnification claims to a general federal judgment fund. § 15, 7 U.S.C. § 136m.

d. Regulation of Pesticides in Food

Pesticides in foods are regulated under the Food Drug and Cosmetic Act, 21 U.S.C. § 301 et seq., ("FDCA"). Under this statute, EPA may set "tolerances," or acceptable levels, for pesticide residues on unprocessed or raw agricultural products. In setting tolerances, EPA must consider, in addition to health effects, the effects on the food supply from canceling the pesticide.

The "Delaney" clause of the FDCA may prohibit the inclusion of any pesticide found to be a carcinogen in any processed food. This difference in treatment of pesticides on processed and unprocessed foods is a major issue in the regulation of pesticides.

4. Toxic Substances Control Act

Most federal laws deal with toxic substances as wastes (CWA, CAA, RCRA, CERCLA), others deal with exposure in a limited context such as the workplace (OSH Act) or one class of chemical products such as pesticides (FIFRA). The Toxic Substances Control Act of 1976, 15 U.S.C. § 2601 et seq., ("TSCA"), operates on a different, and broader, principle. The general policy expressed in TSCA is that manufacturers of chemicals have a duty to test product safety and that the government (EPA) has the power to control and even to stop production or use of chemicals that present an unreasonable risk. TSCA is a complicated statute, and its broad authority has not been used extensively by EPA.

TSCA covers all "chemicals and mixtures" with the exception of pesticides, tobacco, nuclear material, certain food, food additives, drugs and cosmetics. TSCA also contains separate provisions dealing with the use and disposal of polychlorinated biphenyls ("PCBs") and asbestos in schools.

a. Testing Requirements

Section 4 authorizes EPA to require testing of new and existing substances for their effects on health and the environment when it finds that the manufacturing, distribution, processing, use or disposal of the substance "may present an unreasonable risk of injury to human health or the environment." **§ 4(a)(1), 15 U.S.C. § 2603(a)(1)**. This information is to be used by EPA in determining whether to take regulatory action under other sections of TSCA. EPA has issued "test rules" under this authority which require testing of certain chemicals.

b. Premanufacture Notification

Section 5 of TSCA requires manufacturers to notify EPA before manufacturing a new chemical substance or putting an existing chemical substance to a significant new use. **§ 5, 15 U.S.C. § 2604**. Premanufacture notification ("PMN") includes, in some cases, submission of test data relating to health and environmental effects. Although Section 5 requires submission of existing data, EPA may, in some cases, act to prohibit manufacturing or use of the chemical if additional data are necessary.

c. Regulation of Chemical Substances

Section 6 of TSCA authorizes EPA to place a variety of limitations on the use, marketing, labeling or disposal of chemical substances. EPA may impose such restrictions if it concludes there is a "reasonable basis to conclude" that the substance "presents or will present an unreasonable risk of injury to health or the environment." **§ 6(a), 15 U.S.C. § 2605(a)**. The restrictions may be adopted "to the extent necessary to protect adequately against such risk using the least burdensome requirements."

d. Reporting and Recordkeeping

A major goal of TSCA is to expand, systematize and assemble existing information on chemicals and their exposure effects. Section 8 contains the reporting and recordkeeping requirements. **§ 8, 15 U.S.C. § 2607**. With the exception of small businesses, anyone who obtains information "which reasonably supports the conclusion" that a chemical presents a "substantial" risk of injury to health and the environment must immediately notify EPA. EPA may issue rules for selected chemicals requiring detailed recordkeeping and reporting to enable the Agency to monitor and regulate a chemical throughout its life cycle. Industry is required to keep records of significant adverse health reactions caused by any chemical for 30 years and of environmental damage for 5 years.

CHAPTER 11

Regulation of Natural Resources, Regulation of Land Use and Regulatory Takings

■ ANALYSIS

There are a large number of federal and state laws and common law doctrines that affect the development and preservation of natural resources. These laws frequently act by placing limitations on the development of private lands. The "takings clause" of the Fifth Amendment may operate to limit such government regulation.

A. Regulation of Wetlands Under Section 404 of the Clean Water Act

Wetlands are increasingly seen as critical aspects of the ecosystem that not only support wildlife, but also purify water and limit flooding. Section 404 of the Clean Water Act is perhaps the primary federal provision that acts to protect the destruction of wetlands. Section 404 of the Clean Water Act, CWA § 404, 33 U.S.C. § 1344, prohibits the discharge of "dredge or fill" material into "navigable waters," including wetlands, without a permit. A section 404 permit may be required, for example, before a developer may begin construction in a wetland. The permits are issued by the U.S. Army Corps of Engineers based on criteria established by the Environmental Protection Agency.

1. Jurisdiction

Section 404 requires a permit for the discharge of dredge or fill material into "navigable waters" which EPA and the Corps of Engineers has defined to include "wetlands." One of the most controversial aspects of the section 404 program has been identification of the areas included within the definition of wetlands. In *United States v. Riverside Bayview Homes*, 474 U.S. 121, 106 S.Ct. 455, 88 L.Ed.2d 419 (1985), the Supreme Court upheld the government's definition of wetlands that focused on a biological assessment of the capacity of the wetlands to support types of plant life characterized by living in saturated soils.

The Supreme Court has issued a series of opinions that address the scope of waters that may be regulated as wetlands. These cases are discussed at 5.B.2.c above.

2. The Section 404 Permit Program

Section 404 permits are issued by the Army Corps of Engineers based on criteria established by the EPA. Persons seeking a permit may apply for an individual permit applicable to their activities. The Corps of Engineers has also issued "general permits" that apply to classes of activities. Persons may be authorized under the general permits without the requirement to apply for individual permits. The scope of these general permits has been controversial, and they have been modified several times.

3. Assessment of Alternatives

The section 404 regulations require an assessment of the availability of "practicable alternatives" that have less adverse impact on wetlands. This may involve an assessment of the purpose of the project for which the applicant seeks the 404 permit and whether alternative non-wetland property is available to the applicant.

4. Mitigation

Applicants for 404 permits may, as a condition of a permit, be required to mitigate the loss of wetlands. One controversial element of mitigation has been the ability of applicants to justify destruction of wetlands by committing to construct or restore replacement wetlands. Additionally, mitigation requirements has led to "wetlands banking" in which wetlands are created or restored to compensate for future development activities that may destroy wetlands.

B.   Endangered Species Act

The Endangered Species Act is the primary federal statute that protects endangered and threatened plant and animal species. In *Tennessee Valley Authority v. Hill*, 437 U.S. 153, 98 S.Ct. 2279, 57 L.Ed.2d 117 (1978), the Supreme Court interpreted the statute broadly to prohibit the federal government from taking actions that jeopardize the continued existence of an endangered species regardless of the cost. As a result of the case, the federal government ceased funding of the nearly completed Tellico Dam because operation of the dam might destroy an endangered species of snail darter, a small fish. Although the Endangered Species Act was subsequently modified to allow the government to jeopardize endangered species in limited cases based, in part, on cost considerations, the ESA is still seen as a statute that generally elevates its environmental goal of species preservation above economic considerations.

1.   Listing of Endangered and Threatened Species and Designation of Critical Habitat

Under section 4 of the ESA, the Secretary of the Interior (terrestrial and freshwater species) and the Secretary of Commerce (marine species) are responsible for designating species as "endangered" or "threatened." **ESA, § 4, 16 U.S. C. § 1533**. The Act of listing a species as "endangered" triggers the regulatory obligations contained in sections 7 and 9 of the Act. Once a species is designated as "endangered" or "threatened" the ESA also imposes a requirement for the designation of "critical habitat" where the critical habitat can be determined and designation is "prudent." Critical habitat has been designated for only a few of the many listed species.

2. Prohibitions on "Taking" Endangered Species

Section 9 of the ESA prohibits any person, both private parties and the government, from "taking" an endangered species. **ESA, § 9, 16 U.S.C. § 1538.** The word "take" is a defined term in the ESA and should not be confused with regulatory "takings" under the Fifth Amendment. Under the ESA, "take" means "to harass, harm, pursue, hunt, shoot, would, kill trap, capture, or collect, or to attempt to engage in any such conduct." **ESA, § 3(19), 16 U.S.C. § 1532(19)**. At a minimum, the prohibition on "taking" extends to the intentional killing of a member of an endangered species. In *Babbitt v. Sweet Home Chapter of Communities for a Great Oregon*, 515 U.S. 687, 115 S.Ct. 2407, 132 L.Ed.2d 597 (1995), the Supreme Court upheld a definition of "take" promulgated by the Department of Interior that included "significant habitat modification or degradation" which results in the actual death of an endangered species.

3. Limitations on Actions of the Federal Government

Under section 7 of the ESA, the federal government is prohibited from undertaking any action that "jeopardizes" the continued existence of an endangered species or results in the destruction of "critical habitat." **ESA, § 7(a)(2), 16 U.S.C. § 1536(a)(2)**. Section 7 also requires federal agencies that are considering actions that may jeopardize an endangered species to engage in consultation with the Department of the Interior. The Department of the Interior may make comments and recommendations about the proposed action, but it cannot veto the action.

In addition to precluding federal actions that may jeopardize the existence of an endangered species, federal agencies are also subject to the prohibition in section 9 from "taking" an individual member of an endangered species. Section 7(b)(4) of the ESA, however, allows the Secretary of the Interior to authorize a federal agency to undertake an action that may "take" an endangered species if, among other things, the taking is "incidental," unlikely to jeopardize the continued existence of the species, and the agency has taken steps to minimize the impact on the endangered species. **ESA, § 7(b)(4), 16 U.S.C. § 1536(b)(4)**.

4. Limitation on Actions by Private Actions

There are two situations in which the ESA may apply to the actions of private parties.

a. Private Actions that Constitute a "Take"

(1) Section 9

Section 9 of the ESA prohibits private parties from "taking" an endangered species. ESA, § 9(a)(1), 16 U.S.C. § 1538(a)(1). As discussed in B.2 above, "taking" includes not only the intentional killing or harming of endangered species, but also the destruction or modification of habitat that results in the actual death of a member of an endangered species. Thus, land development in an area potentially containing an endangered species raises the possibility of violation of the ESA.

(2) Incidental Takes and Habitat Conservation Plans

The impact of the section 9 prohibition on land development is reduced by section 10(a) of the ESA. Section 10(a) allows the Secretary of the Interior to permit "incidental" takes by a private party if the party minimizes the impact of the taking and the action will not "appreciably reduce the likelihood of the survival and recovery of the species in the wild." **ESA, § 10(a), 16 U.S.C. § 1539(a).** This is a similar standard for authorization of "incidental takes" by the federal government under section 7(b)(4). Authorization for incidental takes is implemented through a "habitat conservation plan" developed by the private party and approved by the Secretary of the Interior.

b. Private Actions Requiring Government Approval

Although Section 7 of the ESA only applies to actions of the federal government, it may indirectly be applied to actions of private parties if the private action requires approval by the federal government. Thus, if a private party needs a wetlands permit under section 404 of the Clean Water Act, section 7 may apply to government approval of the permit. In this case, the government may authorize an "incidental take" under section 7(b)(4).

C. Public Trust Doctrine

The Public Trust Doctrine provides that certain lands, primarily water bodies and land submerged under or tidal land adjacent to water bodies, are subject to a "public trust" possessed by the federal and state governments. In *Illinois Central Railroad Co. v. Illinois*, 146 U.S. 387, 13 S.Ct. 110, 36 L.Ed. 1018 (1892), the U.S. Supreme Court voided the grant by the Illinois legislature of submerged lands based on a conclusion that the Public Trust Doctrine prohibited the state from totally relinquishing its interest in the land.

Among other things, the Public Trust Doctrine has been used to justify government regulation of marine, wetlands and beachfront property and to limit the possibility that private landowners can claim a Fifth Amendment regulatory taking when the government limits use of property subject to the Public Trust.

D. Federal Land Policy

It is frequently said that one-third of the nation's land is owned by the federal government. Perhaps the greatest issue in public lands management is balancing the competing objectives of economic development of resources with preservation of the public lands. There are a number of different statutes that affect management decisions on federal lands; these statutes have been adopted at different times and reflect different policies. There is, unfortunately, no comprehensive statutory approach to management of federal lands.

The federal Mining Law of 1872 gives the person who locates certain hardrock minerals (the statute does not apply to oil and gas or coal) on federal lands certain mining rights. The statute gives the federal government little authority to limit the mining of those minerals. Under both the Mineral Leasing Act and the Outer Continental Shelf Lands Act, the federal government has broader authority to regulate federal lands that are leased for oil and gas development.

Under the Federal Lands Policy and Management Act, most federal lands are to be managed to promote "multiple use." Similarly the Multiple§ Use Sustained Yield Act provides for multiple use decisions in national forests.

Certain federal lands are subject to restricted development. National Parks are subject to stringent development limits. The National Park Service was created in 1916 to manage national parks. Under the Wilderness Act, federal lands can be designated as "wilderness areas" in which development is limited. The President also has power to withdraw federal lands. In 1976, Congress imposed certain legislative constraints on the President's authority to withdraw lands from development.

E. Takings

1. Regulatory Takings

The Fifth Amendment to the U.S. Constitution prohibits the taking of private property for public use without just compensation. This is the "takings clause," and it is the basis of a constitutional limitation on the government's authority to regulate the use of private property. In *Pennsylvania Coal v. Mahon*, 260 U.S. 393, 43 S.Ct. 158, 67 L.Ed. 322 (1922), the Supreme Court held that a law that regulated the use of property could constitute a "taking" under the Fifth Amendment even if the government did not acquire title or physically invade the property. Pennsylvania Coal is the seminal case in establishing the concept of "regulatory takings."

Landowners claiming a regulatory taking typically argue that limitations on the use of their property so diminish its value that the government has effectively "taken" their land. The remedy if such a taking were found would include compensation to the landowners for the lost value and/or invalidation of the regulation. In the environmental context, takings claims have been asserted, for example, for limitations established under the wetlands protection provisions of section 404 of the Clean Water Act.

2. Takings Tests

In *Pennsylvania Coal, supra*, the Supreme Court stated that the government can regulate private land use, but if a regulation goes, in the Court's words, "too far" it will constitute a taking. The Supreme Court has struggled to develop an appropriate legal test for determining when a regulation goes too far in limiting the use of private property. The Court has essentially established two limited "per se" rules in which a taking will almost always be found. In most cases, however, the Supreme Court has employed an "ad hoc" or case-by-case balancing of a variety of factors in assessing whether a regulation constitutes a taking.

a. Per Se Tests

(1) Physical Invasion

The Supreme Court has held that any regulation that results in a direct "physical invasion" of a landowner's property will constitute a taking. In *Loretto v. Teleprompter Manhattan CATV Corp.*, 458 U.S. 419, 102 S.Ct. 3164, 73 L.Ed.2d 868 (1982), for example, the Court held that a regulation that required apartment owners to allow cable companies to run cable lines to tenants' apartments constituted a taking.

(2) Total Deprivation of Value

In *Lucas v. South Carolina Coastal Council*, 505 U.S. 1003, 112 S.Ct. 2886, 120 L.Ed.2d 798 (1992), the Supreme Court stated that, with one exception, regulations that result in a total deprivation of value will constitute a taking. Thus, a regulation that reduced the value of the regulated property to "zero" would constitute a per se taking. The only exception would be if the regulation prohibited some class of activity that would constitute a nuisance at common law. Since the landowner never had a property right to commit a nuisance, such a regulation would not deprive the landowner of a recognized property right.

b. Ad Hoc Balancing Tests

The Supreme Court has not been able to develop a clear, predictable test for regulatory takings in situations that do not satisfy either of the two per se tests. In the common situation where a regulation limits the use of property but does not require a physical invasion or totally deprive the land of value, the Court has applied an ad hoc, case-by-case balancing of a variety of factors. There is no set list of factors, but factors the Court has referred to have included 1) the magnitude of the loss, 2) the extent to which the regulation interfered with "distinct investment-backed expectations" of the landowner, 3) the extent to which the regulation prevents a public harm, 4) the extent to which the regulation imposed reciprocal benefits and burdens on property, and 5) whether the regulation is a proper application of the states' police powers by being rationally related to the protection of health, welfare and morals. The rationale and application of each of these factors is the subject of dispute.

c. Remedies

In *First English Evangelical Lutheran Church of Glendale v. Los Angeles County*, 482 U.S. 304, 107 S.Ct. 2378, 96 L.Ed.2d 250 (1987), the Supreme Court held that once a taking has been found compensation must be paid for the time the regulation is in effect. Thus, not only might a taking claim result in the regulation being removed, but the landowner will be entitled to compensation for the "temporary taking" that occurred during the period when the regulations was in effect.

*

CHAPTER 12

International Environmental Law

■ **ANALYSIS**

The area of environmental law is increasingly focusing on the global nature of environmental problems. A number of United Nations Conferences, including the 1972 Conference on the Human Environment in Stockholm and the 1992 Conference on the Environment and Development in Rio de Janeiro, brought attention to international environmental issues and adopted "Declarations" of environmental principles.

A. Sources of International Law

International public law recognizes a variety of sources of international law. These include:

1. Treaties

Treaties are documents that establish express obligations among the consenting parties to the treaties. Several major international environmental issues, including ozone depletion and global warming, have been the subject of international treaties. Treaties are generally adopted and implemented in a multi-step process. First, the language of treaties is "adopted" when, in most cases, at least two-thirds of the parties vote for adoption. A treaty will not, however, be binding on individual countries until they "ratify" the treaty. In many cases, a treaty will not finally enter into force until a specified number of countries have ratified the treaty. In the United States, treaty ratification must proceed through a legislative process of "advice and consent" by the Senate.

2. Custom

A "customary rule of international law" can establish binding norms on nations. Identification of accepted "customary rules" of international law can be ambiguous and requires that the rule generally be part of "consistent state practice" and that the practice is a part of a perceived legal obligation. Certain environmental principles, such a principle that countries not act in ways that inflict harm outside of their territory or the "precautionary principle" that justifies regulation in the face of uncertain, but potentially significant, environmental risks, have been advocated as possible candidates as customary international law.

3. General Principles of Law Recognized by Civilized Nations

There may be classes of legal doctrines that are widely recognized among legal systems and that can rise to the level of binding "general principles of law." Like customary law, identification of general principles is ambiguous.

It may include a principle such as "res judicata" specifically incorporated in many legal systems or more general principles of "natural law."

4. Judicial Decisions and Writings of Highly Qualified Publicists

In some cases, prior decisions by international tribunals or writings by "publicists" or international law experts, may be used to determine international law.

B. International Environmental Law Institutions

There are a number of institutions that have a role in the implementation of international environmental law.

1. International Tribunals

In some cases, disputes involving environmental issues are resolved by international tribunals. The International Court of Justice is the principal judicial office of the United Nations for resolving disputes among nations. The ICJ has had only limited involvement in environmental disputes. Other tribunals may be available depending on the nature of the dispute. The International Tribunal for the Law of the Sea exists to resolve disputes under the United Nations Convention on the Law of the Sea. Trade disputes may, as discussed below, be resolved by the World Trade Organization.

2. United Nations Organizations

The United Nations has a number of institutions that are directly related to environmental protection. The United Nations Environment Programme (UNEP) is involved in research, dissemination of information, and facilitating treaty negotiation in a number of environmental areas. There are a number of other U.N. institutions that also have environmental responsibilities.

3. World Trade Organization

The World Trade Organization (WTO) is the entity established in 1994 to implement the international trade agreements that began as the General Agreement on Tariffs and Trade (GATT). Among other things, the WTO has issued several important rulings on the relationship between domestic environmental laws and international trade requirements.

4. International Financial Institutions

A number of international organizations such as the World Bank are involved in funding of national projects that have environmental consequences. The extent to which international financial institutions consider environmental consequences as a part of their funding decisions is a growing area of focus.

5. Non–Governmental Organizations

There are a large number of private organizations that are active in the area of international environmental law. These are referred to as "non-governmental organizations" or NGOs, and they play a variety of roles in the formulation and enforcement of international environmental law.

C. Issues in International Environmental Law

There are numerous environmental issues that are the focus of international attention. These include, among many others, control on the trade in endangered species, maritime pollution, trade in hazardous wastes and water resource allocation. The following are three issues that are frequently addressed in law school courses.

1. Transboundary Pollution

Control of pollution that crosses international borders is addressed in a variety of different ways. The United States has a number of statutes and treaties that address international pollution issues. As noted in Chapter 6.M.1, the Clean Air Act has provisions that may address transboundary air pollution in certain cases. Customary international law may provide some remedies where one country asserts injury from transboundary pollution. The *Trail Smelter Arbitration*, although based on a treaty between the U.S. and Canada, has been widely seen as milestone case in international law that may have recognized an international obligation to prevent serious environmental injury arising from transboundary pollution.

2. Ozone Depletion

In the mid–1970's, evidence began to emerge that stratospheric ozone, levels of ozone in the upper atmosphere that act to shield the earth from cosmic radiation, were being destroyed by human produced chemicals called "chlorofluorocarbons" ("CFCs"). One response to this concern was the adoption in 1987 of the Montreal Protocol, an international agreement that required a phase-out of designated ozone-depleting CFCs. The provisions of the Montreal Protocol have been amended and strengthened since its initial adoption. One of the important elements of the Montreal Protocol is its recognition of the special status of developing countries. Developing countries, unlike the more developed countries that have used virtually all of the CFCs in the past, are allowed greater authority to use CFCs for "basic domestic needs." The Montreal Protocol has been implemented in the United States through provisions of the Clean Air Act discussed in Chapter 6.M.2.

3. Global Warming

Mounting evidence indicates that human activities, primarily the emission of carbon dioxide from the burning of fossil fuels, are contributing to a rise in global temperatures. This "global warming" may arise as a result of the "greenhouse effect" in which certain chemicals in the atmosphere allow energy from the sun to reach the earth's surface but prevent its reflection back into space. These greenhouse gases include carbon dioxide and methane. A growing consensus indicates that global warming may have significant environmental effects on the planet over the next few hundred years.

One international response to global warming was the adoption of the 1997 Kyoto Protocol under the 1992 United Nations Framework Convention on Climate Change. The Kyoto Protocol, among other things, established a targeted set of reductions on the emission of greenhouse gases by a group of developed countries. Several aspects of the Kyoto Protocol have been controversial including the imposition of specific reductions on developed, but not undeveloped countries, and the ability to use implementation mechanisms such as marketable pollution rights to achieve compliance.

Although the U.S. ratified the UNFCCC, the U.S. has refused to ratify the Kyoto Protocols. The future of international cooperation in control of global warming is unclear.

D. International Trade and Environmental Law

A growing focus of international environmental law is the relationship between domestic environmental laws and international trade agreements that seek to eliminate discriminatory bars to international trade. Several major disputes have arisen over the application of the World Trade Organization Agreement, a continuation of the General Agreement on Tariffs and Trade, (GATT/WTO) to certain U.S. environmental laws. Under Articles I, III and XI of the GATT/WTO, "like products" of "most favored nations" are to be treated the same and most import restrictions are prohibited. Article XX(b) and (g), however, establishes exceptions to the requirement of "like treatment" of imported products if the import restrictions relate to protection of human, animal or plant life or relate to the conservation of exhaustible natural resources. In a series of rulings, earlier dispute resolution panels under GATT narrowly construed the exemptions and ruled that U.S. bans on the importation of tuna caught in ways that injured dolphins violated the trade agreement. In 1996, the dispute resolution panel of the WTO held that EPA regulations adopted under the Clean Air Act that treated foreign petroleum refineries differently from domestic refineries also violated WTO/GATT.

*

Answers to Review Questions

■ CHAPTER 4—NEPA

1. F. Although EPA may make a determination (when it reviews an EIS under the authority of section 309 of the Clean Air Act) that a proposed action is environmentally unsatisfactory, it has no authority to prohibit the federal agency from taking that action.

2. F. NEPA does not contain a citizen suit provision. Citizens have sought judicial review of the adequacy of EIS's under general federal question jurisdiction.

3. F. Congress, by statute, has provided that no action of the Administrator of EPA under the Clean Air Act will be classified as a "major federal action" for purposes of NEPA. 15 U.S.C. 4057 793(c)(1).

4. F. In some cases, federal agencies must collect new information. The CEQ regulations require agencies to develop information

that is "essential" to a reasoned choice among alternatives if "the overall costs of obtaining it are not exorbitant."

5. F.   Unless a proposed action is subject to a categorical exclusion, a federal agency may be required to undertake an "environmental assessment" of a proposed action in order to determine whether the proposed action is a "major federal action significantly affecting the quality of the human environment."

6. F.   In some cases, a private activity must be assessed in an EIS where federal approval is necessary in order to undertake the private action.

7. F.   The Supreme Court has indicated that NEPA is "essentially procedural" and that an agency does not violate NEPA if it does not take mitigation measures identified in an EIS.

8. T.

9. F.   In some cases, an agency may be required to prepare a "supplemental EIS" which addresses new information that is "substantial" or "significant."

10. F.   An agency is required to begin the EIS process only at the point where it has formulated a "proposal" for action.

■ CHAPTER 5—CWA

1. F.   Discharges of pollutants not covered by an NPDES permit are generally considered not to violate the Clean Water Act and are protected by the permit shield provision in section 402(k).

2. F.   Unless the facility is violating water quality standards-based effluent limits in its NPDES permit, discharges that cause water quality criteria to be exceeded in the stream do not violate the

CWA. Water quality problems may, however, be a basis for modifying the permit to include water quality standards-based effluent limits that will ensure that criteria are not exceeded.

3. F.   POTWs, like other direct dischargers, are required to obtain an NPDES permit.

4. T.   If EPA has not proposed and thereafter promulgated NSPS effluent limitation guidelines, no facility can meet the definition of new source in section 306(a)(2). A newly constructed facility would be subject to the requirements applicable to existing sources.

5. F.   A permit writer may develop BAT limits on a case-by-case basis when EPA has not promulgated BAT effluent limitation guidelines. These case-by-case limits would be based on "best professional judgment" or BPJ.

6. F.   New Sources are subject to technology-based "new source performance standards." These limits are not subject to the BCT cost tests.

7. F.   The upset defense does not apply to violations of water quality standards-based effluent limits.

8. F.   In *Solid Waste Agency of Northern Cook Cty v. United States Army Corps of Engineers,* 531 U.S. 159, 121 S.Ct. 675, 148 L.Ed.2d 576 (2001), the Supreme Court held that the term "navigable waters" did not include isolated, intermittent bodies of water that might be used by migratory birds.

9. T.   Pretreatment limits may be based on either technology-based "categorical" limits promulgated by EPA or the general prohibition on the introduction of pollutants that cause a POTW to violate limits in its NPDES permit.

10. F.   Under Sections 301(l) and 301(n) FDF variances may be granted from BAT limits on toxic pollutants.

11. T.   Section 509(b)(1)(F) authorizes judicial review of EPA issued permits in U.S. Courts of Appeals. A citizen would have to

satisfy "standing" requirements to obtain judicial review.

12.   F.   Generally national effluent limitations guidelines can only be challenged within 120 days of their promulgation. They cannot subsequently be contested in a suit challenging issuance of a permit.

13.   F.   EPA has taken the position that states must set designated uses at levels that constitute "fishable/swimmable" waters unless the state can demonstrate that those uses are not attainable.

14.   F.   Water quality criteria are not directly included in NPDES permits as effluent limitations. When based on Total Maximum Daily Loads and Waste Load Allocations, a water quality standards-based effluent limitation may be at concentrations that are greater than water quality criteria. Additionally, EPA allows states to establish "mixing zones" surrounding the point source discharge. Water quality within the mixing zones may exceed water quality criteria.

15.   F.   In *Pronsolino v. Nastri*, 291 F.3d 1123 (9th Cir. 2002), the court upheld EPA's authority to require TMDLs on waters that failed to meet water quality standards solely as a result of non-point source pollution.

■ CHAPTER 6—CAA

1.   F.   States are not generally free to establish more stringent auto emission standards. Only California may establish more stringent standards, and oterh states may only adopt the California standards.

2.   T.   Even if a state changes a provision in an approved SIP, it remains federally enforceable until EPA approves and promulgates the change.

3. F. MACT standards are technology-based standards that are generally set without consideration of the health effects of the emission. "Residual risk" standards for HAPs under section 112(f) will be set based on human health considerations.

4. T. Under section 110(c)(1), EPA may promulgate a Federal Implementation Plan. Under section 179(b), EPA also has the authority to withhold certain federal highway grants or increase the offset ratio applicable in non-attainment areas.

5. F. The program applies to "new" or "modified" major stationary sources.

6. T. NSPS apply to "new" or "modified" major stationary sources.

7. F. Section 123 essentially prohibits meeting of NAAQS through the use of tall stacks for purposes of dispersion. The effect of dispersion can only be considered based on a stack height that represents "good engineering practice."

8. F. The Title V permit program does not require all industrial sources of air pollution to obtain a permit. Section 502(a) specifies the types of sources that are subject to the permit program.

9. F. The permit shield may not protect a facility from enforcement for violation of requirements not contained in its permit unless the permit writer specifically makes a determination that other requirements are not applicable.

10. F. Although EPA may set primary NAAQS to protect "sensitive" groups of people, the NAAQS is not set at a level that ensures that every person is protected.

11. F. In *Whitman v. American Trucking Associations*, 531 U.S. 457, 121 S.Ct. 903, 149 L.Ed.2d 1 (2001), the Supreme Court confirmed that Primary NAAQS are to be based on scientific evidence relating to the health impacts of a pollutant without consideration of the economic costs of compliance.

12. T.

13. F.   In *Union Electric v. EPA*, 427 U.S. 246, 96 S.Ct. 2518, 49 L.Ed.2d 474 (1976), the Supreme Court held that EPA may not consider the economic or technological feasibility of state SIP provisions when determining whether to approve a SIP.

14. F.   EPA does not promulgate enforceable, nationally applicable RACT standards. It does, however, publish "Control Technology Guidance" that is used by the states in establishing RACT requirements.

15. F.   In a moderate ozone non-attainment area, sources must obtain offsets of at least 1.15 to 1. Therefore, the source must obtain offsets of 11.5 tons of VOCs.

■ CHAPTER 7—RCRA

1. F.   RCRA does not require a generator to obtain a TSDF permit unless the generator disposes of waste on site or if the generator treats or stores wastes on-site for longer than allowed by the applicable accumulation rule.

2. F.   The generator must notify the EPA if the generator does not receive a copy of the manifest signed by all transporters and the TSDF within 45 days of shipment of the waste by the initial transporter.

3. T.   A generator must determine if the waste is a listed waste by checking EPA regulations to determine if the waste is contained on a hazardous waste list. If the waste is not a listed waste, the generator must determine if the waste exhibits any of the four hazardous waste characteristics.

4. F.   Mixtures of "listed" hazardous waste and non-hazardous waste are classified as hazardous waste under the mixture rule. The mixture is classified as a hazardous waste regardless of whether it exhibits a hazard characteristic.

5. F. The remediation waste would be classified as hazardous under EPA's contained-in interpretation. The mixture rule only applies to when non-hazardous and hazardous wastes are mixed together.

6. F. EPA does claim the authority to regulate at least some materials that are to be recycled. EPA Subtitle C regulations specifically define "solid waste" to include some types of secondary materials that are recycled by being reclaimed, used as a fuel, applied to the land, or speculatively accumulated.

7. F. Under the "land ban," hazardous wastes may be disposed of at a landfill only if 1) the facility receiving the waste has been granted a "no migration" petition or 2) the waste has been treated to meet EPA's BDAT pre-treatment requirements.

8. F. Non-hazardous solid waste may be regulated under a variety of provisions of RCRA. Subtitle D, for example, prohibits the open dumping of solid wastes. Under the "land ban," wastes that no longer exhibit a hazard characteristic may still be subject to disposal restrictions. Additionally, sections 7002 and 7003 apply where there is an imminent and substantial endangerment from "solid or hazardous wastes."

9. F. Discharges that are regulated under an NPDES permit are not classified as a solid waste (and therefore not hazardous waste) under RCRA. This exclusion is found in EPA regulations and the definition of solid waste under RCRA.

10. F. Wastes discharged into a sewer leading to a POTW that treats sewage are not classified as a solid waste (and therefore not hazardous waste) under RCRA. This is the domestic sewage exclusion found in EPA regulations and the definition of solid waste under RCRA. Wastes discharged into a sewer are subject to the pretreatment program under the Clean Water Act.

11. F. A generator is not obligated to run laboratory analysis to determine if its waste is hazardous. To determine if a waste is a "listed" waste, the generator needs to check the regulatory lists. To determine if a waste is a "characteristic" waste, the generator may rely on its "knowledge of process" to determine if the waste exhibits a hazard characteristic. If the generator improperly concludes that the waste is not hazardous, the generator may be in violation of RCRA.

12. F.   States may be delegated authority to issue TSDF permits.

13. F.   Facilities obtaining a TSDF permit may be required to cleanup non-hazardous solid waste at their facility under the corrective action provisions of section 3004(u) and section 3008(h).

■ CHAPTER 8—CERCLA

1. T.   The release reporting provision of section 103(a) only requires reporting if the person in charge has knowledge of the release of a reportable quantity of a hazardous substance. There is no reporting obligation, however, if it is "federally permitted release" such as a discharge in compliance with an NPDES permit under the Clean Water Act.

2. F.   Under § 107(a)(1), the current owner of a facility is a PRP even if he or she was not in any way responsible for the release of the hazardous substance. Owners who undertook "all appropriate inquiry" prior to purchasing the property may, in some cases, have defenses to liability such as the innocent landowner or bona fide prospective purchaser defenses.

3. F.   To establish the "innocent landowner" defense, the owner must not only establish that he or she purchased without knowledge but also that he or she undertook "all appropriate inquiry" prior to purchasing the property.

4. F.   Petroleum is not a hazardous substance even if it contains a hazardous substance as long as the hazardous substance is a

normal constituent of petroleum and is present at concentrations normally found in petroleum. Additionally, EPA and the courts have stated that petroleum is not a hazardous substance even if it contains hazardous substances, like lead, that are typically added as part of the refining process.

5. F.   Lenders may become PRPs if they "participate in management" while they hold the security interest.

6. F.   A citizen suit may be brought against a PRP for violation of a requirement of CERCLA, but release of a hazardous substance is not a violation of CERCLA. The citizen suit provision of § 7002(a)(10(B) of RCRA may, however, be available to obtain injunctive relief where a person has contributed to an "imminent and substantial" endangerment from disposal of solid or hazardous waste.

7. T.   Section 113(f)(2) provides "contribution protection" for persons entering approved settlements with the government. In *United States v. Atlantic Research,* ___ U.S. ___, 127 S.Ct. 2331, 168 L.Ed.2d 28 (2007), however, the Supreme Court indicated that "contribution protection" will not protect a settling PRP from a private cost recovery action brought under § 107(a)(4)(B).

8. T.   Plaintiffs in section 107(a)(4)(B) have the burden of proof to establish the cleanup was consistent with the NCP.

9. F.   Generally, a generator is liable as a PRP if the generator sent a hazardous substance to a site and a hazardous substance of any type is released from the site.

10. F.   CERCLA establishes strict liability for PRPs and compliance with law is not a defense. Section 107(b)(3) establishes a limited statutory defense to liability for releases caused by "third parties" with whom the defendant had no direct or indirect contractual relationship.

11. F.   Under section 113(h) there is no "pre-enforcement" review of a 106 order. The person must either violate the order and risk

enforcement or comply with the order and later seek recovery of its costs.

12. F.   Persons who once owned property at which there has been a release of hazardous substances can still be PRPs. Under section 107(a)(2), they can be PRPs if they owned the property at the time of disposal of hazardous substances.

13. F.   Under section 107(e), persons cannot by contract avoid CERCLA liability. They may, however, enter a contract to be indemnified if they are forced to incur costs under CERCLA.

14. F.   In *Cooper Indus. v. Aviall Servs., Inc.*, 543 U.S. 157, 125 S.Ct. 577, 160 L.Ed.2d 548 (2004), the Supreme Court held that PRPs who voluntarily clean up property cannot seek contribution under § 113(f). In *United States v. Atlantic Research*, ___ U.S. ___, 127 S.Ct. 2331, 168 L.Ed.2d 28 (2007), however, the Supreme Court later held that PRPs who voluntarily cleanup their property may sue for cost recovery under Section 107(a)(4)(B).

APPENDIX B

Practice Exam Questions

The following practice examination consists of three questions. Give it a try without referring to this Blackletter, but you should always have access to the applicable statutes when answering questions about environmental law.

I (One Hour)

Baloney Coldcut Co. operates a meat processing facility that discharges its wastewater into the Southfork River. Baloney has an NPDES permit, issued by the U.S. Environmental Protection Agency, that limits the discharge of biological oxygen demanding substances (BOD), Total Kjeldahl Nitrogen (TKN), total suspended solids (TSS) and oil and grease. The limitations on BOD and TKN are more stringent than required by the national effluent limitation guideline for the meat processing industry. The permit requires Baloney to monitor its discharge and report to EPA in a discharge monitoring report (DMR).

From October 1984 through May 1989, Baloney violated its discharge limits for BOD, TSS, oil and grease and TKN over 35 times. Most of these violations were the result of heavy rainfalls that caused the facility's biological treatment system to exceed capacity. In the DMR, Baloney noted that they were caused by "excessive rainfall." In June 1989, the company began installation of increased capacity in its treatment system and alteration of the configuration of the system to improve control of TKN. The Environmental Resource Defense Committee, (ERDC), a national environmental group, is considering filing a citizen suit under section 505 of the Clean Water Act against Baloney. They have heard that EPA is interested in bringing an action for administrative penalties against Baloney, but, as of yet, EPA has taken no action.

Advise ERDC about the issues it will likely face if it chooses to bring a citizen suit. Discuss 1) any procedural and jurisdictional issues that ERDC would face in bringing a citizen suit, 2) any substantive issues ERDC would face including the elements of its cause of action and any defenses that Baloney might assert, and 3) the remedies ERDC might obtain.

II (One Hour)

The Owner Company (TOC) owns an industrial park which it leases to a variety of companies. One lessee, Lessee Inc. (LI), operated a kitchen cabinet manufacturing business in one building at the park. As part of the business, LI spray painted wood with oil based paints. Approximately six months ago, LI's lease ended, and it vacated the property.

Two months ago, neighbors of the park noticed a chemical smell and saw what looked like oily water collecting in puddles on the industrial park. When they notified TOC, the company investigated and found smelly chemicals were collecting in small pools. Near the area that LI leased, TOC found abandoned drums of oil paint and spent solvents with labels that identified them as LI's. TOC also learned from other tenants that LI had buried drums of paint wastes and spent solvents on the property. The drums are apparently leaking, and chemicals are leaching into groundwater, and rising to the surface in the pools.

As soon as TOC learned these facts, it hired a contractor. The contractor dug up the buried drums and tested their contents. The waste paint and spent solvents in the drums exhibited the Toxicity Characteristic under RCRA and were thus hazardous wastes. The contractor, complying with the requirements of RCRA, had the buried drums and abandoned drums shipped off-site for disposal.

Considerable amounts of chemicals still remains in the soil, and the contractor can not give an estimate of the cost of removing all of the contamination without doing extensive, and expensive, groundwater monitoring. However, even without the monitoring the contractor has advised TOC that the cost of a full remediation of the site will be very high.

At this point, TOC comes to your law firm for advice. It has already spent a considerable amount to remove the drums, and it wants LI to pay for a full cleanup and to reimburse the company for its past costs. The partner in charge wants you to prepare a memorandum discussing possible federal statutory causes of action against LI by TOC. At a minimum, she wants you to describe possible causes of action under CERCLA and RCRA. Make sure you discuss the elements of any cause of action, the possible relief that TOC may be able to obtain, and any defenses that LI might assert.

III (One and ½ Hours)

You are counsel to WidgeCo., a company that manufactures metal widgets. Due to the increased demand for widgets, WidgeCo is planning to open a new facility. Current plans call for the new facility to be located in an urban area with high levels of unemployment. The company believes that providing jobs in such an area is good social policy and good business.

A candidate location has been identified in the southern portion of a large city. The area had previously been the site of a petroleum refinery, but the refinery structures were removed in the early 1970's. The property now has a large warehouse and parking lot. If the company purchases the property, it will tear down the warehouse and construct a new building to house the widget manufacturing equipment. Everything about the location is perfect. Construction would be simple. It is near both supply and distribution centers. The workforce is available. And the price is right.

Management, however, has environmental concerns. Widget manufacturing produces a number of pollutants and wastes. Based on their consultant's evaluation of the process, they anticipate that the operations would result in emission of 120 tons per year of volatile organic compounds ("VOCs") and 20 tons per year of toluene. Additionally, there will be significant quantities of wastewater that would contain lead, zinc and quantities of organic substances with high biological oxygen demand ("BOD"). Finally, the process would also produce over 200 kilograms per month of halogenated spent solvents. The current plans call for disposal of the wastewater into the city sewer system, and disposal of the spent solvents at a disposal facility permitted to receive hazardous wastes.

If the company decides not to purchase the urban property, they have alternative plans to construct the facility in a previously undeveloped tract of land in a largely rural area. If this rural tract is used, the current plans for facility operations would be essentially unchanged except that the wastewater would be discharged into a permanent stream that flows into a major river.

The president of WidgeCo would like you to prepare a memo discussing the environmental consequences associated with construction on the urban and rural tracts. She wants to know, in general, what environmental requirements would apply to operation of the facility, but she particularly wants to know what differences in requirements might apply if one or the other tract were selected. She would also like you to identify any other environmental issues that might affect selection of one or the other tracts.

Research reveals the following potentially relevant information;

- VOCs react to form ozone in the atmosphere, and VOCs are regulated as a criteria pollutant under the Clean Air Act.

- The urban area is classified as a "moderate" non-attainment area for ozone. Among other things, the Clean Air Act requires offsets of 1.15 to 1 for VOCs in these areas.

- Toluene is listed as a "hazardous air pollutant" under section 112(b) of the Clean Air Act.

- Halogenated spent solvents are a "listed" hazardous waste under RCRA.

If there is additional information that you need to respond properly to the president's questions, please identify what information you need.

IV (One Hour)

As you now know, environmental law is full of acronyms and catch-phrases. Give a brief description of the following terms, including their meaning, statutory basis and significance.

1) Domestic Sewage Exclusion

2) BCT

3) Individual Control Strategy

4) MACT

5) National Contingency Plan

6) Land Ban

7) NAAQS

8) ARAR

9) TSDF

10) BDAT

11) National Priorities List

*

APPENDIX C

Sample Answers to Practice Exam

I

a.   Procedural/Jurisdictional Issues

ERDC will have to satisfy certain procedural requirements prior to bringing its citizen suit.

Notice. Section 505(b) requires that a plaintiff give notice of intent to file a citizen suit to the State in which the violation occurs, the alleged violator, and to the Administrator of EPA. ERDC must wait until at least sixty days after sending its notice letter before it can file its complaint. The complaint can be filed in the federal district court in the district in which the source is located.

Government Prosecution. If the state or federal government commences and "diligently prosecutes" a civil or criminal action in federal or state court before the end of the sixty day period, ERDC will be precluded from bringing its citizens suits under section 505(b)(1)(B). If a government enforcement action were brought in federal court, ERDC could move to intervene as of right.

If EPA or the State seeks administrative penalties against Baloney before Baloney files its complaint, ERDC will be able to bring its citizen suit as long as ERDC's complaint is filed within 120 days from the date it gave notice. A state action for administrative penalties will bar a citizen suit only if it is brought under a "comparable" state law. This provision is contained in section 309(g).

Standing. ERDC must establish that it has "standing" to bring the citizen suit. Section 505(g) defines a "citizen" as a person or persons having an interest which is or may be adversely affected. In order to establish "organizational" standing, ERDC will be required to allege and ultimately prove, that is has members who individually meet the test for standing, that the interests it is protecting are germane to its organizational purpose and that the participation of individual members is unnecessary.

To prove that individual members have standing, ERDC will typically be required to allege, and ultimately prove, that it has members who are injured by the alleged violation. This might be satisfied by identifying members who live near to and use the water body into which Baloney discharges. They must also establish that the injury was "caused" by the acts of the defendant and that the court can "redress" the injury. Redressability is typically satisfied by seeking an injunction to force the defendant to cease the violation or it may also be satisfied by an award of civil penalties payable to the federal government that may deter future violations by the defendant.

A citizen suing under the "citizen suit" provision will satisfy the "zone of interest" requirements applicable to standing.

Jurisdiction and Gwaltney. Section 505(a)(1) gives federal courts jurisdiction over citizen suits' that allege a defendant is "in violation" of its permit. In *Gwaltney of Smithfield v. Chesapeake Bay Foundation*, the Supreme Court held that federal courts do not have jurisdiction if the alleged violation is "wholly past." ERDC must initially make a good faith allegation in its complaint that Baloney, as of the date the complaint is filed, is either currently in violation of its permit or that the past violations are likely to recur. At some point, ERDC may be required to prove these allegations.

Baloney will argue that the improvements in its treatment system will prevent any future violations. ERDC will have to argue that, as of the date of filing of the complaint, the past violations are likely to recur. ERDC might also be able to argue that the improvements will correct problems in controlling some, but not all, of the pollutants that are subject to effluent limits.

b.   Substantive Issues

Violation of an Effluent Standard or Limitation. Section 505(a)(1) of the Clean Water Act authorizes "citizen suits" against any person who is alleged to be in violation of an "effluent standard or limitation." Section 505(f) defines an effluent standard or limitation to include a condition of an NPDES permit. Baloney's DMRs establish that Baloney has exceeded the limits in its permit, and this evidence should be enough to establish a violation.

Upset Defense. Baloney may attempt to assert the "upset" defense. The upset defense is an affirmative defense, and the burden of proof would be on Baloney. To assert the upset defense, an upset provision must be in Baloney's NPDES permit. All permits issued by EPA are required to have an upset provision, and this permit was issued by EPA.

To satisfy the upset defense, Baloney must prove, among other things, that it had properly installed and operated adequate pollution control equipment, that it had given notice of the upset within 24 hours, and that the violation occurred for reasons beyond its reasonable control. Given the number of violations, the upset defense would be extremely difficult to establish.

Beyond elements of proof and notice, the upset defense only applies to violation of "technology-based" limitations. The facts indicate that the limits on BOD and TKN are more stringent than national effluent limitation guidelines. This strongly suggests that they are based on water quality standards. A review of the administrative record of the permit will show the basis for the limitations. If the BOD and TKN limits are "water quality standards-based" the upset defense is simply not available.

c. Relief

Relief. If ERDC is successful, it will only be able to obtain injunctive relief and civil penalties paid to the federal government. The court is also authorized to award attorney's fees to any prevailing or substantially prevailing party.

II

The Owner Company (TOC) may be able to recover its past and future costs of cleaning up the property under CERCLA. In *United States v. Atlantic Research*, the Supreme Court held that PRPs who voluntarily clean up their property could bring an action for cost recovery under section 107(a)(4)(B). In *Cooper Indus. v. Aviall Services, Inc.*, the Supreme Court held that a PRP who voluntarily cleaned up property could not bring an action for contribution under § 113(f) of CERCLA.

To recover its cleanup costs under § 107(a)(4)(B), TOC will have to plead and prove the following:

Release or threat of release of hazardous substances from a facility. TOC should have no difficulty in establishing that there was a release from a facility. TOC must establish that the waste paint and spent solvents are "hazardous substances." Since these appear to be hazardous wastes under RCRA, they also meet the definition of hazardous substances under CERCLA.

LI is a PRP. TOC must establish that LI is among the class of "potentially responsible parties" identified in section 107(a). TOC should be able to establish that LI is a PRP under section 107(a)(2) since LI was an "operator" of a facility at the time of disposal. Since the lease has terminated and LI no longer occupies the site, it probably is not a current "operator" under section 107(a)(1).

TOC incurred response costs. TOC must plead and prove that it has already incurred "costs of response." The cost of removal of the drums should constitute response costs.

Consistency with the NCP. TOC must also plead and prove that it has incurred response costs in a manner that was "consistent with the National Contingency Plan." This could be a problem for TOC. The National Contingency Plan requires that private party cleanups need only meet "substantially compliance" with the technical requirements of the NCP. At a minimum, however, this might require that TOC provide for some public notice and public participation in its cleanup. It also may require TOC to prepare some document that explores alternatives to the cleanup. The extent of the requirements for complying with the NCP vary depending on whether the cleanup is classified as a short term "removal" or long term "remedial" action. TOC will have fewer problems in establishing that its actions were consistent with the NCP if it can prove that its cleanup is a removal action.

TOC should ensure that all future cleanup actions are taken in a manner that is consistent with the NCP (including giving public notice of its cleanup) in order to increase its chance of recovery.

Future Costs. TOC can spend money completing the cleanup and hope that it is able to recover all its costs from LI. TOC should, however, bring an action immediately. If TOC wins the action, it can obtain a declaratory judgment that LI is responsible for future costs and LI will be more likely to participate in the cleanup.

Injunctive Relief under CERCLA. The citizens suit provision in CERCLA does not authorize a court to issue an order compelling LI to cleanup the property.

Injunctive Relief under RCRA. TOC may, however, be able to sue LI under section 7002(a)(1)(A) alleging that LI violated RCRA by disposing hazardous wastes without a permit. TOC may also be able to sue LI under section 7002(a)(1)(B) alleging that LI is a past generator who has contributed to an "imminent and substantial endangerment." The federal district court can issue an injunction under section 7002(a) requiring cleanup. There are certain procedural requirements (e.g., filing of notice of intent to sue) that TOC would have to satisfy.

III

A. Industrial Location

1. Air Concerns

The facility will have numerous potential obligations under the federal Clean Air Act.

General SIP Requirements. First, it will be subject to any general obligations contained in the State Implementation Plan (SIP). These will be federally enforceable and enforceable by citizen suit if the SIP provisions were approved by EPA through its notice and comment process. Section 110(a)(2) contains the general requirements that state must include in SIPs. These general requirements include, among other things, an obligation for states to adopt enforceable emission limitations and other control measures necessary to meet the requirements of the Act. States must adopt SIPs after EPA promulgates national ambient air quality standards (NAAQS) under section 109 of the CAA. Primary NAAQS are established by EPA at a level that is "requisite to protect the public health" with an "ample margin of safety." In *Whitman v. American Trucking Ass'n*, the Supreme Court recently confirmed that primary NAAQS are to be set without consideration of the economic costs of compliance. The CAA establishes specific compliance deadlines for attainment of primary NAAQS. Secondary NAAQS are established to protect the "general welfare" that is defined in section 302 of the CAA to include, among others, non-human health related, environmental effects on animals and economic effects. The CAA requires only SIPs ensure that secondary NAAQS will be met within a reasonable time.

Non-attainment Requirements. Since the area is non-attainment for ozone, the facility will be subject to both the general requirements for non-attainment areas found in Subpart D of the CAA and the specific SIP requirements applicable to ozone non-attainment areas adopted in the 1990 amendments to the CAA. The general requirements include, among others, obligations that apply to a "new or modified major stationary source." These sources are required to obtain a permit, must obtain applicable "offsets", and must use of technology representing "lowest achievable emission rates" (LAER) for non-attainment pollutants. LAER is defined in section 171(3) as the rate of emissions that 1) reflects the most stringent limit found in any SIP unless the limit is proved to be not achievable or 2) is the most stringent emission limit achievable in practice by any class or category of such sources. The more stringent of the two levels applies.

Under section 302(j), the general definition of "major stationary source" is any source that emits or has the potential to emit more than 100 tons per year of any pollutant. In moderate ozone non-attainment region the 100 tons per year limit also applies to the definition of "major stationary source." The term "potential to emit" requires assessment of the quantity of pollutants that may be emitted after installation of pollution control equipment. In this case, the facility may meet this definition because it is newly constructed (therefore there is no issue of modification and the application of any bubble rule) and it has the potential to emit more than 100 tons per year of any pollutant after use of control requirement. If the amount of pollutants indicated in the facts are before application of pollution control equipment, the facility may not, in fact, meet the threshold for classification as a major stationary source. Also, if the plant can be redesigned to reduce the amount of emissions of any pollutant to under 100 tons it may escape regulation as a new major stationary source. Since the facility will be located in a "moderate" ozone non-attainment region, it must obtain offsets of at least 1.15 to 1 for VOC, an ozone precursor. In other words, it must ensure that existing sources obtain permanent and enforceable reductions of their existing emissions of at least 1.15 tons of VOCs for every new ton of emission by the facility.

PSD Requirements. Assuming that the area is either in attainment or unclassifiable with respect to other criteria pollutants, the facility will also be subject to the Prevention of Significant Deterioration new source review requirements. These requirements apply to a new or modified "major emitting facility." Section 169(1) defines a major emitting facility as one that has the potential to emit more than 100 tons per year of any pollutant if it is among a list of specific industrial sources or 250 tons per year from any other source. It does not appear that "widget manufacturing" is listed among the enumerated industrial classifications, and if it is not, the facility will not be a major emitting facility since it emits less than 250 tons per year of any one pollutant. It will also be necessary to determine the amount of pollutants being emitted after installation of pollution control equipment. If the facility does meet the definition of "major emitting facility," it facility would be subject to a requirement to employ "best available control technology." BACT is generally developed on a case-by-case basis any applies to any pollutant. The "increment" limits that apply for various classes of PSD areas only apply to emissions of sulfur dioxide and particulates.

NSPS Requirements. The facility may also be subject to New Sources Performance Standards under section 111 of the CAA. NSPS are uniform, national technology-based limitations on the emission of any air pollutant that EPA establishes for classes or categories of facilities. NSPS apply to "new or modified stationary sources." There is no size limit for the definition of stationary sources, but a source is only newly constructed or modified if it commences construction or modification after the date of proposal of NSPS by EPA. Thus, it is necessary to determine if NSPS have been proposed and promulgated to see if NSPS are applicable.

NESHAP Requirements. Section 112 requires EPA to establish National Emission Standards for Hazardous Air Pollutants (NESHAPs) that apply to the defined list of Hazardous Air Pollutants. This section requires that "major sources" of hazardous air pollutants be subject to a technology-based standard known as "maximum achievable control requirements" or MACT. A major source is defined as one that has the potential to emit more than 10 tons per year of any single HAP or 25 tons per year of any combination of HAPs. In order to determine if this facility meets this definition, it is necessary to determine whether the projected emissions of toluene are before or after use of pollution control equipment. MACT is applicable to both new and existing sources. Section 112(d) requires EPA to develop new source MACT based on the operation of the best controlled similar source; existing source MACT is generally to be based on the average emission limitations achieved by the best performing 12% of an industrial subcategory. In the absence of a federally promulgated MACT standard, permit writers may develop MACT on a case-by-case basis.

Title V Permit. If the facility is a "major stationary source," a "new or modified major stationary source" under the non-attainment program, a "major emitting facility" under the PSD program or is subject to NSPS or NESHAPs it must have a Clean Air Act permit as established under Title V of the CAA.

2. Water Concerns

Since the facility will be discharging into a sewer connected to a "publicly owned treatment works," it would be described as an "indirect discharger" and not subject to the NPDES permit requirement. It will, instead, be subject to the pretreatment requirements under section 307(b) of the Clean Water Act. Indirect dischargers are treated differently under the Act since their wastes will be subject to treatment by the POTW. The pretreatment standards are designed to ensure that the indirect discharger's wastes do not interfere with treatment by the POTW, pass through the POTW without treatment, or contaminate the sludge generated by the POTW in ways that prohibit the sludge from being put to beneficial use.

EPA has established several general classes of pretreatment requirements to which this facility might be subject. First, EPA has established uniform, national "categorical" standards that apply to indirect dischargers in specific industrial categories. EPA establishes a categorical standard by determining the technology-based standard that would apply (both new source and existing source) if the facility were a direct discharger; EPA then subtracts from this otherwise applicable limit, the amount of treatment that would be expected from a typical POTW. These categorical standards will only apply if EPA has promulgated a pretreatment standard for the industrial category of the facility in the problem. Second, the facility will be subject to the "general prohibition" that applies to all indirect discharger. The general prohibition prohibits a facility from discharging wastes that either a) cause the POTW to violate the discharge limits in the POTW's NPDES permit or b) violate the sewage sludge standards that are also in the NDPES permit. EPA has promulgated sewage sludge standards under section 405 of the CWA; these standards establish limits on the concentrations of pollutants that may be present in sewage sludge, and they vary depending on the use to which the sludge is to be put. Finally, there may be local limits on discharges to POTWs that are established by local authorities.

3. Hazardous Waste Concerns

The spent solvents will be classified as a hazardous waste under RCRA and subject to a variety of requirements. Under RCRA, hazardous wastes are defined as a subset of solid waste; thus, it is necessary to determine if a material is a "solid waste" before determining if it is hazardous. EPA has established regulatory definitions of solid waste that apply for determining what materials will be subject to regulation as hazardous waste under Subtitle C of RCRA. Under the regulatory definition, a material is a solid waste if, among other things, it is "discarded" either by being abandoned, recycled or classified as "inherently waste like." In this case the spent solvents are being sent to a RCRA permitted disposal facility, and this would constitute abandonment. Thus the spent solvents would be classified as a waste.

A solid waste can be a hazardous waste either by being listed or by exhibiting one of the four hazardous waste characteristics: ignitability, reactivity, corrosivity or toxicity. In this case, the facts indicate that spent solvents are a listed waste. Therefore they are classified as a hazardous waste under RCRA.

Under RCRA, a generator is not required to obtain a federal permit unless the generator engages in storage, disposal or treatment by keeping the waste on-site past the allowed accumulation period. The generator must, however, ensure that the hazardous waste is sent to a permitted facility and must prepare a manifest that contains information about the waste and the designated permitted facility. The wastes must be transported by a transporter who has an EPA ID number. The manifest must be signed by the generator, the transporter and the final facility that receives the waste. The facility must send a signed copy of the manifest back to the generator. If the generator does not receive the copy of the manifest within 45 days, it must notify the government. This manifest system is intended to ensure that the wastes are not illegally dumped by the transporter.

Although the generator does not need a permit, it does have obligations in addition to the manifest requirements. The generator in this case would, among other things, be responsible for determining whether the material is a hazardous waste, obtaining an EPA ID number, complying with certain recordkeeping obligations, and ensuring proper on-site storage.

Since the facility will produce more than 100 kilograms per month of hazardous waste, it is not exempt from many requirements as a "conditionally exempt small quantity generator." Since it produces less than 1000 kilograms per month of hazardous waste it is a "small quantity generator" and may store on-site for 180 days. Generators that generate more than 1000 kilograms per month are allowed only 90 days of on-site storage.

4. Property Contamination

CERCLA Liability. Purchase of property always raises concern about potential liability under the Comprehensive Response Compensation and Liability Act (CERCLA) and RCRA for contamination on the property. In this case, the fact that the urban property was formerly a petroleum refinery makes these concerns particularly significant. Under section 107(a)(1) of CERCLA, the current owner or operator of a facility is generally among the class of "potentially responsible parties" (PRPs) who can be liable for paying all or part of the costs of cleanup that are incurred, consistent with the National Contingency Plan, by the government or other PRPs. Additionally, a PRP may be subject to a cleanup order issued by EPA by section 106. Therefore, buying the property has the potential to subject the new owner to substantial liability for cleanup of the property.

There may be several bases on which the company might not be liable under CERCLA. First, liability of PRPs only applies to the cleanup of "hazardous substances." CERCLA defines hazardous substances by reference to other statutes; this includes toxic substances under the Clean Water Act, hazardous air pollutants under the Clean Air Act and most hazardous wastes designated under RCRA. CERCLA does, however, exclude crude oil and petroleum from classification as a hazardous substance unless the oil or petroleum has been specifically listed or designated as hazardous under those statutes. This is the "petroleum exclusion" under CERCLA, and there, any petroleum contamination on the property may not subject the owner to CERCLA liability.

The petroleum exclusion does not apply, however, if the material has been specifically listed or designated as hazardous a hazardous substance. EPA and the courts have interpreted the petroleum exclusion to apply even if the oil or petroleum contains constituents, such as benzene, that are themselves designated as hazardous under other applicable statutes (at least if those constituents are naturally occurring and are at concentrations that occur naturally). EPA has also stated that the petroleum exclusion applies to gasoline containing constituents, such as lead, that are added during the refining process. If, however, the oil itself has been listed as a hazardous waste or it exhibits a hazard characteristic, it may be classified as a hazardous substance. Certain types of oil wastes at petroleum refineries, such as sludges produced from the treatment of oil wastes, have been listed as hazardous wastes under RCRA. Therefore, some oil on the property may be a hazardous substance depending on where the oil came from.

Second, the company may not be liable under CERCLA if it can establish one of a number of defenses. CERCLA contains a new "bona fide prospective purchaser" defense to liability as an owner under § 107(a)(1) for property purchased after January 2002. If the company undertakes "all appropriate inquiry" prior to buying the property it should have a defense to liability even if it discovers contamination. If the government later cleans up the property, the property may be subject to a "windfall lien" that is based on the increased value to the property as a result of the cleanup. Additionally, if the company undertakes "all appropriate inquiry" prior to purchase and does not discover contamination it may be entitled to assert the "innocent landowner" defense or, if the contamination is coming from adjacent property, the "contingous landowner" defense.

For property purchased after November 2006, EPA has promulgated regulations that establish the requirements for "all appropriate inquiry." In general, these require that before buying the property the company should hire a "qualified environmental professional" to undertake a Phase I environmental audit that includes an inspection of the property, a title search to determine prior owners and a check of government records and inquiry of the current landowner.

RCRA Liability. An owner may also potentially be subject to an order under RCRA to cleanup the property if there is an "imminent and substantial endangerment" from the presence of hazardous or solid waste. This liability comes from sections 7003 (government order) or section 7002(a)(1)(B)(citizen suit) of RCRA. There is no petroleum exclusion to liability under RCRA.

5. Environmental Justice

The fact that the property is located in an urban area with high levels of unemployment at least suggests that the company should investigate any environmental justice implications. On the one hand, the government has indicated a policy of encouraging development of contaminated urban property to provide jobs. This policy is generally reflected in a variety of "brownfields" programs. On the other hand, there is increasing concern about discrimination that may arise if environmentally harmful activities are disproportionately located in minority or poor communities. This concern is generally referred to as "environmental justice." There are several possible legal actions that residents may have to fight the location of the facility on environmental justice grounds if it needs a permit (as under the Clean Air Act) to operate. First, if a plaintiff could prove a discriminatory intent in issuance of a permit by a state government, there might be potential violations of the fourteenth amendment. Second, EPA has adopted regulations under the federal Civil Rights Act that prohibit parties, primarily states receiving federal funds, from having policies, such as permitting policies, that produce a discriminatory effect. Parties may petition EPA to cut off funding to states that violate these regulations. It is now unlikely that a plaintiff would have a direct cause of action against the state or polluter for violation of EPA environmental justice regulations.

II.   Rural Location

1.   Air Concerns

Although it is not clear in the facts, I will assume that the rural area is not "non-attainment" for any criteria pollutant. In that case, the facility would not be subject to the special requirements that apply in non-attainment regions. It would still be subject to any general requirements in the SIP, PDS requirements, new source performance standards that have been proposed under section 111 and NESHAP requirements under section 112. The SIP requirements might be the same in the rural area; the PSD, NSPS and NESHAP requirements will be the same. The facility might, or might not, be subject to the Title V permit requirement depending on the whether it is subject to PSD, NSPS, NESHAP or meets the definition of "major stationary source."

2.   Water Concerns

At the rural area, the facility would be subject to the requirement to obtain a National Pollutant Discharge Elimination System (NPDES) permit. An NPDES permit is required under section 301(a)(1) for any discharge of a pollutant. This is defined in section 502, as the addition of any pollutant to navigable waters from a point source. Navigable waters are further defined as "waters of the US." The Supreme Court has said that this may not include intrastate, non-navigable, intermittent bodies of water in which jurisdiction is based solely on the presence of migratory birds. Although the facts relating to the stream would need to be explored, it is likely that it would be classified as a tributary to navigable water and therefore a "water of the U.S." Therefore, the discharge of industrial wastes from a pipe into the stream would trigger the NPDES requirement. The permit would be issued by the EPA unless the state has been delegated NPDES permit issuance authority.

The NPDES will contain substantive restrictions on the quantities or concentrations that the facility may discharge from the pipe and certain other reporting requirements. The substantive restrictions may be either "technology based" or "water quality standards based."

Technology based Limitations. The facility would be classified as a new source if it commenced construction after promulgation by EPA of national "new source performance standards." If EPA has promulgated these NSPS, the permit must contain these NSPS limitations. NSPS limits do not differ depending on the classification of the pollutant as toxic, non-toxic or conventional. There are also no variances for achieving NSPS.

If no NSPS have been promulgated, the facility will be an existing source. There are several different types of technology based limits that apply to existing sources. Limits based on "best practicable technology" were to be met by all existing sources by 1989. BPT limitations are the floor; all existing source must meet these limits. BPT limits do not vary based on the type of pollutant. Only the "fundamentally different factors" (FDF) variance applies to BPT limits.

Additionally, existing source will be subject to limits based on "best available technology"(BAT) and "best conventional technology"(BCT). BAT limits apply to both toxic and non-toxic/non-conventional pollutants. Only FDF variances apply to BAT for toxic pollutants. BAT limits for non-toxic, non-conventional limits may be subject to the FDF variance, the economic variance in section 301(c) and the water quality variance in 301(g). BCT limits apply to a designated class of "conventional" pollutants. BCT limits are subject to a stricter cost test than BAT limits. There are only limited variances, including FDF, that apply to BCT limitations.

Water Quality Standards Based Limits. In addition to any technology based limits, the permit may also contain limits necessary to achieve water quality standards under section 301(b)(1)(C) of the Clean Water Act. Water quality standards, established under section 303 of the CWA, include a "designated use" of the water. In most cases, states required to set the designated use to achieve the "fishable/swimmable" goals of the Act unless the state can demonstrate that the goal is unattainable either on environmental or economic grounds. Water quality standards also include "criteria." Criteria are typically numerical concentrations of specific pollutants that can exist in the water without preventing attainment of the designated use. Criteria may also be based on bioassays (or tests of toxicity on aquatic critters) or narrative (no discharge of toxic pollutants in toxic amounts). Water quality standards also contain an "antidegradation" provision that prevents worsening of existing water quality in certain cases.

Water quality standards are translated into specific permit limitations through a series of steps that include identification of a "total maximum daily load," (TMDL) and a waste load allocation among sources of the TMDL. Additionally, states may authorize the use of a "mixing zone" in developing water quality standards based limits to ensure that the criteria are not exceeded outside of a "mixing zone" around the point of discharge. The mixing zone is used to calculate the permit limitation, but the limitation applies at the end of the pipe, not at the edge of the mixing zone.

3. Hazardous Waste Concerns

These would be the same in the rural as in the urban area.

4. Property Contamination

Although the possibility of contamination is greater in the urban area, potential CERCLA or RCRA liability still exists in the rural area and an environmental audit that satisfies the requirements for "all appropriate inquiry" should be performed.

E. Environmental Justice Concerns

Although these concerns are more likely to arise in an urban setting, there is still the possibility that environmental justice concerns might arise in a rural area depending on the demographics of the area and the existence of other environmentally harmful facilities in the area.

(With only slight modification, this was an actual student answer the question).

IV

1) Domestic Sewage Exclusion. The definition of solid waste in section 1004(27) of RCRA excludes domestic sewage. Under EPA regulations, this exclusion

applies to virtually all wastes that are put into a sewer connected to a municipal sewage treatment plant (Publicly Owned Treatment Works). Since the materials are excluded from being solid wastes, they cannot be hazardous wastes. This means that materials that would otherwise be classified as hazardous wastes can be dumped into a sewer without violating RCRA. Any federal restrictions on placing materials into the sewer will arise under the pretreatment program of the Clean Water Act.

2) BCT. Best Conventional Technology. Under section 301(b)(2)(E), existing point sources (other than POTWs) must meet BCT effluent limits on "conventional" pollutants. Section 304(b)(3) specifies the factors that EPA considers in setting BCT limits. BCT requires consideration of two cost tests that do not apply to BAT limits. BCT may be no less stringent that BPT and no more stringent than BAT.

3) Individual Control Strategy. Under section 304(l) of the Clean Water Act, states are required to identify certain stream segments that are not meeting water quality standards for toxic pollutants. States are also required to identify the point sources discharging toxic pollutants that are contributing to the problem. The state must adopt an "individual control strategy" ("ICS") that will reduce the discharge of toxic pollutants from listed point sources which, together with other controls, are sufficient to ensure the segment meets water quality standards. The ICS is typically the NPDES permit requirements for the identified point source.

4) MACT. Maximum Achievable Control Technology. Under section 112(d) of the Clean Air Act, EPA must promulgate technology-based emission limits on hazardous air pollutants. These limits are known as MACT. MACT apply to categories of industrial sources, and they may vary in stringency between new and existing sources. MACT must be met by "major sources" as defined in section 112(a)(1).

5) National Contingency Plan. The "National Contingency Plan" ("NCP") contains substantive and procedural requirements relating to the cleanup of hazardous substances by the government and private parties. The portions of the NCP relating to the cleanup of hazardous substances were adopted by EPA under section 105 of CERCLA. Section 107(a) limits the recovery of costs from PRPs if the cleanup was not consistent with the NCP.

6) Land Ban. Under sections 3004(d)-(g) of the RCRA, the land disposal of hazardous wastes is generally prohibited. Hazardous wastes can only be disposed of in landfills if 1) EPA has determined that there will be no

migration of the wastes from the landfill or 2) the hazardous waste has been pretreated to levels established by EPA under section 3004(m).

7) NAAQS. National Ambient Air Quality Standards. NAAQS are established by EPA under section 109 of the Clean Air Act. Primary NAAQS are set at a level, with an adequate margin of safety, requisite to protect the public health. Secondary NAAQS are set at a level requisite to protect public welfare. NAAQS must be established for pollutants for which EPA has published criteria under section 108. Promulgation of a primary NAAQS triggers the states' requirements to prepare a State Implementation Plan.

8) ARAR. Applicable, Relevant and Appropriate Requirements. ARARs are standards for the cleanup of hazardous substances under section 121(d) of CERCLA. ARARs are standards derived from other statutes that are either "applicable" to the cleanup or are "relevant and appropriate" for use in setting cleanup levels. ARARs might include, for example, water quality criteria published under the Clean Water Act.

9) TSDF. Treatment, Storage, and Disposal Facilities. Facilities that treat, store or dispose of hazardous waste are required to have a permit under RCRA. TSDFs must satisfy stringent requirements before they are issued a final permit. The standards applicable to TSDFs are contained in section 3004 of RCRA. Section 3005 of RCRA contains requirements for permit issuance.

10) BDAT. Best Demonstrated Available Technology. EPA may promulgate technology-based levels or methods of treatment under section 3004(m) of RCRA. These limits are known as BDAT. Under the Land Ban, hazardous wastes may be disposed of in landfills if they have first been pretreated in compliance with BDAT.

11) National Priorities List. The National Priorities List ("NPL") is a national list of the worst sites containing hazardous substances. EPA ranks sites for inclusion on the NPL through use of its "hazard ranking system." EPA publishes the NPL under section 105 of CERCLA. EPA has adopted regulations that limit EPA's ability to spend money for a remedial action that will result in the long-term cleanup of the site that is not on the NPL.

12) Bona Fide Prospective Purchaser. A new exclusion from liability under section 107(r) of CERCLA that applies to persons who purchase property after January 2002 with knowledge that the property is contaminated. In order to qualify as a bona fide prospective purchaser, the person must have undertaken "all appropriate inquiry" prior to purchase and satisfy a number of other conditions after purchase.

*

APPENDIX D

Acronyms

A

ALJ—Administrative Law Judge. Person presiding over most adjudicatory hearings required under the APA.

APA—Administrative Procedure Act. Establishes administrative procedures for federal agency rulemaking and adjudication. 5 U.S.C. Chapter §§ 551–559. Also contains provisions dealing with judicial review of agency actions. 5 U.S.C. §§ 701–706.

AQCR—Air Quality Control Region. Areas designated under section 107 of the CAA as either attainment, non-attainment or unclassifiable with respect to NAAQS.

ARAR—Applicable Relevant and Appropriate Requirements. Requirements for the level of cleanup at CERCLA sites that are derived from other statutes. The requirement to meet ARARs is contained in section 121(d) of CERCLA.

ATSDR—Agency for Toxic Substances and Disease Registry. Federal agency responsible, among other things, for undertaking health assessments at Superfund sites under section 104 of CERCLA.

B

BAT or BACT—Best Available Technology or Best Available Control Technology. Technology-based effluent limitations applicable to toxic and non-toxic/non-conventional pollutants under the CWA. BAT limits were to be met by 1989 under section 301(b)(2)(C), (D) and (F). Factors used in establishing BAT are specified in section 304(b)(2).

BADT—Best Available Demonstrated Technology. Technology-based levels applicable to new sources under section 111 of the CAA and section 306 of the CWA. Also known as NSPS or New Source Performance Standard.

BCT or BACT—Best Conventional Technology or Best Available Conventional Technology. Technology-based effluent limitations applicable to conventional pollutants under the CWA and which are to be met by 1989 under section 301(b)(2)(E). Factors used in establishing BAT are specified in section 304(b)(4).

BDAT—Best Demonstrated Available Technology. Technology-based pretreatment limits for hazardous wastes under section 3004(m) of RCRA. Hazardous wastes meeting BDAT may be land disposed without violating the RCRA land ban prohibition.

BMP—Best Management Practice. Methods for controlling non-point sources of pollution under the CWA that are contained in an area-wide management plan.

BOD—Biological Oxygen Demand. A method for specifying the amount of organic material in wastewater by measuring the amount of oxygen that will be removed from water as microorganisms consume the organic material. BOD is a conventional pollutant under the CWA.

BPJ—Best Professional Judgment. A case-by-case determination of a facility's effluent limitations under the CWA that is typically performed when national effluent limitations guidelines have not yet been promulgated.

BPT or BPCT—Best Practicable Technology or Best Practicable Control Technology. Technology-based effluent limitations applicable to all types of pollutants under the CWA and which are to be met by 1977 under section 301(b)(1)(A). Factors used in establishing BAT are specified in section 304(b)(1).

C

CAA—Clean Air Act, 42 U.S.C. §§ 7401 to 7671q. The primary federal statute dealing with the control of air pollution.

CERCLA—Comprehensive Environmental Response, Compensation, and Liability Act, 42 U.S.C. §§ 9601 to 9675. [Also known as Superfund]. The primary federal statute dealing with the cleanup of sites contaminated with hazardous substances.

CEQ—Council on Environmental Quality. Office with primary responsibility for establishing policies for implementation of NEPA, including promulgation of general NEPA regulations. Established under section 202 of NEPA.

CFC—Chlorofluorocarbon. Class of chemicals that cause depletion of stratospheric ozone. Regulated under Title VI of the CAA and the international agreement known as the Montreal Protocol.

CFR—Code of Federal Regulations. Annual compilation of federal regulations.

GHG—Greenhouse Gas. The group of chemicals, including carbon dioxide and methane, that contribute to global warming by the greenhouse effect. The Kyoto Protocols designate a number of substances as GHGs including carbon dioxide, methane, nitrous oxide and certain fluorinated gases.

CO—Carbon Monoxide. A odorless and poisonous gas. Carbon monoxide has been designated a criteria pollutant under section 108 of the CAA and has an

NAAQS under section 109 of the CAA.

CTG—Control Technology Guidance. Guidance documents issued by EPA that are used to establish RACT requirements under the CAA.

CWA—Clean Water Act, 33 U.S.C. §§ 1251 to 1387. [Also known as the FWPCA or Federal Water Pollution Control Act]. The primary federal statute dealing with the control of water pollution.

CZMA—Coastal Zone Management Act, 16 U.S.C. §§ 1451 to 1464. Federal statute which, among other things, requires planning for activities that affect coastal areas.

D

DMR—Discharge Monitoring Report. Facility's report on the amount of pollutants that are discharged. They are used to evaluate compliance with NPDES permit requirements.

DO—Dissolved Oxygen. The amount of oxygen found in water. Greater levels of dissolved oxygen are beneficial for many types of aquatic life.

DOE—Department of Energy.

DOI—Department of the Interior.

E

EA—Environmental Assessment. Document prepared under NEPA to determine whether an EIS must be prepared.

EDF—Environmental Defense Fund. A private, public interest environmental organization.

EIS—Environmental Impact Statement. Document required under section 102(2)(C) of NEPA for "major federal actions significantly affecting the quality of the human environment."

EPA—Environmental Protection Agency. Federal agency with primary responsibility for implementation of the major federal pollution control statutes.

EPCRA or EPCRTKA—Emergency Planning Community Right-to-Know Act, 42 U.S.C. §§ 11001 to 11050. Portion of CERCLA adopted in 1986 that requires, among other things, reporting of the presence of certain hazardous substances to local planning officials and annual reporting of the amount of hazardous substances that have been released.

ESA—Endangered Species Act, 16 U.S.C. §§ 1531 to 1544. Primary federal statute dealing with actions that affect endangered or threatened species.

F

FDF—Fundamentally Different Factors variance. A variance from effluent limitations guidelines (other than NSPS) established under the CWA. FDF variances are authorized under section 301(n) of the CWA.

FIFRA—Federal Insecticide Fungicide Rodenticide Act, 7 U.S.C. §§ 136 to 136y. Federal statute regulating the sale, labeling and use of pesticides.

FIP—Federal Implementation Plan. Federal plan promulgated by EPA under the CAA when a State fails to prepare an adequate SIP.

FOIA—Freedom of Information Act, 5 U.S.C. § 552. Federal statute requiring release of most types of documents in the possession of the federal government.

FONSI—Finding of No Significant Impact. A determination under NEPA that an EIS does not need to be prepared.

FWPCA—Federal Water Pollution Control Act, 33 U.S.C. §§ 1251 to 1387. [Also known as the CWA or Clean Water Act]. The primary federal statute dealing with the control of water pollution.

G

GATT—General Agreement on Tariffs and Trade. An international agreement addressing the free trade in goods that was originally adopted in 1948. GATT was incorporated into the international agreement that established the World Trade Organization in 1995 and is now known as GATT/WTO.

H

HAP—Hazardous Air Pollutant. Hazardous air pollutants designated under section 112 of the CAA.

HC—Hydrocarbons. A class of chemicals that are involved in creation of ground level ozone and formation of smog.

HCP—Habitat Conservation Plan. The plan to minimize and mitigate impacts on endangered species that is required under section 10 of the Endangered Species Act in order to obtain authorization for the incidental "take" of endangered species.

HRS—Hazard Ranking System. Procedures used in identifying sites for inclusion in the NPL under CERCLA.

HSWA—Hazardous and Solid Waste Amendments. Major amendments to RCRA adopted in 1984.

I

ICS—Individual Control Strategy. Control measures required under section 304(l). They are applied to certain point sources in order to assure that streams will meet water quality standards for toxic pollutants.

I/M—Inspection and Maintenance. Requirements for inspection of air pollution control equipment on automobiles in areas that are non-attainment for ozone under the CAA.

L

LAER—Lowest Achievable Emission Rate. Emission limitation applicable to new or modified major sources in non-attainment areas under section 173(a)(2) of the CAA.

LDR—Land Disposal Restrictions. Restrictions established under RCRA to implement the "land ban."

LEV—Low Emission Vehicles. Types of low polluting vehicles that will be required in certain areas that are non-attainment for ozone under the CAA.

LUST—Liquid Underground Storage Tanks.

M

MACT—Maximum Achievable Control Technology. Technology-based emission limit for major sources of hazardous air pollutants under section 112 of the CAA.

MSDS—Material Safety Data Sheet. Document containing information about certain toxic chemicals that employees must be provided under the OSH Act.

MSWLF—Municipal Solid Waste Landfills. Municipal landfills receiving solid waste (and hazardous wastes from small quantity generators and households) subject to special requirements under Subtitle D of RCRA.

N

NAAQS—National Ambient Air Quality Standards. Ambient concentrations of certain designated criteria pollutants under section 109 of the CAA. Primary NAAQS are established to protect "public health." Secondary NAAQS are established to protect "public welfare."

NCP—National Contingency Plan. Federal regulations establishing requirements for, among other things, the cleanup of hazardous substances under CERCLA.

NEPA—National Environmental Policy Act, 42 U.S.C. §§ 4321 to 4370d. Federal statute that, among other things, requires federal agencies to prepare EISs.

NESHAP—National Emission Standards for Hazardous Air Pollutants. General term for restrictions on the emission of hazardous air pollutants under section 112 of the CAA.

NGO—Non-governmental Organization. Private organizations that are involved in the formation and implementation of international environmental policy.

NOx—Nitrogen Oxides. A class of chemicals that are involved in production of smog. Nitrogen dioxide has been designated a criteria pollutant under section 108 of the CAA and has an NAAQS under section 109 of the CAA.

NPDES—National Pollutant Discharge Elimination System. Permit system under the CWA that is applicable to point sources of pollutants. Issuance of NPDES permits is governed by section 402 of the CWA.

NPL—National Priority List. List established under section 105 of CERCLA of the worst sites containing hazardous substances.

NRDC—Natural Resources Defense Council. A private, public interest environmental organization.

NSPS—New Source Performance Standards. Technology-based levels applicable to new sources under section 111 of the CAA and section 306 of the CWA. Also known as BADT or Best Available Demonstrated Technology.

NWF—National Wildlife Federation. A private, public interest environmental organization.

O

O₃—Ozone. A highly reactive form of oxygen containing three oxygen atoms.

Ozone at ground level has adverse effects on human health and the environment. Ozone in the stratosphere is important in blocking ultraviolet radiation. Ozone has been designated a criteria pollutant under section 108 of the CAA and has an NAAQS under section 109 of the CAA.

OCS—Outer Continental Shelf. Offshore area around U.S. coasts that extends to the point where the ocean floor drops sharply.

OMB—Office of Management and Budget. Executive office with certain responsibilities to review activities of regulatory agencies that have major affects on the U.S. economy.

OPA—Oil Pollution Act, 33 U.S.C. §§ 2701 to 2761. Act adopted in 1990 which, among other things, establishes a CERCLA type liability system for the cleanup of oil released into navigable water.

OSHA—Occupational Safety and Health Administration. Agency in the Department of Labor with responsibilities for protection of worker health and safety under the OSH Act.

OSH Act—Occupational Safety and Health Act, 29 U.S.C. § 651 et seq. Federal statute that, among other things, provides for the establishment of occupational safety and health standards for toxic pollutants in the workplace.

P

PCB—Polychlorinated biphenyls. Class of hazardous chemicals that are regulated under TSCA.

pH—A measure of the acidity and alkalinity of a substance. pH is a conventional pollutant under the CWA. pH is also used to measure the corrosivity characteristic under RCRA.

PM—Particulate matter. PM has been designated a criteria pollutant under section 108 of the CAA and has an NAAQS under section 109 of the CAA. PM–10 includes particulates that are less than 10 microns in diameter. PM–2.5 includes particulates that are less than 2.5 microns in size.

POTW—Publicly Owned Treatment Works. Municipal sewage treatment plants under the CWA.

PRP—Potentially Responsible Parties. Class of persons who are responsible for the cleanup of hazardous substances under section 107(a) of CERCLA.

PSD—Prevention of Significant Deterioration. Program, established in Part C of the CAA, regulating air pollution in areas with air quality than is better than that required by NAAQS.

PSES—Pretreatment Standards for Existing Sources. Technology-based standards applicable to existing sources that discharge pollutants to POTWs under section 307(b) of the CWA.

PSNS—Pretreatment Standards for New Sources. Technology-based standards applicable to new sources that discharge pollutants to POTWs under section 307(b) of the CWA.

R

RACM—Reasonably Available Control Measures. Control requirements applicable to existing sources in non-attainment areas under the CAA.

RACT—Reasonably Available Control Technology. Technology-based control requirements applicable to existing sources in non-attainment areas under the CAA.

RCRA—Resource Conservation and Recovery Act, 42 U.S.C §§ 6901 to 6992k. The primary federal statute dealing with the management and disposal of hazardous waste.

RFP—Reasonable Further Progress. Requirement under the CAA that states make incremental progress toward meeting NAAQS in non-attainment areas prior to the final compliance date.

RI/FS—Remedial Investigation/Feasibility Study. A preliminary assessment performed under the Comprehensive Environmental Response, Compensation and Liability Act to determine the proper level and means of cleanup of a site contaminated with hazardous substances.

ROD—Record of Decision. A final document prepared under the Comprehensive Environmental Response, Compensation and Liability Act that documents EPA's decision on the proper level and means of cleanup of a site contaminated with hazardous substances.

S

SARA—Superfund Amendments and Reauthorization Act. Major amendments to CERCLA that were adopted in 1986.

SDWA—Safe Drinking Water Act, 42 U.S.C. §§ 300f to 300j–26. Federal statute regulating chemicals in public drinking water supplies. It also contains the separate UIC program.

SEPA—State Environmental Policy Acts. Term for state laws that are modeled after NEPA.

SIP—State Implementation Plan. State plan required by section 110 of the CAA that specifies state requirements for achieving NAAQS.

SOx—Sulfur oxides. Class of chemicals that, among other things, are involved in production of acid rain. Sulfur oxides have been designated a criteria pollutant under section 108 of the CAA and has an NAAQS under section 109 of the CAA.

SWMU—Solid Waste Management Unit. An area where solid or hazardous wastes were disposed of that may be subject to cleanup obligations under the corrective action provisions of RCRA.

T

TC—Toxicity Characteristic. One of the four characteristics for classifying hazardous wastes under RCRA.

TCLP—Toxicity Characteristic Leachate Procedure. Procedure for extracting leachate from a solid waste to determine whether it exhibits the toxicity characteristic under RCRA.

TMDL—Total Maximum Daily Loads. TMDLs identify the total amount of a pollutant that can be discharged into a stream segment without causing a violation of WQS under the CWA. States are required to develop TMDLs under section 303(d) of the CWA.

TRI—Toxic Release Inventory. Database containing information on releases of hazardous substances that has been submitted under section 313 of EPCRA.

TSCA—Toxic Substances Control Act, 15 U.S.C. §§ 2601 to 2692. Federal statute regulating the production and use of toxic substances.

TSDF—Treatment Storage and Disposal Facility. Facilities handling hazardous waste that are required to have a Subtitle C permit under RCRA.

TSS—Total Suspended Solids. A measure of the amount of particulates in water. TSS is a conventional pollutant under the CWA.

U

UIC—Underground Injection Control. The UIC program, contained in the SDWA, regulates the disposal of materials into wells.

UST—Underground Storage Tanks.

V

VOC—Volatile Organic Compounds. Class of air pollutants that are involved in the generation of ozone in the atmosphere.

W

WLA—Waste Load Allocation. Amount allocated to a point source that is its portion of the total amount of waste that may be discharged into a water body without violating WQS. May be used in establishing water-quality standards based effluent limits in an NPDES permit.

WQA—Water Quality Act. Amendments to the CWA that were adopted in 1987.

WQS—Water Quality Standards. Standards specifying the use and quality of water in a state required under section 303 of the CWA.

WTO—World Trade Organization. International organization established in 1995 that is involved in the implementation of certain agreements regarding international trade.

APPENDIX E

Casebook Cross–Reference Table

Doremus, Lin, Rosenberg & Schoenbaum Environmental Policy Law: Problems, Cases, and Readings 5th Ed., 2008 (Foundation Press)

Geltman, Modern Environmental Law 1997 (West)

Grad & Mintz, Environmental Law, 4th Ed. 2000 (Lexis)

Percival, Schroeder, Miller & LEape, Environmental Regulation: Law, Science and Policy 5th Ed., 2006 (Aspen)

Plater, Abrams, Goldfarb, Graham, Heiinzerling & Wirth, Environmental Law and Policy: Nature, Law and Society 3d Ed., 2004 (Aspen)

**Ruhl, Nagle & Salzman, The Practice and Policy of Environmental Law 2008
(Foundation Press)**

*

APPENDIX F

Table of Cases

APPENDIX G

Table of Statutes

POPULAR NAME ACTS

ADMINISTRATIVE PROCEDURE ACT

CIVIL RIGHTS ACT OF 1964

CLEAN AIR ACT